Using Windows Draw™

STEPHEN W. SAGMAN

Using Windows Draw

Copyright© 1993 by Que® Corporation

Library of Congress Catalog No: 92-63324

ISBN: 1-56529-121-2

96 95 94 93   4 3 2 1

Interpretation of the printing code: the rightmost double-digit number is the year of the book's printing; the rightmost single-digit number, the number of the book's printing. For example, a printing code of 93-1 shows that the first printing of the book occurred in 1993.

The figures reproduced in this book were created with Collage Plus from Inner Media, Inc., Hollis, NH.

Publisher: Lloyd J. Short

Associate Publisher: Rick Ranucci

Operations Manager: Sheila Cunningham

Book Designer: Scott Cook

Production Analyst: Mary Beth Wakefield

Graphic Imaging Specialist: Dennis Sheehan

Figure Specialist: Wilfred Thebodeau

Production Team: Debra Adams, Jeff Baker, Julie Brown, Claudia Bell, Paula Carroll, Brad Chinn, Jeanne Clark, Michelle Cleary, Tim Cox, Mark Enochs, Brook Farling, Tim Groeling, John Kane, Bob LaRoche, Tom Loveman, Sean Medlock, Caroline Roop, Linda Seifert, Suzanne Snyder, Marcella Thompson, Suzanne Tully

For Sarah and Andy, two perfect symbols whom only nature could draw.

With all my love,

Uncle Steve

xxxooo

CREDITS

Title Manager
Shelley O'Hara

Product Director
Steven M. Schafer

Acquisitions Editor
Sarah Browning

Production Editor
Anne Owen

Copy Editors
William A. Barton
J. Christopher Nelson
Christine Prakel
Colleen Totz

Editorial Assistance
Elizabeth D. Brown
Jill L. Stanley

Technical Editor
Matthew D. Lee

Composed in *Cheltenham* and *MCPdigital* by Que Corporation

Stephen W. Sagman is the president of a New York City-based company that creates user documentation and provides training, courseware, and user interface consulting. Mr. Sagman writes about personal computing in *PC/Computing*, *PC Week*, and *PC Magazine* and gives classes and seminars in desktop publishing, graphics, and multimedia.

Prior to technical writing, Mr. Sagman edited *MIDI Marketer*, an electronic musical instrument marketing newsletter, and served as marketing manager at several high-technology companies.

Mr. Sagman graduated from Hamilton College and has an M.B.A. from the City University of New York. He is also the author of *Using Harvard Graphics 3.0* and *1-2-3 Graphics Techniques* from Que, and *Getting Your Start in Hollywood*.

He can be reached via CompuServe (72456,3325), MCI Mail (SSAGMAN), or at 140 Charles St., New York, NY 10014.

ACKNOWLEDGMENTS

The author would like to thank Kenny Driver and Jack Davis at Micrografx for their technical assistance, and Matthew D. Lee at Micrografx for his thorough technical editing and for the many useful tips and suggestions he offered during the creation of this manuscript.

The author would also like to thank Sarah Browning for acquiring him for this book, Steve Schafer for his careful attention and many invaluable suggestions, Anne Owen for her consummate production editing and care, and Wilfred Thebodeau for his fine work in enhancing the figures.

TRADEMARK ACKNOWLEDGMENTS

CONTENTS AT A GLANCE

TABLE OF CONTENTS

Introduction

Prepare for a treat when you use Windows Draw. Draw isn't just another business productivity tool. Draw is one of the world's most popular software programs because it's easy to use, powerful, and—best of all—fun. In a very short time, you can create drawings, logos, and designs with Draw's easy-to-understand and easy-to-use tools. And you don't have to be an artist to get impressive results from Draw.

One key to Draw's versatility is the program's library of 2,600 ClipArt symbols. With this sizable assortment of ready-made pictures at your disposal, you may never need to actually draw a picture of your own with Windows Draw. Instead, you can borrow the appropriate art from the library, add your own text, and enjoy results that would make a professional artist proud.

Another key is Draw's extensive and logically organized toolbox of tools and controls. These tools provide you with all the capabilities you need in a drawing program, from creating simple shapes such as lines, boxes, and circles to fine-tuning the shapes of complex curves. The toolbox, located along the left border of the Draw window, is available to you at any point in the program, as is Draw's extensive color palette, from which you can pick any of a multitude of colors.

Menus located at the top of the Draw window offer a host of additional commands that endow Draw with many of the capabilities of far more costly and complicated illustration programs.

Whether you need to create a logo for a new company, a poster promoting an event, an advertisement for a product, or a masthead for a newsletter, Draw enables you to accomplish the job easily and professionally. Draw also enables you to turn drawings into files that can be incorporated into other programs. After you create a drawing for a newsletter, for example, you can easily transfer the drawing to a desktop publishing program. After you create a logo, you can transfer the logo to a presentation graphics program, to appear on every slide you create. Because Draw is an application written for Microsoft Windows, Draw works especially easily in conjunction with other Windows applications. Draw can, however, create files for import into other, non-Windows programs as well.

What Is in This Book?

The chapters that follow contain complete information about using all of Draw's tools and commands. You also can find in these pages many tips and ideas for creatively using Draw's many capabilities to accomplish special tasks.

The topics in this book are organized to present the information you need as quickly as possible.

Chapter 1, "Guided Tour," takes you on a comprehensive tour of the program's various capabilities and features. Exercises show you how to design a poster and a logo and then how to use the logo to embellish the poster, as well as any other drawings you may create later.

Chapter 2, "Getting Started," explains the Draw screen, along with several essential concepts that can facilitate your work in Draw. Additional information to help you get started using Draw also is included in the chapter, such as how to get on-screen help and how to set up a drawing.

Chapter 3, "Using ClipArt," outlines how to use the 2,600 selections of clip art in Draw's ClipArt catalog. You can learn how to browse and search through the catalog, pull out the pictures you need, and even how to add images you create to the library so that your custom images are available for other projects.

Chapter 4, "Working with Text," discusses how to incorporate text into a drawing and how to edit and change the appearance of text already in place. This chapter also shows you how to create special text effects such as placing text on a curve, filling text with a color gradient, and creating drop shadows. You can even create a text logo in a complete and detailed exercise.

Chapter 5, "Adding Symbols," explains how to use Draw's drawing tools to create new graphic shapes and designs.

Chapter 6, "Changing the Appearance of Symbols," instructs you on how to use Draw's extensive editing tools and commands to change the fill and line styles of symbols, change the shape of symbols, and use special tools such as Slant and Rotate.

Chapter 7, "Arranging Symbols on the Page," shows you how to arrange and rearrange the symbols you place on the page, combining and connecting symbols, aligning symbols, blending symbols, and creating special patterns of symbols on the page.

Chapter 8, "Working with Color Palettes," gives you information on how to modify the colors in the default color palette, load a different color palette, and save a combination of colors you create in a new color palette.

Chapter 9, "Printing Your Work," provides instructions for creating printed copies of your work with a standard desktop printer and creating an output file to send to a service bureau for printing on a high-resolution image setter. This chapter also includes information on Windows fonts and font technologies.

Chapter 10, "Exporting and Importing Graphics," explains how to transfer drawings you create to other programs and how to incorporate graphics created in other applications into your drawing. Chapter 10 also discusses a method of sharing information (including drawings) new to Windows 3.1: Object Linking and Embedding.

Appendix A, "Installing Draw," provides detailed instructions for installing and running Draw on your computer system.

Appendix B, "Draw's Fonts," lists the fonts that come with Windows Draw.

Appendix C, "Draw Keyboard Shortcuts," lists all the keyboard combinations you can use as shortcuts to Draw commands.

Who Should Use This Book?

The thorough discussions and step-by-step procedures and exercises in this book have been designed to help anyone learn Windows Draw. You don't need to be an artist to use Draw, and this book assumes no special artistic experience on the part of the reader. A prior familiarity with Microsoft Windows, however, is beneficial to your effective use of Draw and this book. This book does not teach you the basics of Windows, however. If you have never used a Windows program before,

Que's *Using Windows 3.1, Easy Windows,* or other books about the Windows operating environment may prove helpful to your full understanding of *Using Windows Draw*. Following the steps in *Using Windows Draw* will help you become accustomed to the way Windows programs work. Chapters 1 and 2 introduce many of the concepts you need to know for using Windows while you learn about Draw.

How To Use This Book

Try to set some time aside to relax at your computer with this book. The step-by-step exercises throughout the book enable you to try for yourself the procedures described. Don't attempt to finish the entire book in one sitting, however. The best way to learn anything is to do so in frequent, small doses.

After you initially finish *Using Windows Draw*, keep the book handy for use as a ready reference. The book's comprehensive table of contents and index can help you quickly find the necessary information whenever you need a quick refresher on how to accomplish a specific task.

Guided Tour

The best way to quickly become familiar with Windows Draw is to try the program hands-on. Experience is the best teacher, so the series of exercises in this chapter lets you practice using Draw to create some real drawings. This chapter helps you set up drawings, add text and graphic elements, then refine them with Draw's editing tools.

Each of these exercises builds on the previous exercises, so you have a solid overview of Draw's features when you're done. Real expertise comes in later chapters when you learn the nuts and bolts of using Draw.

If you haven't already installed Draw, you should follow the instructions in Appendix A, "Installing Draw." Then return to this chapter with an hour or two of uninterrupted time. Windows Draw offers fun, innovative opportunities, especially if your experience with computers has been mainly word processing, database management, or spreadsheets.

Using the Mouse

If you're unfamiliar with using a mouse, take a few moments to get acquainted with it. Windows Draw relies on using the mouse to move the pointer on-screen, so you will need to become comfortable with it.

Some people seem at ease with their mouse instantly, and others find controlling a mouse awkward at first. Overcoming mouse phobia is purely a matter of a little practice. These tips will make using the mouse easier.

First, make sure to clear a little space on the desk for the mouse. If you're left handed, clear some space on the left side of the keyboard. Too many people try to use a mouse that's wedged in among piles of papers, coffee cups, and other desk paraphernalia. Rest the heel of your hand on the desk just in front of the mouse and let your fingers fall naturally across the top of the mouse. Your index finger should land on the mouse button and your thumb should rest against the side of the mouse. You should be able to move the mouse a few inches in any direction on the desk by moving your wrist without picking up your hand from the desk. You only need these few inches to move the pointer on-screen.

Starting Draw

When Microsoft Windows starts, the Program Manager window appears on-screen. Within this window are program group windows that hold icons. There's an icon for each of the programs that you can run. One of the program group windows is labeled Micrografx at the top. Inside this window is an icon labeled Windows Draw 3.0. If you don't see the Micrografx window open on-screen, find the icon in the Program Manager window labeled Micrografx (it's probably in the lower left corner of the window) and then double-click it.

To start Windows Draw, position the pointer on the Windows Draw 3.0 icon and double-click the left mouse button (click the left button twice quickly). Figure 1.1 shows the Program Manager window, the Micrografx program group window, and the Windows Draw icon.

When you double-click the Windows Draw icon, the Windows Draw window opens. You may want to maximize this window so it fills the screen. To maximize the window, click the up-arrow button in the upper right corner of the window. Figure 1.2 shows how the Draw window looks.

Getting To Know the Draw Window

Across the top of the window is the *Title bar* which reads Windows Draw (refer to fig. 1.2). Below the Title Bar, the *Menu bar* (with the words File, Edit, Change, and so on) holds Draw's menus of commands. You can choose any of these words to pull down a menu. The menu closes when you choose a command or click elsewhere on the screen.

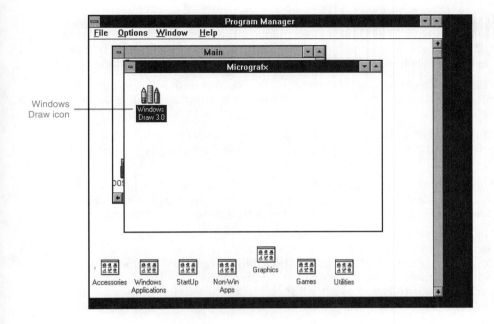

Fig. 1.1

The Windows Draw icon in the Micrografx group window.

Windows Draw icon

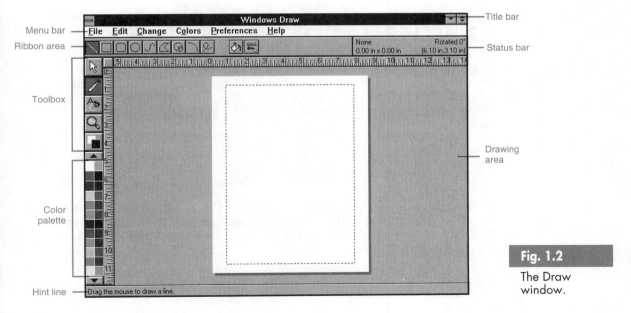

Menu bar

Ribbon area

Toolbox

Color palette

Hint line

Title bar

Status bar

Drawing area

Drag the mouse to draw a line.

Fig. 1.2

The Draw window.

Just below the Menu bar are the *Ribbon area* on the left and the *Status bar* on the right. The Ribbon area displays buttons you can use to draw different shapes and change the fill and line styles of symbols. The Status bar shows helpful information you can use as you work in Draw.

The left side of the window contains the *Toolbox* and *Color palette*. You choose tools from the Toolbox and colors for objects from the Color palette.

At the bottom of the screen, the *Hint line* gives you suggestions for actions and describes the purpose of tools and buttons as you work in Draw.

The rest of the screen is the *Drawing area*. Within the Drawing area, you see a blank page surrounded by gray. You can gauge the current size of the page by examining the rulers that border the Drawing area.

Try moving the pointer across the window by moving the mouse. As you position the pointer on each tool in the Toolbox, each color in the Color palette, and each button in the Ribbon area, the Hint line provides information. As you move the pointer across the Drawing area, the Status bar tells you exactly how far from the top left corner of the page the pointer is.

Exercise 1: Creating a Poster

In this first exercise, you can create a poster that the Hamptons Visitors Bureau will use to publicize its upcoming bicycle race. With a little guidance, you can create a full-color 8 1/2-by-11-inch drawing to be printed later in a large poster size. Figure 1.3 shows the completed poster.

Setting Up the Page

Your first task when beginning a new drawing is to ensure that the page is set up the way you want. You can choose a page size and page orientation by choosing the **P**age command from the **P**references menu. To set up the page, follow these steps:

1. From the **F**ile menu, select **N**ew to start a new drawing.

2. Choose **P**references from the Menu bar to pull down the Preferences menu.

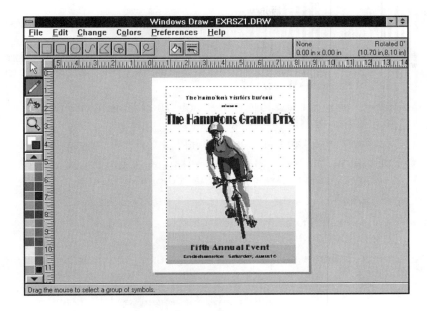

Fig. 1.3

The completed
poster.

NOTE You can choose **P**references by clicking the word
"Preferences" in the Menu bar or by pressing the Alt
key and the underlined letter in the word **P**references
(the P). The boldfaced letters in these instruction
steps are the hotkeysyou can press in conjunction with
the Alt key to select a command.

3. Choose **P**age, and the Page dialog box appears, as shown in figure 1.4.

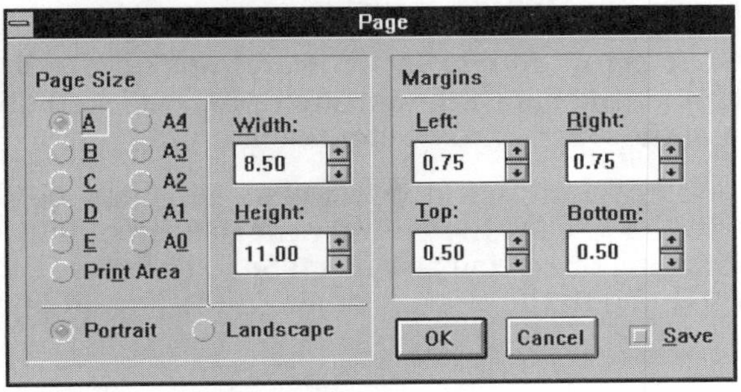

Fig. 1.4

The Page dialog
box.

Try choosing each of the Page Size settings. Notice that each setting changes the Width and Height numbers.

4. Make sure that the Page Size is set to **A** and the orientation is set to Portrait, as shown in figure 1.4. If not, click the buttons next to each of these settings.

5. Make sure that the margins are set to the following numbers: Left: .75, Right: .75, Top: .50, Bottom: .50.

   You can press Tab to move the highlight within the dialog box.

6. Choose OK. The Page dialog box disappears and you see an 8 1/2-by-11-inch portrait page within the Drawing area.

You also should check the Ruler settings by following these steps:

1. Choose **P**references from the Menu bar to pull down the Preferences menu.

2. Choose **R**ulers, and the Rulers dialog box appears, as shown in figure 1.5.

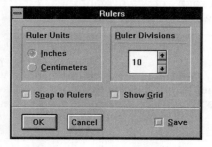

3. Make sure that Ruler Units is set to **I**nches. If Ruler Units is set to **C**entimeters, choose **I**nches instead.

4. Click the up-arrow and down-arrow buttons next to the Ruler Divisions number to change the setting to 10. This step divides each inch along the rulers into 10 increments.

5. Make sure that both the **S**nap to Rulers and Show **G**rid options are turned on. If not, click the button next to each option. When you're drawing or editing an object, **S**nap to Rulers causes the pointer to jump to the nearest point on the page that lines up with

division marks on both the horizontal and vertical rulers. Show **G**rid causes a pattern of tiny dots to appear across the page. You can use these dots to visually align objects on the page.

6. Choose OK to close the Rulers dialog box.

Now you're ready to create the poster by adding text and graphic objects to the page. To add these elements, you use the Text and Drawing tools in the Toolbox. The next section explains how to use these tools.

Adding Text to the Page

You begin the design by adding text to the page. After the text is on the page, you can modify its size, position, and appearance.

To add text, click the Text tool in the Toolbox. When you click the Text tool, the pointer changes to a *text cursor* (an arrow with an ABC design next to it). The Ribbon area also displays special controls that enable you to change the appearance of the text you're about to place on the page. If you know exactly how you want the text to look, you can change these settings now. If not, you can come back later to change text you have already placed on the page.

In this case, you already have decided on the typeface, so you can select it before entering the text by following these steps:

1. Click the down-arrow button next to the Font list box in the Ribbon area. A scrollable list of font names appears.

2. Scroll down the list by clicking the down arrow on the scroll bar at the right. Find the font name *Broadway*.

3. Choose Broadway from the font list.

Move the pointer back onto the page. As you move the pointer, notice that a pair of markers moves within the rulers. Use these markers to position the pointer about an inch from the top of the page and about 2 inches from the left. Click the mouse button to place a flashing text cursor on the page. Type **The Hamptons Visitors Bureau**. Then double-click the mouse to enter the text you have just typed. Your page should look like the one shown in figure 1.6.

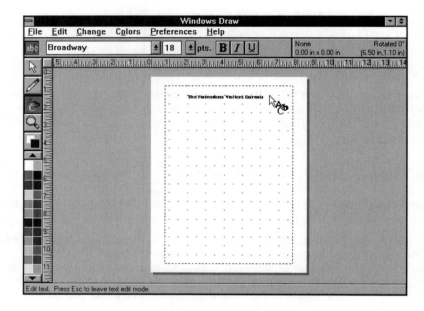

Fig. 1.6

The page with
the first line of
text.

Adding More Text

Now you can enter a second line of text. Move the cursor just below the
first line and click once to place a flashing text cursor on the page.
Type **Presents** and double-click the mouse.

Now move the pointer down to about 2 1/2 inches from the top of the
page. Click the mouse once to place a text cursor, then type **The
Hamptons Grand Prix**. Double-click the mouse. Move the pointer down
about 9 1/2 inches from the top of the page, type **Fifth Annual Event**,
and double-click the mouse. Now move the pointer about 1/2 inch
lower, click the mouse to place a text cursor, and type **Bridgehampton
Saturday, August 6**.

You have finished entering text, so press the Esc key. The pointer becomes a standard pointer without the ABC icon, meaning you are no
longer in text entry mode. Figure 1.7. shows the page as it should look.

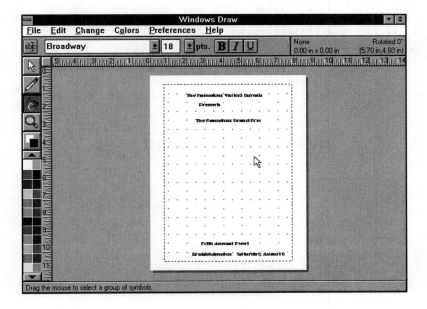

Fig. 1.7

The page with all
the text added.

Formatting the Text

Now take a few moments to resize and reposition the text so it fits the design you have in mind.

Try placing the pointer on a line of text and clicking the left mouse button once. You can select each line of text separately in this manner. Selected text is surrounded by a set of eight handles that mark the borders of the text block. Figure 1.8 shows a magnified view of a selected text block surrounded by handles.

When you position the cursor anywhere within the borders of a text block, the pointer displays a four-way arrow. This arrow indicates that you can move the text block by pressing and holding the mouse button and then moving the mouse. Try this technique by following these steps:

1. Position the pointer on the first line of text on-screen. The pointer should display a four-way arrow.

2. Press and hold the mouse button.

3. Move the mouse to the right a little. A rectangle marking the boundaries of the text block moves in correspondence with the mouse.

4. Release the mouse button to drop the text block at the current position.

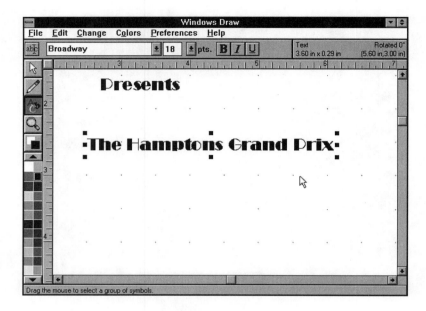

Fig. 1.8

A selected text
block.

When you position the pointer directly on one of the handles, the cursor changes to a double arrow. This arrow indicates that you can move the handle to stretch the text block. To move a handle, position the pointer on it, press and hold the mouse button, and then move the mouse. When you move a handle on one of the block's sides, you can change the height or width of the text, stretching its shape. When you move a handle at one of the block's corners, you make the size of the text proportionately larger or smaller without stretching its shape.

Try changing the text size by following these steps:

1. Position the cursor on the lower left corner handle of the text block you just moved.

2. Press and hold the mouse button.

3. Move the mouse diagonally down and to the left a little. (Because you're moving a corner handle, the handle will only move diagonally).

4. Release the mouse button.

The Font Size list box in the Ribbon area displays the point size of the currently selected text block. After you change the size of a text block, the Font Size shows the new text size. Using the Font Size display as a guide, try changing the size of the first line of text to 20 points by dragging the lower corner of the text block. If you find this task difficult, you may want to try another method. Click the text block and then click the current point size in the Font Size list box, highlighting the current setting. Type 20 to replace the highlighted text and press Enter. The text in the selected text block is now 20 points. Then change the size of the second line of text (the word "Presents") to 14 points.

Next, drag each side handle of the text block "The Hamptons Grand Prix" toward the sides of the page so the block rests against the dotted blue margin lines. This step stretches the text and distorts its shape considerably. Now drag the top handle toward the top of the page until the text is approximately 55 points high.

Click the text block "Fifth Annual Event" to select it. Then click the current point size in the Font Size list box, highlighting the current setting. Type 30 to replace the highlighted text and press Enter. The text in the selected text block is now 30 points. Select the last text block on the page and change its size to 18 points using the same method. The page should now look like the page shown in figure 1.9.

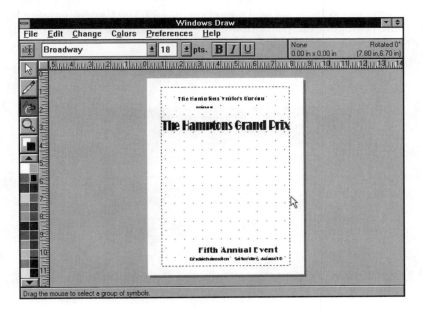

Fig. 1.9

The page with the text sized properly.

The last step in placing the text properly is to center it on the page. Draw comes with a set of special commands for aligning objects with each other or against the page. To try this command, follow these steps:

1. Click the first text block on the page to select it.

2. Choose **A**lign from the **C**hange menu.

3. Choose Page C**e**nter from the Align menu. This command centers the selected object in the horizontal center of the page.

4. Select the other text blocks one at a time and use the **A**lign Page C**e**nter command. Instead of using the Page C**e**nter command from the menu, you can press Ctrl-F9 (the shortcut key combination for the command).

Adding ClipArt to the Page

A large area remains in the center of the page. Now you can fill the area with a drawing to represent the bike race. If you're a great artist, you can now use the drawing tools to draw a bicycle racer. But if you're like most of us, you will be happy to know you can choose from among thousands of pre-drawn pictures, called *ClipArt symbols*. These symbols are contained in Draw's ClipArt catalog. In fact, the ClipArt catalog has an entire category of sports-related ClipArt symbols. To find a cyclist symbol, follow these steps:

1. Choose **C**lipArt from the **F**ile menu. The Find ClipArt dialog box opens, as shown in figure 1.10.

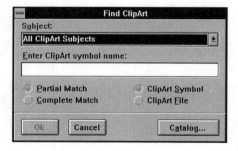

The Find ClipArt dialog box.

2. Click the down-arrow button next to the S**u**bject text box to see a scrollable list of subjects.

3. Use the scroll bar to the right of the subject list to scroll to Sports, then click it.

4. Click in the text box under **E**nter ClipArt symbol name.

5. Type **cyclist** into the text box and press Enter. When Draw informs you that the keyword "cyclist" has multiple matches, choose OK. The ClipArt Catalog dialog box appears, as shown in figure 1.11.

Fig. 1.11

The ClipArt
Catalog dialog
box.

Within the dialog box, you see the "SPORTS09.DRW" file selected in the **F**iles section. In the **C**lipArt Symbols section, you see three symbols that contain the word "cyclist" highlighted in red. These three symbols are selected (the buttons next to them are highlighted). The fourth symbol is not selected.

6. Choose **P**review to see the selected symbols. The preview should look like figure 1.12.

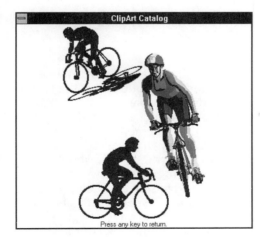

Fig. 1.12

The preview of
the selected
symbols.

The colorful symbol of a female cyclist would be ideal for your poster. Press any key to return to the ClipArt Catalog window.

7. Click the symbol named "Cyclist, female." This symbol should now be the only one with a highlighted button.

8. Choose OK to place the symbol on the page.

9. Drag the upper left corner handle toward the center of the symbol so the symbol slightly overlaps the text block, as shown in figure 1.13.

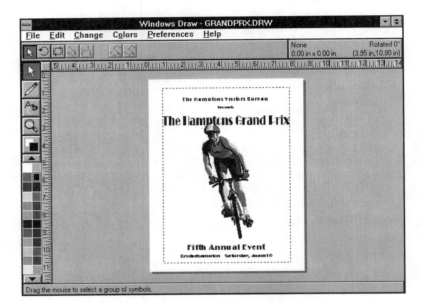

Fig. 1.13

The ClipArt symbol correctly positioned.

NOTE   Notice that the ClipArt symbol overlaps the text block because the symbol was added after the text block. Each new symbol you add to the page, whether it's a ClipArt symbol, a text symbol, or a graphic symbol, is drawn on top of other symbols it overlaps. Remember this detail when you construct a drawing. Try to place the background symbols first and then draw the symbols that should be on top. Don't worry if you need to place a new symbol behind other symbols or if you need to move a background symbol to the front. Draw provides a special pair of commands for changing the order of symbols on the page. You have the chance to try one of these commands later in this chapter.

Now would be a good time to save your work on disk. In fact, just about any time is a good time. You need to get in the habit of saving your work early and saving it often. To enter a name for the file, choose **S**ave from the File menu. When the Save File dialog box appears, type **GRANDPRX** into the Save File As text box. Then, choose **S**ave to save the file.

Adding a Gradient Background

The poster is beginning to take shape. The text and the ClipArt symbol are informative and colorful, but the poster could be enhanced by a background that is a little more interesting than pure white. To change the background, you can draw a rectangle and fill it with a *color gradient*, an area of color that gradually changes from one hue to another. Then place the rectangle in the background of the drawing.

To draw the rectangle, follow these steps:

1. Click the Draw tool in the Toolbox.

2. Click the Rectangle button in the Ribbon area. The Rectangle tool displays a picture of a rectangle.

3. Position the pointer against the dotted blue left margin line about even with the handle bars of the bicycle.

4. Press and hold the mouse button.

5. Drag the pointer diagonally down and to the lower right part of the page, to the intersection of the bottom and right margin lines.

6. Release the mouse button.

A rectangle appears on the page, but it doesn't contain the proper fill color. In fact, the rectangle is unfilled and contains no color at all. To modify the fill of the rectangle, follow these steps:

1. Click the Pointer tool in the Toolbox.

2. Click somewhere on the rectangle, away from the ClipArt symbol and the text. You should see handles surround the rectangle to indicate that it's selected.

3. Click the Draw tool in the Toolbox.

4. Click the Fill Style button in the Ribbon area. The Fill Style menu appears, as shown in figure 1.14.

5. Choose **G**radient from the Fill Style menu. The Gradient dialog box appears (see fig. 1.15).

   The Gradient dialog box displays a variety of gradient patterns from which you can choose. This dialog box also provides controls you can use to create your own gradient patterns.

6. Choose the first gradient in the upper left corner. This gradient changes color from top to bottom.

7. Choose OK. The Gradient dialog box closes and a white-to-black gradient appears within the rectangle, as shown in figure 1.16.

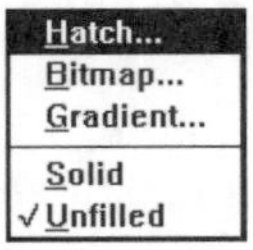

Fig. 1.14

The Fill Style menu.

Fig. 1.15

The Gradient dialog box.

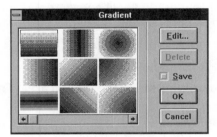

Fig. 1.16

The rectangle with a gradient.

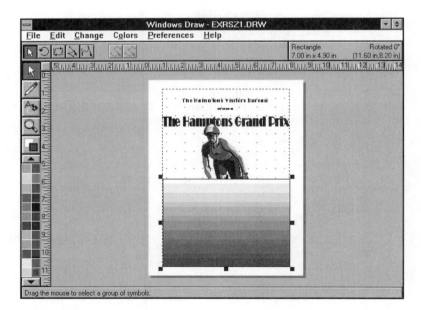

Change the colors for the gradient by following these steps:

1. Click the Color tool in the Toolbox.

2. Click the first button on the pop-out menu of buttons (the Fill Color button). The color you choose from the Color palette when this button is selected is the ending color of the gradient.

3. Move the pointer across the green colors on the left side of the Color palette and look at the Hint line at the bottom of the screen, which identifies each color (see fig. 1.17). Click the color Aquamarine. (You may need to scroll down the list of colors by clicking the down arrow at the bottom of the Color palette.)

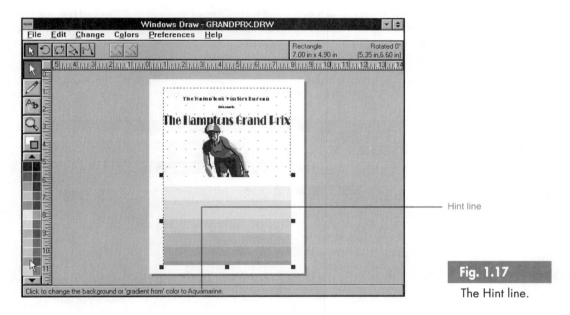

— Hint line

Fig. 1.17

The Hint line.

The rectangle is attractive, but it's surrounded by a thin black line. Remove the line by following these steps:

1. Click the Pointer tool in the Toolbox.

2. Click the rectangle you have just created to select it.

3. Click the Draw tool in the Toolbox.

4. Click the Line Style button in the Ribbon area. The Line Style menu appears, as shown in figure 1.18. This menu displays a collection of line styles you can choose from and provides other commands for changing the width and endings of a selected line.

5. Choose Invisible from the Line Style menu.

Fig. 1.18

The Line Style
menu.

Sending the Background to the Back

The white-to-green gradient now covers the text at the bottom of the
page and part of the cyclist ClipArt symbol. To fix this problem, move
the rectangle with the gradient behind the other symbols by following
these steps:

1. Choose the **O**rder command from the **C**hange menu. The Order
   pop-out menu appears, as shown in figure 1.19.

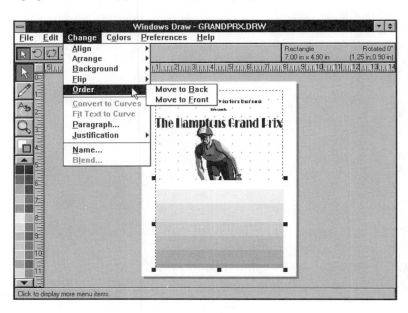

Fig. 1.19

The Order
pop-out menu.

2. Choose Move to **B**ack from the Order pop-out menu. Click somewhere on the gray area of the screen to deselect the rectangle.
The poster should now look like the drawing in figure 1.20.

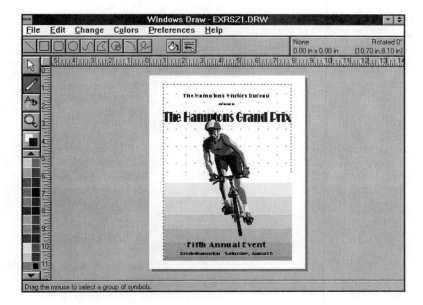

Fig. 1.20

The drawing with
the gradient
rectangle in the
back.

Changing the Headline to Curves

You can apply a few finishing touches to the elements you have put
together to form the poster. The text blocks are still all black. You may
want to choose a more interesting color for them. First, try changing
the top two text blocks to a red shade. To accomplish this step, select
both text blocks, then click a red shade in the Color palette.

One way to select more than one item on-screen is to select the first
item, press and hold the Shift key, and then select the next item. Another way is to draw a *rubber band box* around all the items you want to
select. Try this second method by following these steps:

1. Click the Pointer tool in the Toolbox.

2. Position the pointer above and to the left of the text block "The
Hamptons Visitors Bureau."

3. Press and hold the mouse button.

4. Move the pointer below and to the right of both text blocks, as shown in figure 1.21.

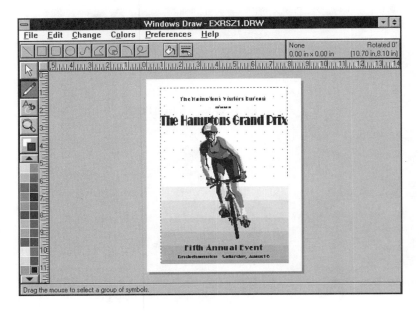

Fig. 1.21

Using a rubber band box to select two symbols.

5. Release the mouse button. You see one set of handles surround both symbols, and the Status bar near the upper right corner of the window tells you that Multiple Symbols are selected (see fig.1.22).

Find and choose the color Scarlet from the second column of colors in the Color palette. (Remember, look at the Hint line to see the name of each color.) Try using the same technique to change the rest of the text on the page to the same color.

Placing a Gradient in the Headline

Another finishing touch is to place a color gradient within the headline "The Hamptons Grand Prix." You have learned to change the color of a text block by selecting the text block and choosing a color from the Color palette. But to fill a symbol with a gradient, you must choose **G**radient from the Fill Style menu. Because text symbols have no fill, you cannot fill them with a gradient unless you convert them to graphic objects that can have fills.

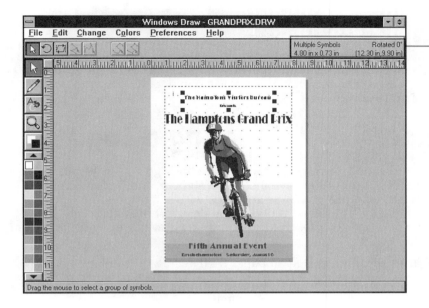

Status bar

Fig. 1.22

The Status bar.

Draw provides a simple method to convert text to graphic objects. To try the conversion, follow these steps:

1. Choose the Pointer tool from the Toolbox.

2. Click the "The Hamptons Grand Prix" text block to select it.

3. Choose **C**onvert to Curves from the **C**hange menu. This command converts the text to a series of graphic shapes called curves.

Now you can fill the curves with a gradient by following these steps:

1. Choose the Draw tool from the Toolbox.

2. Click the Fill Style button in the Ribbon area.

3. Choose the gradient that appears on the Fill Style menu. The Fill Style menu always displays your most recent selections as a convenience. The letters will now be filled with the gradient.

4. Click the Color tool and then click the third button on the pop-out menu, the Background Color tool. Now you can choose a starting color for the gradient from the Color palette.

5. Choose Red from the Color palette.

6. Click the Color tool again and then click the first button on the pop-out menu, the Fill Color tool. Now you can choose an ending color for the gradient from the Color palette.

7. Choose Mahogany from the Color palette (just to the right of Red).

Saving the File

To resave the poster you have just created, choose Save **As** from the File menu. Then enter the name **Grandprx** into the Save File As text section and choose OK.

Exercise 2: Creating a Logo

In this second exercise, you will create the logo for Mr. Weinberg's new pizza restaurant. You have met Mr. Weinberg, and he has communicated to you that his pizzas are made with sun-dried tomatoes and goat cheese. Therefore, the logo you design should keep with Mr. Weinberg's vision of a crisp, contemporary, even trendy Italian restaurant.

You sketch out a design on paper then decide to re-create it in Draw. Follow these steps to create a new page on which to work:

1. Choose **New** from the **File** menu.

2. Choose **Page** from the **Preferences** menu.

3. Make sure the Page Size is set to **A** (8 1/2-inches-by-11-inches) and the orientation is set to Portrait.

4. Leave the default margins and choose OK to return to the page.

Creating the Background Design

First, you can create some of the graphic elements you need. You decide to place the text "Weinberg's" and "Pizza" on some geometric shapes that represent the kind of design Mr. Weinberg would like. To begin creating the shapes, follow these steps:

1. Click the Draw tool from the Toolbox.

2. Click the Rectangle tool in the Ribbon area.

3. Use the readings on the Status bar and the rulers to position the pointer at approximately one inch from the left side of the page and 6.5 inches down from the top.

4. Press and hold the mouse button and drag diagonally to the right. Create a rectangle that is approximately 6.5 inches wide and 1 inch tall. Again, use the Status bar to check the size of the rectangle as you draw it (see fig. 1.23).

5. Release the mouse button to place the rectangle on the page.

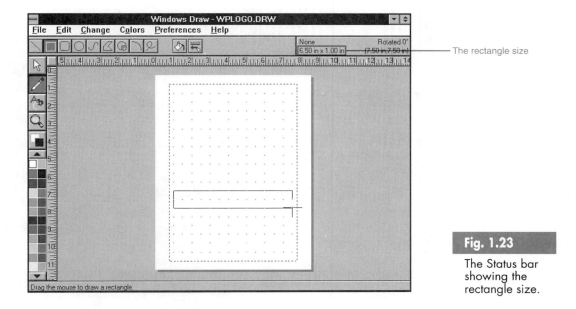

The rectangle size

Fig. 1.23

The Status bar showing the rectangle size.

Before you proceed, you can make the rectangle a little more contemporary by following these steps:

1. Click the Pointer tool in the Toolbox.

2. Click the Fill Style button in the Ribbon area.

3. Choose **B**itmap from the Fill Style menu. The Bitmap dialog box opens, as shown in figure 1.24.

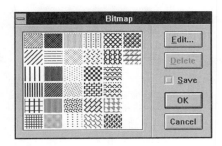

Fig. 1.24

The Bitmap dialog box.

4. Choose the fourth bitmap down in the third column by clicking it once and then choosing OK. The rectangle is filled with a herringbone pattern of black dots on a white background.

Now you can choose a more interesting combination of colors.

1. Click the Color tool in the Toolbox.

2. Click the third button on the pop-out menu (the Background Color button) and then click Russet from the Color palette. Russet is one of the shades of violet in the second column of colors. (You may need to scroll down the colors to find Russet by clicking the down-arrow button at the bottom of the Color palette.)

3. Click again on the Color tool and click the first button on the pop-out menu (the Fill Color button).

4. Click White in the Color palette. Now you have set the pattern of dots to white against a russet background.

5. Click the Line Style button and choose **Invisible** from the Line Style menu to remove the rectangle's outline. Figure 1.25 shows the rectangle.

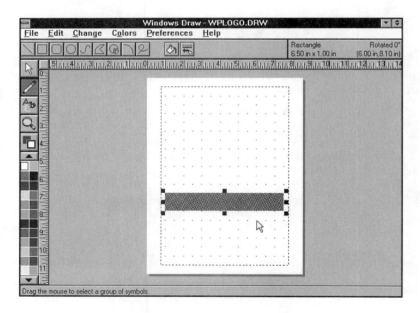

Fig. 1.25

The rectangle with color added and its outline made invisible.

Now you can duplicate the rectangle to create a stair-stepped pattern.

1. Choose the Pointer tool from the Toolbox.

2. Press and hold the Shift key.

3. Position the pointer on the rectangle.

4. Press and hold the mouse button.

5. Drag a duplicate of the rectangle up 1/2 inch. (Use the Status bar to tell how far you're moving the duplicate.)

6. Release the mouse button to drop the rectangle.

7. Position the pointer on the right side handle of the rectangle.

8. Press and hold the mouse button again.

9. Drag the mouse to the left 1/2 inch so the rectangle is now approximately 6 inches wide rather than 6.5 inches. (Use the Status bar to tell the rectangle's width.) The two rectangles should now look like the two shown in figure 1.26.

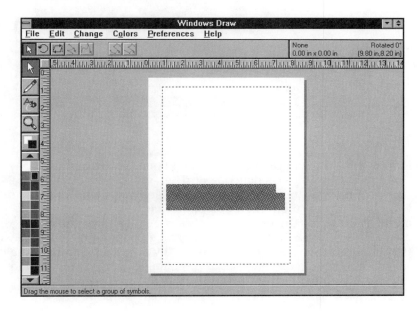

Fig. 1.26

The original rectangle and a duplicate.

10. Repeat steps 2 through 6 to drag a duplicate of this second rectangle up another 1/2 inch.

11. Reduce the width of the duplicate another 1/2 inch (approximately 5.5 inches wide).

12. With the Pointer tool, select the rectangles by drawing a rubber band box that completely encloses all three. (The Status bar should read Multiple Symbols.)

13. Choose **A**lign from the **C**hange menu.

14. Choose **C**enter from the Align pop-out menu. The three rectangles appear in a stair-stepped pattern, as shown in figure 1.27.

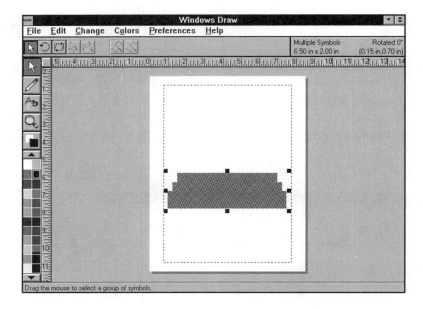

Fig. 1.27

The three
rectangles in a
stair-stepped
pattern.

TIP

Before going on, you can use the **Group** command to assemble the
three rectangles into a single object. Then you can enjoy the convenience of moving and resizing the rectangles as a single object
without worrying about their positions changing relative to one
another. To group the rectangles, choose Arrange from the **Change**
menu. Then choose **Group** from the **Arrange** pop-out menu. Because
the three rectangles still are selected, they are grouped into a single
object. You always can ungroup the rectangles later if you need to
change one of them.

Now you can continue the background design by drawing a perfect
square on the page. But this time, you know in advance how you want
the square to look. You can change the fill and line settings before
drawing the rectangle by following these steps:

1. If the three rectangles are still selected, click on a blank portion of
    the page to deselect them.

2. Choose the Draw tool from the Toolbox.

3. Click the Fill Style button and choose **S**olid from the Fill Style
    menu.

4. Click the Line Style button and choose **I**nvisible from the Line
    Style menu.

5. Choose Turquoise from the Color palette, a blue-green shade in the second column of colors. Remember, move the pointer across the Color palette and look at the Hint line at the bottom of the screen to see the color names.

Now you're ready to draw the rectangle.

1. Position the pointer 2 inches from the left side of the page and 2 inches down.

2. Press and hold the Ctrl key and press and hold the mouse button while dragging diagonally down and to the right. Draw a square 4.5 inches wide. Holding the Ctrl key while you draw a rectangle forces the rectangle to be a perfect square.

3. Release the mouse button. The square should fill with turquoise.

Just for fun, add a small lavender rectangle that sits on top of the square. Follow these steps:

1. Choose Lavender from the first column in the Color palette.

2. Position the cursor at the top left corner of the turquoise square.

3. Press and hold the mouse button and drag diagonally up and to the right to create a rectangle that is 1/2 inch tall and the same width as the square. Your drawing should now look like the drawing shown in figure 1.28.

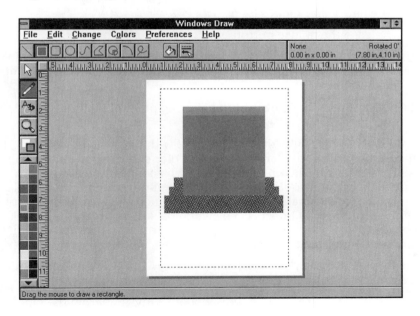

Fig. 1.28

The drawing with additional graphic shapes.

Adding More Graphic Elements

The design is taking shape. But a logo for a pizza restaurant is not complete without a representation of a pizza slice. You can begin by drawing a triangle that you will later convert to a slice.

1. Click the Draw tool from the Toolbox.

2. Click the Polyline tool in the Ribbon area.

3. Position the cursor in the gray area just to the right of the page. You will perfect this part of the drawing there before bringing it onto the page.

4. Follow the ruler at the top of the drawing area and position the cursor at the 10-inch mark and about halfway down the page.

5. Press and hold the Ctrl key and the mouse button while dragging the pointer to the right 2 inches to the 12-inch mark.

6. Release the mouse button but don't move the pointer.

7. Make sure that the pointer is positioned at the end of the line you just drew and then press the mouse button again.

8. Drag the pointer diagonally down and to the left to draw the second side of the triangle. Move the pointer so it aligns with the 11-inch mark on the top ruler. The Status bar should indicate that the line is 2.51 inches long.

9. Release the mouse button but don't move the pointer.

10. Draw the third side by connecting the ends of the first two sides. Be careful to finish the third side at exactly the starting point of the first side.

11. Click the mouse button at the starting point of the first side to finish the shape.

If you have successfully drawn a triangle with three sides that meet, the triangle fills with lavender, the last Fill Color chosen. If the sides do not meet, the triangle will not fill with color. To connect the three sides, choose the Pointer tool, draw a rubber band box around the triangle, and then choose Arrange from the Change menu. On the Arrange pop-out menu, choose Connect. Then switch back to the Draw tool, click the Line Style button, and choose Invisible from the Line Style menu to remove the lines and leave the fill.

You may need to work on the triangle a bit to convert it to a pizza slice. Use the Zoom button to zoom in on the triangle by following these steps:

1. Click the View tool in the Toolbox.

2. Click the first button in the View pop-out menu, the Zoom button. Then draw a rubber band box around the triangle. The program zooms in on the portion of the drawing you have enclosed (see fig. 1.29).

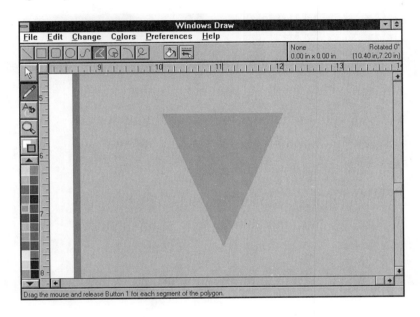

Fig. 1.29

The zoom view of the triangle.

Reshaping the Triangle

Every graphic object you draw can be reshaped, resized, and repositioned. When you reshape an object, you can independently move all the line and curve segments that make up the object. You also can change the degree of curve segments.

The triangle you just finished drawing has straight sides, but you will see how easily you can make them curve. By curving one side, you can make the triangle look more like a pizza slice.

To try curving a side, follow these steps:

1. Choose the Pointer tool from the Toolbox and then click the triangle.

2. Click the Reshape Bézier button in the Ribbon area.

When you choose the Reshape Bézier button after selecting an object, points appear along the object's border at the ends of the line or curve segments that compose the object. These points are called *anchor points*. You can move these points to move the segments. Figure 1.30 shows an object with its anchor points visible.

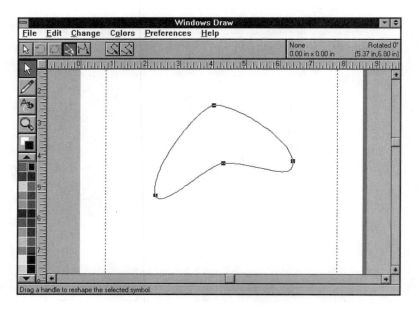

Fig. 1.30

An object with anchor points.

On the sides of each anchor point are *control points* that you can move to change the curvature of the lines as they approach the anchor points. Figure 1.31 shows the same object with anchor points and control points visible.

Notice that the triangle has small *x*'s at each corner. These *x*'s are actually control points sitting right on top of the anchor point. Try moving one of the control points by following these steps:

1. Position the cursor on the *x* at the upper right corner of the triangle.

2. Press and hold the mouse button.

3. Move the mouse diagonally up and to the left approximately 3/4 inch. (Use the Status bar to see how far you have moved the mouse.) This step changes the angle at which the line approaches the anchor point, bending the line into a curve (see fig. 1.32).

4. Release the mouse button.

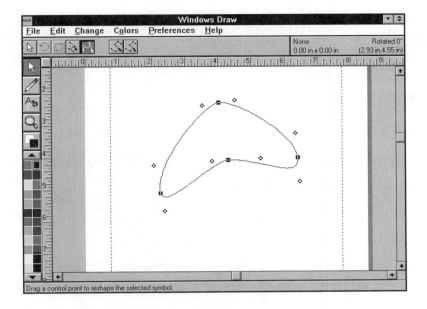

Fig. 1.31

An object with anchor and control points.

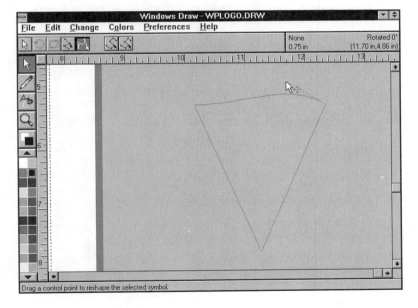

Fig. 1.32

Moving one of the triangle's control points.

5. Position the pointer on the x at the upper left corner of the triangle.

6. Press and hold the mouse button.

7. Move the mouse diagonally up and to the right the same distance (approximately 3/4 inch).

8. Press Esc to finish reshaping the object. The object now looks like the example shown in figure 1.33.

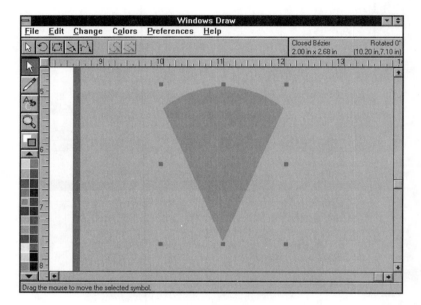

Fig. 1.33

The reshaped triangle.

While the object is still selected, click Red in the left column of the Color palette.

Next you can duplicate the shape and use the duplicate to add to the design.

1. Click the Select button in the Ribbon area.

2. Press and hold the Shift and Ctrl keys. This action copies the graphic and contains the movement of the pointer to horizontal or vertical.

3. Position the pointer on the triangle.

4. Press and hold the mouse button.

5. Drag a duplicate of the triangle up about 1/3 inch. (The Status bar tells you this number.)

6. Release the mouse button.

7. Choose Russet from the Color palette to change the color of the duplicate.

8. With the duplicate still selected, drag its left handle to the left one ruler division (.10 inch) and its right handle to the right one ruler division (.10 inch).

9. Slide the duplicate down one ruler division to align the two triangles.

10. Choose **O**rder from the **C**hange menu, then from the Order pop-out menu, choose Move to **B**ack. The shapes will be aligned as shown in figure 1.34.

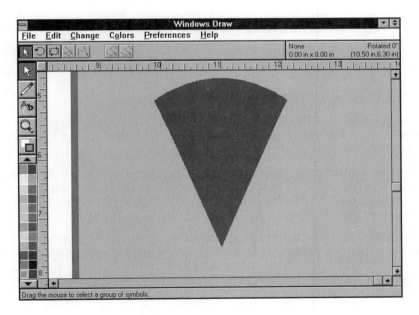

Fig. 1.34

The correct positioning of the two triangles.

You can make a few more modifications to improve the appearance of this part of the design. Follow these steps:

1. Click the red triangle.

2. Click the Draw tool in the Toolbox.

3. Click the Fill Style button in the Ribbon area.

4. Choose the gradient shown on the Fill Style menu.

5. Click the Color tool in the Toolbox.

6. Click the third button on the pop-out menu (the Background color tool).

7. Click Salmon in the Color palette. The resulting gradient is very subtle, but it will enhance the logo considerably.

8. Click the exposed portion of the other triangle to select it.

9. Click the Fill Style button again.

10. Choose the same bitmap you used earlier.

11. Click the Color tool.

12. Click the first button on the pop-out menu and choose White from the Color palette.

13. Click the third button on the pop-out menu and choose Russet from the Color palette.

14. Draw a rubber band box around the two triangles. Make sure that the box completely encloses both triangles and the Status bar reads Multiple Symbols.

15. Choose **A**rrange **G**roup from the **C**hange menu.

Now the two triangles are joined together as a group. When you move one triangle, the other triangle goes along. You don't have to worry about accidentally disturbing their alignment.

Now you can return to a full page view so you can see the entire drawing and arrange the pizza slice on the logo. To switch to a full page view, click the View tool and then click the View Page button to view the entire page.

Drag the pizza slice onto the existing drawing by clicking the slice, holding the mouse button, and dragging the mouse. If the slice goes behind the turquoise box, choose **O**rder from the **C**hange menu and then choose Move to **F**ront. Then drag a corner handle of the slice to increase the slice's size until it fits on the rest of the drawing (see fig. 1.35). The height of the slice should be approximately 4 3/4 inches according to the Status bar.

Adding Text

The final steps in preparing the logo are to add some text. Somewhere you need to incorporate the name of the restaurant, "Weinberg's Pizza," within the logo.

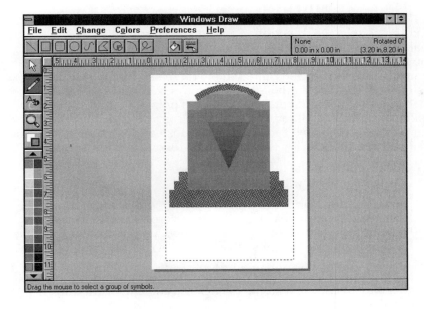

Fig. 1.35

The properly
positioned pizza
slice.

For interest, you can separate the two blocks of text and place them in
different parts of the logo. The word "Pizza" becomes part of the
graphic design. You haven't yet decided how the text should look,
though, so place the text on-screen and then play with a number of
design possibilities until you find a good result.

Begin by entering the word "Pizza" on-screen. Then you can try various
design possibilities, fonts, sizes, and colors for the text. To enter the
text, follow these steps:

1. Click the Text tool in the Toolbox. The pointer now displays the
   ABC design of the Text tool to indicate that Draw is in text mode.

2. Position the pointer in the gray area to the left of the page, near
   the left ruler, and click the mouse button. Because the Text Cursor button is activated when you first choose the Text tool, clicking the page places a text cursor. You have placed the cursor in
   the gray area outside the page so you can work on the text without accidentally disturbing the rest of your drawing.

3. Type the word **Pizza.**

4. Press Esc to finish entering text. If you planned to add more text,
   you can double-click the mouse instead. Double-clicking finishes
   the first text entry but leaves Draw in text mode so you can place
   another text cursor on the page and type another text block.

Notice that the Text tool is still selected in the Toolbox. Because the Text tool is selected, the Ribbon area displays controls you can use to change the appearance of text blocks on-screen. Click the text block you have just entered and then drag its lower right corner handle diagonally down and to the right. When you release the mouse button, the Font Size list box in the Ribbon displays the new size of the text. Change the text size to approximately 140 points tall so it is clearly visible on-screen. Another way to change the size of text is to click the text block with the Text tool and then choose a specific point size from the Font Size list box. Try this method by following these steps:

1. Make sure that the text block is selected. If the block isn't selected, click it with the Text tool.

2. Click the down-arrow button to the right of the current text size setting and then use the scroll bar to scroll down the list to 140. You can see the list only goes to 144 points. To make text larger than 144 points, you must stretch it with the pointer.

3. Click 140. The text changes to 140 points.

Another way to choose a size is to click the current size setting, highlighting the current number. Then type in the new setting (140) and press Enter.

Because the "Pizza" text will be integrated into the graphic design, you want to use a clean-lined font for this text. Appendix B of this book shows the fonts that come with Windows Draw. Follow these steps to choose a font for the text block:

1. Make sure that the text block is still selected.

2. Click the down-arrow button next to the current font name (probably Swiss) to pull down a list of font names.

3. Scroll through the list and choose the font name you want. Try choosing Dom Casual, for example. Dom Casual is a fun font well-suited for many designs, but it's too playful for this design. Perhaps the best selection is Fette Engschrift.

4. Press F on your keyboard to jump to the fonts that begin with the letter *F*.

5. Scroll to Fette Engschrift, then choose it. Your drawing with the text should now look like figure 1.36. Notice the correct font name and font size in the Ribbon area.

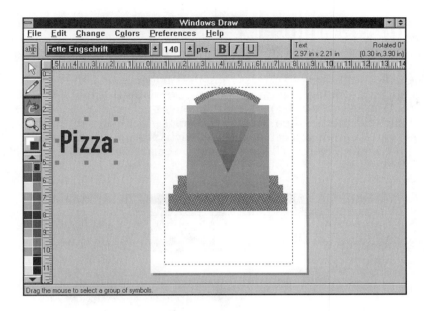

Fig. 1.36

The drawing with
the first text block
added.

Perhaps you're not yet happy with the appearance of the text. If the word looks too ordinary, using all capital letters may help. You can edit text you entered in Draw very easily. To edit the "Pizza" text block, follow these steps:

1. Make sure that the text block is selected. If not, click the block with the Text tool.

2. Click the Text Cursor button in the Ribbon area to place a text cursor in the selected text block.

3. Press the right-arrow key on the keyboard once to move the cursor after the letter *P*.

4. Press and hold the Shift key and then press the End key. This step highlights the rest of the word.

5. Hold the Shift key while you type **IZZA** to replace the highlighted text with new text.

6. Press Esc to finish editing the text.

Now the text is more dramatic and angular, with a better fit for the geometric design you have created. Two more enhancements you may want to try before placing the text on the drawing are a color gradient and a drop shadow. You can create the color gradient first.

Before you can place a gradient in text, you must convert the text to graphic objects that you can fill. The Convert to Curves command on the Change menu is designed for this purpose. To convert the text block to curves, click the block with the Text tool or the Pointer tool. Then choose Convert to Curves from the Change menu. The text does not appear to change, but the Status bar now indicates that Multiple Symbols are selected. If you move the pointer elsewhere on the page and click the mouse, then position the pointer back on the text and click, you find that you can now select each character as a separate graphic shape. Figure 1.37 shows how you can select only the character *P*, for example.

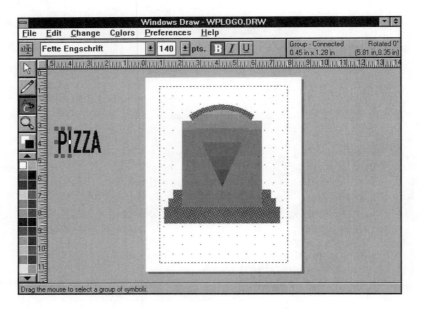

Fig. 1.37

A single character selected after text has been converted to curves.

You want to apply a gradient to all the characters, however, so draw a rubber band box that encloses all the characters. One set of handles surrounds all the text. Then follow these steps to choose a gradient:

1. Choose the Draw tool from the Toolbox.

2. Click the Fill Style button in the Ribbon area. Because you chose the vertical gradient earlier in this exercise, the gradient appears on the Fill Style menu.

3. Click the vertical gradient on the Fill Style menu. The text fills with the currently selected gradient colors.

4. Click the Color tool in the Toolbox.

5. Click the first button on the Color tool pop-out menu, the Fill Color button.

6. Choose Yellow from the Color palette to create a white-to-yellow gradient.

The other effect you may want to try is a drop shadow. A drop shadow gives the object an interesting, three-dimensional appearance. To create the drop shadow, you duplicate the object, place the duplicate behind the object, and then make the duplicate black to look like a shadow. Before you begin, though, you should group the character shapes so you can duplicate the group rather than the individual characters. The result is two groups that you can easily manipulate independently. To group the character shapes, choose Arrange Group from the Change menu. The characters don't appear to change, but the Status bar now indicates that a Group-Composite is selected.

To duplicate the group, follow these steps:

1. Choose the Pointer tool from the Toolbox.

2. Press and hold the Shift key.

3. Position the pointer on the group, press and hold the mouse button, and then drag the mouse diagonally down and slightly to the right. This step drags a copy of the group in this direction.

Here's a way to move any symbol or group of symbols in small increments. Position the pointer on a symbol and then press and hold the space bar. Now you can use the arrow keys to move the symbol in small steps vertically and horizontally.

TIP

Next you want to change the color of the duplicate and position it behind the original. Use this procedure:

1. With the duplicate still selected, click the Draw tool in the Toolbox.

2. Click the Fill Style button in the Ribbon area.

3. Choose **S**olid from the Fill Style menu.

4. Click Black in the Color palette.

5. Choose **O**rder from the **C**hange menu.

6. Choose Move to **B**ack from the Order pop-out menu. The text should look much more interesting now.

One last advisable step is to group the two groups you have just created into a single group. You can create groups within groups whenever you want to create arrangements of objects that can move independently. To group the text group and the drop shadow group, draw a rubber band box around the pair with the Pointer tool and then choose **A**rrange **G**roup from the **C**hange menu. The complete text with a drop shadow appears in figure 1.38.

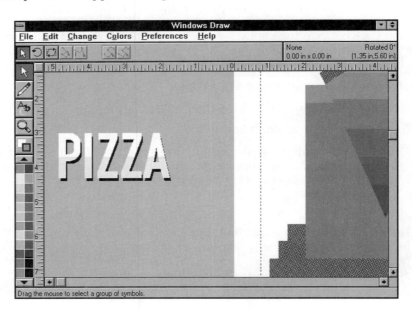

Fig. 1.38

The text with a gradient and drop shadow.

Now position the pointer in the middle of the word "PIZZA" and drag it onto the drawing, centered at the bottom of the Aquamarine box. If the text appears to slip behind the box, use Move to **F**ront to bring the text to the top of the stack of objects.

To make the text more dramatic, drag the top handle of the text group up so the text is almost as tall as the box. Drag the side handles of the group out, as shown in figure 1.39.

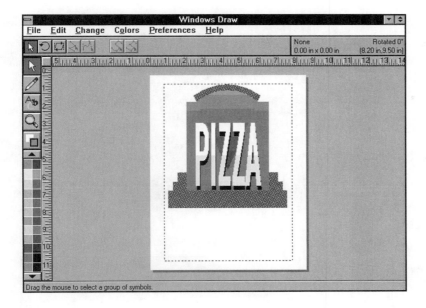

Fig. 1.39

The text placed
on the drawing
and resized.

When you stretched the text, the drop shadow moved proportionately.
The drop shadow is now too far from the text to create a subtle effect.
Fortunately, the text characters and the drop shadow are two separate
groups, so you can move the combined group back onto the gray area
and ungroup the object into two groups. Then you can reposition the
drop shadow group so it's closer to the text group. To try this technique, follow these steps:

1. Click the text group with the Pointer tool and then drag the group
   to the gray area to the left of the drawing.

2. Choose Arrange from the Change menu, then choose Ungroup
   from the Arrange pop-out menu.

3. Click in the gray area away from the text to deselect the text.

4. Click the middle of the text to select the object on top (the group
   with the color gradient).

5. Click again without moving the pointer to select the object
   underneath (the drop shadow).

6. Choose Rulers from the Preferences menu and turn off Snap to
   Rulers by clicking the check box next to Snap to Rulers. If the
   check box is already unchecked, clicking Snap to Rulers turns it
   back on. Then choose OK.

7. Press and hold the mouse button while dragging the drop shadow group closer to the top group, as shown in figure 1.40.

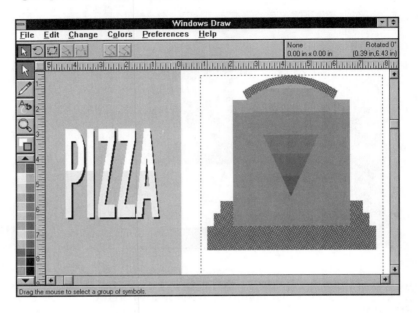

Fig. 1.40

The revised drop shadow positioning.

8. With the Pointer tool, draw a rubber band box around both groups and then use the **G**roup command to regroup them.

9. Drag the text back into position on the drawing.

Adding a Second Text Block

The only remaining task is to add the name of the proprietor, Mr. Weinberg. Choose the Text tool and then click in the gray area to the left of the drawing. Type **WEINBERG** in all caps, hitting the space bar once after each character and three times after the *N*. Then press Esc to finish entering the text. Click the text block and enter 60 points into the Font Size list box. The drawing should appear as shown in figure 1.41.

Choose Bodoni from the Font list box and click the Bold button in the Ribbon area, which displays a bold letter *B*.

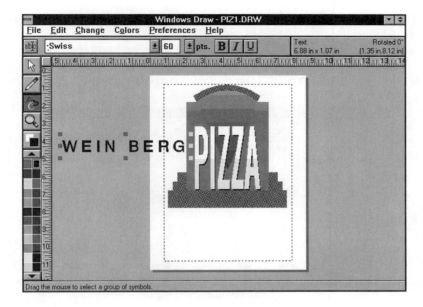

Fig. 1.41

The drawing after typing the second text block.

You can create a drop shadow to give this text a three-dimensional appearance, too, by following these steps:

1. Press and hold the Shift key.

2. Drag a duplicate of the text block diagonally up and slightly to the left of the original.

3. Click White in the Color palette.

4. Enclose the two text blocks with a rubber band box and then use the **G**roup command to group them.

5. Drag the text onto the drawing and position it on the bottom purple rectangle.

6. Drag the left and right handles of the text in to reduce the width of the block so the text fits neatly within the drawing (see fig. 1.42).

For fun, you can finish off the drawing by placing a small square in the remaining space within the second text block. To create the square, follow these steps:

1. Click the Draw tool in the toolbox.

2. Click the Rectangle button.

3. Click Yellow in the Color palette to fill the square you want to draw with yellow.

4. Press and hold the Ctrl key to restrain the rectangle you want to draw to a perfect square.

5. Draw a small square between the *N* and *B* of "WEINBERG."

6. If necessary, reposition the square by dragging it.

The correct font, size, and position for the second text block.

The final step is to group the entire collection of objects you have drawn into one large object. Then you can copy the logo into other designs and move and resize it easily. Draw a rubber band box around the entire logo and then use the **G**roup command.

Your logo is now complete. You can show Mr. Weinberg the result right on the computer screen, or you can print a color copy of the logo with a color printer. If you do not have a color printer, you can create a PostScript output file and send the file to a service bureau that can print the color image for you. You will learn about creating output files and working with service bureaus in Chapter 10, "Exporting and Importing Graphics."

Be sure to save the file the moment you finish by choosing Save **A**s on the **F**ile menu and then entering an eight-character filename such as WPLOGO (for Weinberg's Pizza Logo). Figure 1.43 shows the final logo.

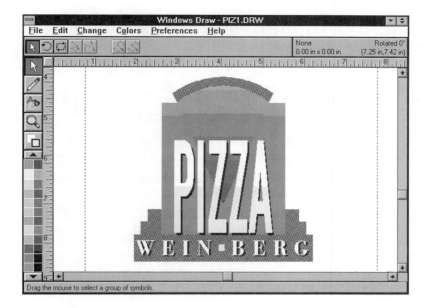

Fig. 1.43

The completed
logo for
Weinberg's
Pizza.

Printing the Logo

After you finish the logo, you can print a copy to see it on paper. If you're lucky enough to have a color printer, you will see a full-color version of the logo; otherwise, you will see a black-and-white rendition.

To print your work, choose **P**rint from the **F**ile menu. A pop-out menu enables you to choose whether to print the entire page, only selected symbols, or the current view. To print the entire page, select **P**age from the pop-out menu. Draw will send your work to the printer.

Exercise 3: Placing the Logo on the Poster

You have just learned that Weinberg's Pizza will be sponsoring the Hamptons Grand Prix bicycle race. As part of the deal, Mr. Weinberg's logo will appear on the hats and T-shirts to be given to all the entrants and on posters and advertisements promoting the event.

Copying the Weinberg's Pizza logo onto the poster you have already created is an easy task in Draw. You can even place the logo into the ClipArt library where it will be available for each advertisement you create for the event.

In this exercise, you can accomplish both tasks quickly and easily. Follow these steps to open the logo file and copy the logo to the Poster:

1. Choose **O**pen from the **F**ile menu.

2. In the Open File dialog box that appears, scroll through the Files section until you find WPLOGO.DRW.

3. Double-click WPLOGO.DRW or click it once and then choose OK. The logo appears on-screen.

4. Click the logo to select it and then choose **C**opy from the **E**dit menu. This step copies the logo to the Windows Clipboard.

5. Choose **O**pen again from the **F**ile menu.

6. Open the file GRANDPRX.DRW (the poster design). The poster design appears on-screen.

7. Choose **P**aste from the **E**dit menu. The logo appears on the page.

8. Drag the logo to the lower right portion of the poster and use a corner handle to reduce its size proportionately to fit the poster. The poster with the logo appears in figure 1.44.

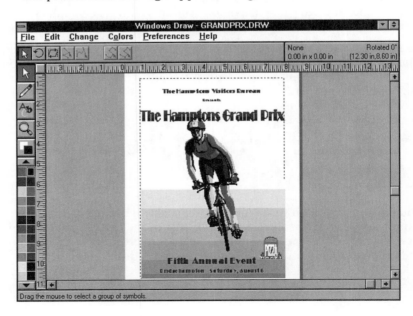

Fig. 1.44

The Hamptons Grand Prix poster with the Weinberg's Pizza logo added.

9. Save the file with the new addition by choosing **S**ave on the **F**ile menu.

Adding the Logo to the ClipArt Catalog

To make the logo easily available for any design you create, you can add it to the ClipArt catalog. Before adding the logo to the ClipArt catalog, name the logo by following these steps:

1. Open the WPLOGO.DRW file.

2. Click the logo to select it.

3. Choose **N**ame from the **C**hange menu. The **S**ymbol Name dialog box appears.

4. Enter **Weinberg's Pizza Logo**, as shown in figure 1.45, and then choose OK.

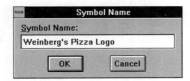

Fig. 1.45

The Symbol Name dialog box.

5. Choose **S**ave from the **F**ile menu to resave the file.

6. Choose **N**ew from the **F**ile menu to open a new file.

Now you can add the file to the ClipArt catalog.

1. Choose **C**lipArt from the **F**ile menu. The Find ClipArt dialog box appears, as shown in figure 1.46.

2. Click the Ca**t**alog button. On the ClipArt Catalog dialog box, choose **A**dd.

3. Into the **S**ubject text section, type **Logos**.

4. Use the scroll bar next to the Files section to find the file WPLOGO.DRW and double-click it, or click it once and choose OK.

5. When the ClipArt Subject Directory dialog box appears, choose OK to accept the current directory. Now you can see the new ClipArt symbol appear on the ClipArt Catalog dialog box, as shown in figure 1.47. Choose **P**review to see the symbol and then press any key to return to the dialog box.

6. Choose Cancel to close the dialog box or choose OK to add the logo to the current blank page.

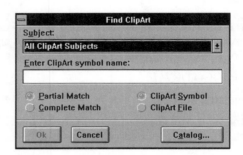

Fig. 1.46

The Find ClipArt dialog box.

Fig. 1.47

The new ClipArt subject and symbol file as they appear in the ClipArt Catalog dialog box.

Now you can place the symbol into any drawing by using the **ClipArt** command on the **F**ile menu.

Summary

In the preceding three exercises, you had the chance to try a wide variety of Draw's commands, tools, and drawing techniques. The rest of this book covers each of these features in detail. The next chapter gives you a thorough lesson on information you should know before creating your own Draw masterpieces.

Getting Started

This chapter serves as a background for your work in Windows Draw. It covers the parts of the Draw window and how to use the controls Draw provides for creating and altering objects. It also explains how to choose tools and menu commands and how to get help when you need immediate information about how a Draw command or procedure works.

Starting Windows Draw

When you install Windows Draw (Appendix A tells you how), the installation program places the Windows Draw icon in a group of icons called Micrografx in the Windows Program Manager. To start Windows Draw, double-click the Windows Draw 3.0 icon in the Micrografx group. Figure 2.1 shows the Windows Draw 3.0 icon in the Micrografx group. When you double-click the icon, the Windows Draw 3.0 window opens. Figure 2.2 shows the Windows Draw window.

NOTE   You may not be using the Windows Program Manager to start your Windows applications if you have installed another Windows shell program, such as Norton Desktop for Windows or Hewlett-Packard's Dashboard for Windows. Check the instructions for these programs to learn how to start Windows Draw.

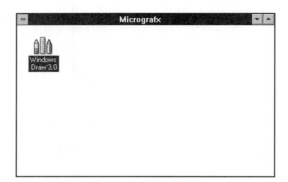

Fig. 2.1

The Windows
Draw icon.

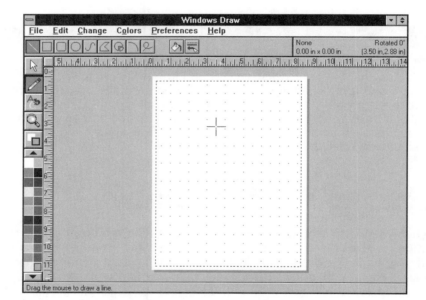

Fig. 2.2

The Windows
Draw window.

Understanding the Draw Window

The Draw window appears on-screen after you start Windows Draw. The *working area* occupies most of the Draw window. You create graphics on the image of a page, called the *drawing area*, that lies within the working area.

Located at the top of the window, the Title bar reads Windows Draw. Below the Title bar, a standard Windows Menu Bar contains the headings **F**ile, **E**dit, **C**hange, **C**olors, **P**references, and **H**elp. The toolbox, running along the upper left side of the window, provides drawing and editing tools. The Ribbon, located below the Menu bar, contains buttons and controls for the tool you are currently using. The color palette, running along the lower left side of the window, provides colors you can select for objects. Figure 2.3 shows these parts of the Draw window along with other parts discussed in detail later in this section.

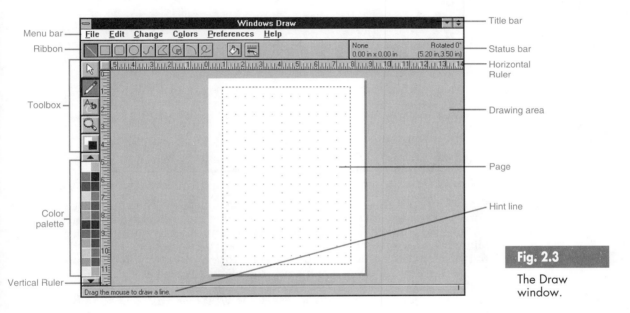

Fig. 2.3

The Draw window.

Because Windows Draw is a Microsoft Windows application, the Draw window has several buttons you can use to control the entire window. If you are familiar with Windows, you already know how to use these buttons.

The down-arrow button at the upper right corner of the Draw window minimizes the window to an icon. You can minimize a window to put it aside temporarily while working in other windows. When you are ready to return to Draw, double-click the icon to open the Draw window again.

The button containing both up and down arrows in the upper right corner of the Draw window is the *Restore button*. When a window fills the entire screen, as the Draw window does in figure 2.3, you can use the Restore button to restore it to a smaller window that occupies only a portion of the screen. The Restore button is then replaced with an up-arrow button you can click to maximize the window so that the window again fills the screen. These buttons are shown in figure 2.4.

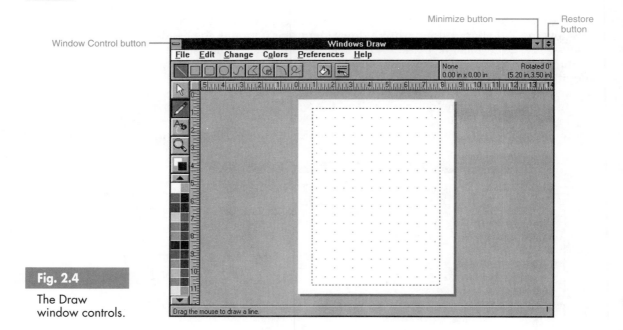

Window Control button

Minimize button

Restore button

Fig. 2.4

The Draw
window controls.

When you click the Window Control button, located at the upper left corner of the window, the Windows Control menu appears giving you options for controlling the window. Menu items enable you to Restore, Minimize, and Maximize the window so that you do not have to use the buttons for those functions. After you restore a window, you also can select the Move and Size commands to change the size and placement of the window on-screen. The Close command exits Windows Draw, and the Switch To command accesses the Windows Task List so that you can switch to another application that is running.

Instead of using the Windows Control menu, however, you can move and resize the window with the mouse. After a window is restored, a border appears around the window. By clicking on this border and holding the mouse button, you can drag the window border to a new position. When you release the mouse button, the window resizes itself within the new border position. By clicking and dragging the Title bar at the top of the window, you can move the entire window.

The Toolbox

The vertical column of five tools above the color palette is the *toolbox* (see fig. 2.5). The toolbox contains the *Pointer tool*, the *Draw tool*, the *Text tool*, the *View tool*, and the *Color tool*.

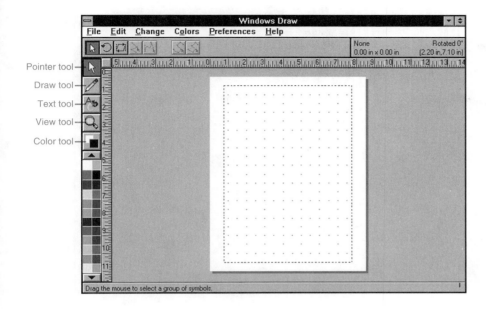

Fig. 2.5

The toolbox.

The first three tools (the *Pointer*, *Draw*, and *Text tools*) enable you to choose one of three working modes in Draw: Edit mode, Draw mode, or Text mode. You always work in one of these modes, so one of these tools is always selected. The buttons displayed in the Ribbon change depending on which mode you choose from the toolbox. When you choose the Draw tool, for example, a group of buttons corresponding to the Draw tool appears in the Ribbon (see fig. 2.6). To choose the type of graphic object you want to draw, choose one of the first nine buttons. To choose the fill that appears within objects and the line style for any lines you draw, choose one of the last two buttons (arranged in a separate group to the right). After you choose another tool from the toolbox, a different set of buttons appears in the Ribbon.

The last two tools (the View and Color tools) enable you to change some of Draw's settings while in the mode you select with one of the first three tools. You can click on these tools without deselecting the currently selected tool to change the view of the drawing area or to designate a different part of a graphic object for a color change.

The ribbon does not change when you choose the View or Color tools. Instead, it shows the buttons and controls for the current mode (determined by one of the first three tools).

Ribbon —

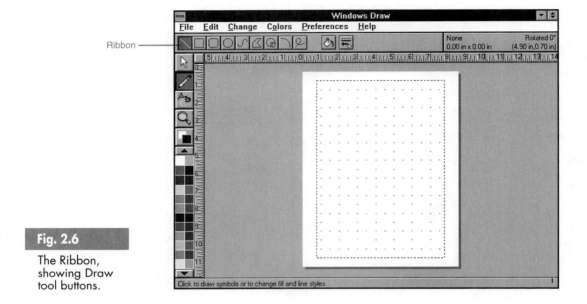

Fig. 2.6

The Ribbon, showing Draw tool buttons.

The following list describes the tools contained in the toolbox.

- The *Pointer tool*, indicated by a picture of a mouse pointer, is for selecting and editing graphic objects and text that you have already created. This tool is one of the three mode selection tools.

- The *Draw tool*, indicated by a picture of a pencil, is for drawing graphic objects on the page. This tool is one of the three mode selection tools.

- The *Text tool*, indicated by the letters ABC, is for placing text on the page. This tool is one of the three mode selection tools.

- The *View tool*, indicated by a picture of a magnifying glass, is for changing the view of the page—zooming in on an area or zooming out to view the full page, for example. You can select this tool while in one of the three modes.

- The *Color tool*, indicated by an overlapping pair of rectangles, is for selecting one of the three parts of an object for which a color is to be selected: the fill, the line, or the background. You can select this tool while in one of the three modes.

The Pointer Tool

After the Pointer tool is selected, Draw is in Edit mode. You can use the buttons that appear in the Ribbon to change the appearance of objects you have already placed on the page with the Draw and Text tools. You can select a rectangle placed on the page as part of a design, for example, and then change its size.

After you select the Pointer tool, the *Pointer tool buttons* appear in the Ribbon. Figure 2.7 shows the Pointer tool buttons.

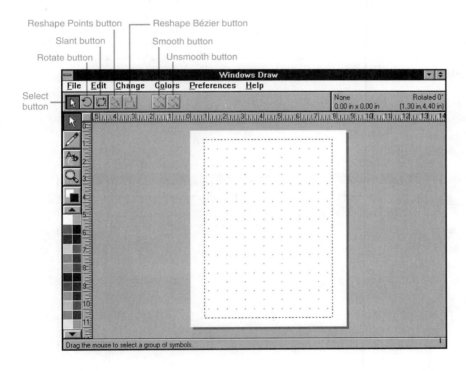

Fig. 2.7

The Pointer tool buttons.

- The *Select button* provides a pointer you can use to select objects.

- The *Rotate button* enables you to rotate objects around a pivot point.

- The *Slant button* slants objects.

- The *Reshape Points button* enables you to add, move, duplicate, delete, or break apart the anchor points that control a curve.

■ The *Reshape Bézier button* enables you to move anchor points and control points to control the shape of a curve.

■ The *Smooth button* causes curve segments to curve through anchor points to give a curve a smooth appearance.

■ The *Unsmooth button* causes curve segments to form straight lines between anchor points to give a curve a jagged appearance.

The Draw Tool

 The Draw tool enables you to add graphic objects to the page to build a drawing. You can add a circle as part of a company logo you are building, for example. After you select the Draw tool, the *Draw tool buttons* appear in the Ribbon. Figure 2.8 shows the Draw Tool buttons.

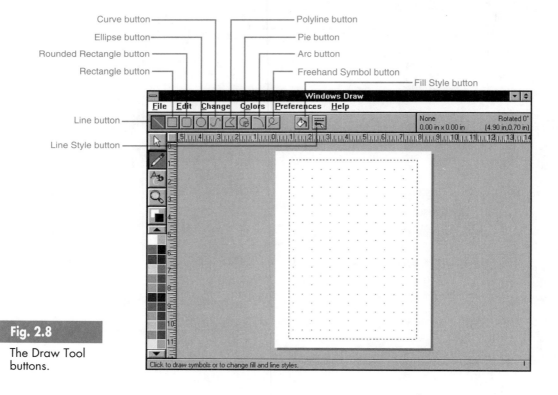

Fig. 2.8

The Draw Tool buttons.

- The *Line button* draws a straight line between two points.

- The *Rectangle button* draws a rectangle or a square.

- The *Rounded Rectangle button* draws a rectangle or square with rounded corners.

- The *Ellipse button* draws an ellipse or circle.

- The *Curve button* draws a Bézier curve.

- The *Polyline button* draws a multisegmented line or a polygon.

- The *Pie button* draws a pie chart.

- The *Arc button* draws an arc or segment of a circle.

- The *Freehand Symbol button* draws a continuous line.

The Text Tool

The Text tool enables you to place individual characters of text, words, lines, or entire paragraphs of text on the page. With the text tool, you can add a company name to a logo, for example. After you select the Text tool, the *Text tool buttons* appear in the Ribbon. Figure 2.9 shows the Text Tool buttons.

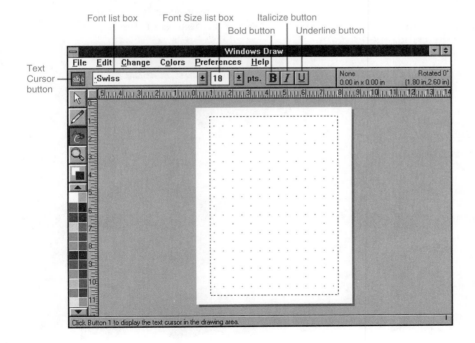

Fig. 2.9

The Text Tool buttons.

- The *Text Cursor button* causes a text cursor to appear within a selected block of text.
- The *Font list box* enables you to select a font for the selected text.
- The *Font Size list box* enables you to select a point size for selected text.
- The *Bold button* makes text bold.
- The *Italicize button* italicizes text.
- The *Underline button* underlines text.

The View Tool

 The View tool, which shows a picture of a magnifying glass, magnifies a part of the page so that you can work with a greater level of detail. This tool is especially useful if your drawing is finely detailed or if the components require very precise adjustment. You can use the View tool with the Draw and Text tools to magnify a portion of a page while you add a graphic or text.

If you choose the Draw or Text tool and then choose the View tool, the Draw or Text tool remains selected, and the View buttons appear on a horizontal pop-out menu of buttons (see fig. 2.10). To see the purpose of each of these buttons, click and hold the mouse button while you drag the pointer to each button. After you choose each button, the hint line describes its function.

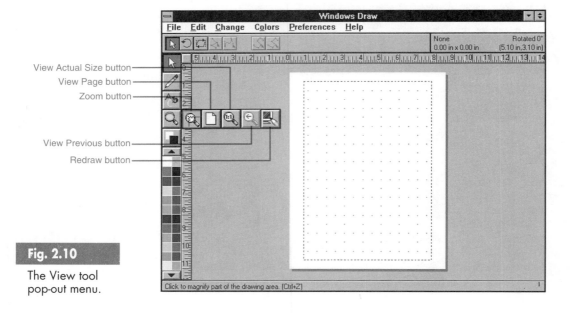

Fig. 2.10

The View tool pop-out menu.

The following list describes the View Tool buttons.

- The *Zoom button* magnifies a portion of the page by drawing a box that encloses it.

- The *View Page button* zooms out so the entire page is visible within the drawing area.

- The *View Actual Size button* displays whatever is on-screen at the actual size it will print.

- The *View Previous button* returns to the last view you were using before you changed the view.

- The *Redraw button* causes Draw to redraw all the objects on the drawing area. You can use this button to clear up the screen if parts of objects you have moved, overlapped, or deleted remain on-screen by mistake.

You also can press F3 to redraw the screen rather than click the View button and then the Redraw button.

TIP

To zoom in on a part of the page, choose the View tool and then choose the Zoom button (the first button on the horizontal pop-out menu). You also can press Ctrl-Z (for "zoom") to zoom in—press and hold the Ctrl key while you press the Z key.

Place the pointer at the upper left corner of the area you want to magnify and then click and hold the mouse button while you drag to the lower right corner. When you release the mouse button, Draw zooms in on the region you have enclosed. Figure 2.11 shows the zoom region enclosed with the Zoom tool. Figure 2.12 shows the zoomed area.

To zoom back out to a normal view of the page, choose the View button again and then choose the Page View button. Draw zooms out so that the entire page fits within the Draw window.

You also can click the View Actual Size button to display objects on-screen at the size they will print out.

You also can click the View Previous button, which shows you the last view you used. If you zoom in to a portion of the page from a full-screen view, you return to the full-screen view. Pressing Ctrl-V is the shortcut key combination for returning to the previous view.

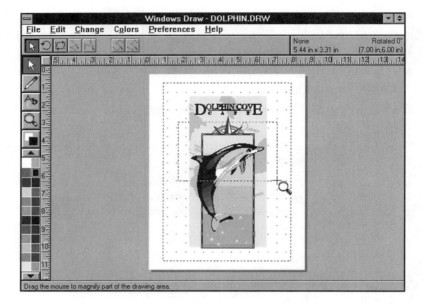

An area enclosed with the Zoom tool.

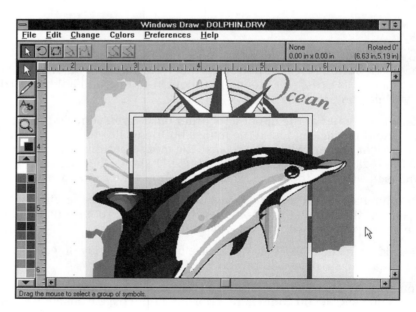

The zoomed area.

The fastest way to zoom in and then zoom back out is to press Ctrl-Z (Zoom) to select an area to zoom in on, followed by Ctrl-V (Previous View) to zoom back out.

TIP

The Color Tool

The fifth tool in the toolbox, the Color tool, also produces a horizontal pop-out menu when you click it. The pop-out menu shows only three buttons that enable you to select a color for text, graphic objects you have drawn, and color gradients. These buttons appear in figure 2.13.

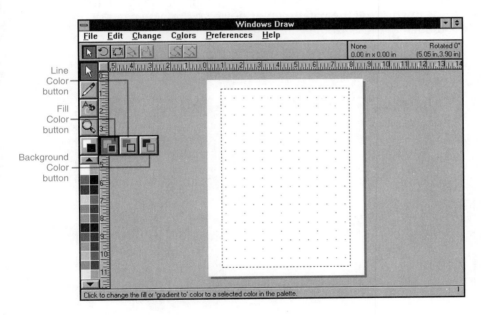

Fig. 2.13

The Color tool pop-out menu.

The following list describes the Color Tool buttons.

■ The *Fill Color button* enables you to select the color of the fill in drawn objects. The fill of a rectangle, for example, is the space in the middle. This button also enables you to select the ending color in a color gradient, which gradually fades from one color at one end to a second color at the other end. The ending color is called the "fade to" color.

- The *Line Color button* enables you to select the color of lines you have drawn or lines that surround objects you have drawn. The lines of a rectangle, for example, are the four straight sides.

- The *Background Color button* enables you to select the color of the background of a symbol or the starting color in a color gradient. The starting color in a gradient is called the "fade from" color.

The Color Palette

The *Color palette*, located at the left edge of the Draw window, contains all the colors available for the current drawing (see fig. 2.14). Because the Color palette is slightly longer than the space available for it, you must use the up and down arrows at the top and bottom of the palette, respectively, to scroll the palette up or down so that you can see the colors hidden at the bottom or top of the palette.

Color palette ⎯

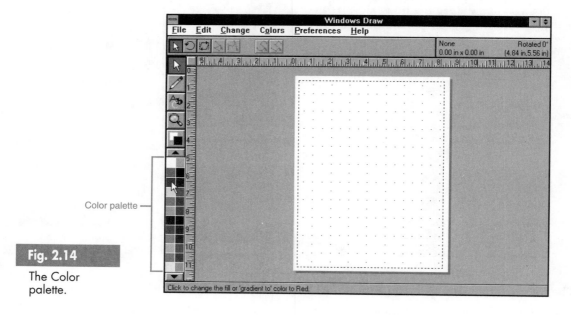

Fig. 2.14

The Color palette.

The default palette has two columns of colors. The left column contains bright colors. The right column contains darker versions of the same colors.

You can edit the color palette and even create and save a new Color palette with your own custom colors. You then can select the Color palette you need for a particular drawing. If you plan to print a drawing on a monochrome printer, for example, you can create a Color palette that contains only shades of gray. If you plan to draw in the style of Monet, for example, you may want to create a Color palette that contains soft pastels. Chapter 8, "Working with Color Palettes," explains how to use Color palettes.

The Status Bar

The *Status bar* is located at the upper right corner of the Draw window (see fig. 2.15). The Status bar displays two lines of information. The first line identifies the type of symbol you have selected and tells you the symbol's degree of rotation. The Status bar also displays how far the pointer has moved during the current operation. By checking the Status bar, you can determine how far you have moved the pointer while you draw a symbol and how long the symbol is to be. You also can tell how far you have moved an object.

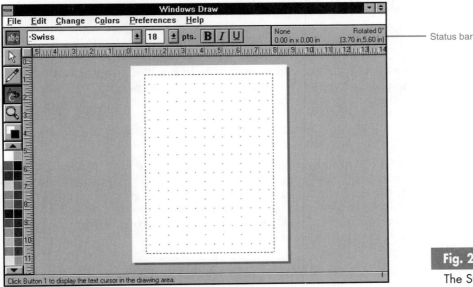

Fig. 2.15

The Status bar.

If you select a symbol you have already drawn, the Status bar tells you the dimensions of that symbol. The Status bar tells you the length and width of a rectangle and the total length of a line. The Status bar even displays the percentage change in the length of a line if you move one of the line's endpoints.

The measurement at the lower right corner of the Status bar shows the current position of the pointer as measured from the upper left corner of the page. The unit of measurement is determined by the unit of measurement you selected for the Ruler by using the Rulers command on the Preferences menu. Chapter 5, "Adding Symbols," explains how to use the Rulers command.

TIP

The yellow "ghost" lines in the horizontal and vertical rulers show the position of your pointer in the ruler. You can turn these off and on by clicking the box where the two rulers come together.

The Hint Line

The *Hint line* is located at the bottom of the Draw window (see fig. 2.16). The Hint line tells you the function of each of the tools and buttons in the toolbox. After you pass the pointer over each tool, the Hint line changes. After you press and hold the mouse button while passing the cursor over each button on one of the View and Color pop-out menus or across the buttons in the Ribbon area, the Hint line describes the function of each button. The Hint line even describes the function of an item you choose from the menu and suggests a keyboard shortcut, if one is available.

When you are not pointing to a tool or a menu item, the Hint line tells you to Drag the mouse to select a group of symbols, which reminds you that you can draw a box around a group of symbols when the Pointer tool is chosen to select more than one symbol at a time. After you select a symbol, the Hint line tells you to Drag the mouse to move the selected symbol.

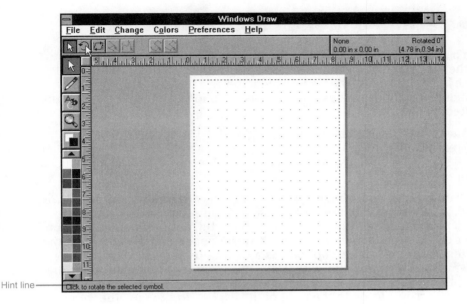

Hint line

Fig. 2.16

The Hint Line.

Selecting a Command or Tool

As you work in Draw, you must select the tools you need and the menu commands you want to use. You must use the mouse to select tools from the toolbox, but as with all Microsoft Windows applications, you can use the mouse or the keyboard to select commands from menus.

Selecting a Tool

To select a tool, place the mouse pointer on the tool and click the left mouse button once. (If you have switched the functions of the mouse buttons, click the right mouse button instead.) To select the Draw tool, for example, place the mouse pointer on the Draw tool and then click the left mouse button once. The Draw tool button appears as if it has been pressed.

Selecting a Menu Command

To select a menu command with the mouse, click the menu name and then click one of the menu items. To use the keyboard, press the Alt key and then press the underlined letter in a menu name. When the menu you choose drops down, press the underlined letter in the menu item you want.

Menu item names that end in three dots lead to dialog boxes. These boxes display several related settings you can change. After you finish changing the settings, you usually click a button labeled OK or Done, or press Enter.

Dialog box options that have round buttons next to them are either/or choices; only one of the options offered can be selected. If an option has a square box next to it (a check box), the option can be turned on or off by clicking on the box. An "X" mark appears in the box when the item is turned on. If an option has a list of alternatives, a list box (a white box with one alternative showing within the box) lies below the option name. Click the current alternative shown in the box or the down-arrow button to the right of the list box to see the other alternatives. Scroll down the list until you find the alternative you want and then click that alternative. If a setting is numeric, the list box displays up and down arrows next to the number. Click the up arrow to increase the number or the down arrow to decrease the number.

Using Keyboard Shortcuts

Draw provides keyboard shortcuts for many operations. When you use the mouse to select a menu item, the Hint line shows you the keyboard shortcut for the command, if a shortcut is available. Appendix C of this book lists the keyboard shortcuts. Keyboard shortcuts make your work speedier and more efficient.

Using Help

Windows Draw has unusually extensive and well-organized on-line help available at the touch of a key or the click of a mouse. You can obtain help on a tool, menu item, or button you are using, or you can browse through the on-line help text information and search for topics of interest.

Getting Context-Sensitive Help

To get specific, context-sensitive help on a tool, button, dialog box, or menu item, press F1 after you select the tool or button, or choose a menu item. A separate help window containing the instructions you need opens (see fig. 2.17). You also can select a tool, click the Help menu, and then choose Current Topic to get context-sensitive help.

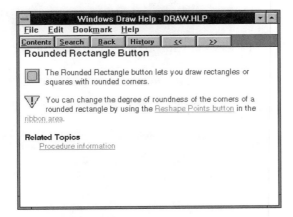

Fig. 2.17

The Help
window.

The Help window first provides a general description of the item you have inquired about. If applicable, the help information includes a numbered, step-by-step procedure you can follow to carry out a task. Special notes or caution items are preceded by an exclamation point icon. Related topics you can access for further relevant material are located at the bottom of the help information.

Certain terms in the help information are underlined with a dotted line. When you click these terms, a small window opens with a definition of the term. Click again to close the window.

Other terms and phrases are underlined with a solid line. These terms are "jump items"; they take you to another part of the help system for further information. When you click an underlined item, the help information about that item appears immediately.

Navigating through the Help System

At the top of the help window are several buttons that help you navigate through the help information. Click the Contents button to see the Master Help Index.

To return to the previous help item, click the **B**ack button near the top of the Help window. The last help information you accessed appears.

Table 2.1 Functions of the Buttons within the Help Window

Button	Function
Contents	Displays the Help contents.
Search	Lists the Help keywords that lead to specific Help topics.
Back	Takes you to the previous Help topic viewed.
History	Shows the last 40 topics viewed. You can select from the list to return to a previously viewed topic.
<<	Displays the previous Help topic in a related series of topics.
>>	Displays the next Help topic in a related series of topics.

Searching For Help Information

At any time, you can click the **S**earch button to display a list of commands and procedures that have help information. To look up a specific term, scroll through the alphabetical list within the Search dialog box to find the term and then double-click the term or click the term once and then click the **S**how Topics button. In the topics list at the bottom of the Search dialog box, you see all the topics that relate to the term. Double-click the topic you want or select the topic and click the **G**o To button. The topic appears on-screen. To print the topic, select Print Topic from the **F**ile menu. To copy the Help topic to the Windows Clipboard to paste into another Windows application, select **C**opy from the **E**dit menu. To add your own comments to the Help topic, perhaps to describe special procedures used at your company, choose Annotate from the **E**dit menu and then type comments into the text box. After you finish typing, click the **S**ave button; a paper clip appears next to the topic name. Now, whenever you click the topic name, your annotations appear.

After you finish reading a topic, you can click the **B**ack button to return to the help information you read before, or you can double-click the Window Control button at the upper left corner of the window to close Help.

Keeping the Help Window on Top

When summoned, Help appears in its own window, separate from the Draw window. This window is actually a separate Windows application that you can switch to when needed. If you are following a procedure step-by-step, however, you may want to keep the Help window on top of other windows so that you can refer to the help information at any time. To do so, choose Always on **T**op from the **H**elp menu within the Help window.

Setting Up a Drawing

Now that you are familiar with some of the basic concepts behind Draw, you can begin a real drawing. To create a drawing, you create graphic objects on the page with the tools in the toolbox. Graphic objects are called *symbols* in Draw. Symbols are drawn objects, text, and ClipArt pictures that you place on the page. Adding drawn objects is covered in Chapter 5, "Adding Symbols." Chapter 4, "Working with Text," explains how to add text symbols. Chapter 3, "Using ClipArt," explains how to add ClipArt pictures.

Each symbol is a separate graphic object. You can select a symbol and then change its fill color or the thickness of the lines surrounding it without changing other symbols. You also can stretch a symbol to change its size, and you can move a symbol to change its position on the page.

To create a complex drawing, you can group symbols of different types and colors. To create an uncomplicated drawing, such as a simple company logo, you can create several symbols, both graphic shapes and text, and then combine them into one finished work. This patient, step-by-step accumulation of symbols creates a drawing, just as many brush strokes form a painting.

This section describes how to begin a new drawing and modify Draw's settings for your needs.

Starting a New Drawing

When you first start Windows Draw, you can begin working immediately on the blank page that appears. You may want to adjust the size and orientation of the page first to match the design you have in mind, however.

If a drawing is already open in Draw, you must choose **New** from the **File** menu to start a new drawing. If you did not save the current drawing, Draw asks whether to Save changes to drawing? Click **Yes** to save the drawing with the changes, or **No** to abandon the changes. If the drawing is already saved on the disk, you lose any changes you made during the current session, but the original file is not erased.

Remember that when you open a drawing in Draw, you copy a file from the disk into the program. The original file remains on the disk until you replace it with a modified version, save a different file with the same name, or delete the file using a DOS command or the Delete command in the Windows File Manager. If you choose **New** and you do not really want to start a new file, click Cancel.

Modifying Preferences

You can modify the way Draw works by using the commands on the **Preferences** menu. You can change these settings at any time while you're working, but you may want to examine the settings briefly before you begin a drawing to be sure that they are set the way you like. Figure 2.18 shows the **Preferences** menu.

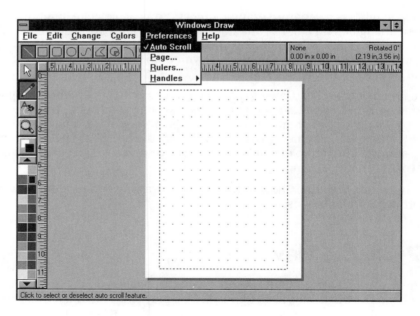

Fig. 2.18

The **Preferences** menu.

Auto Scroll

When the program zooms in to a portion of a picture, you can use Auto Scroll to drag an object beyond the displayed part of the page. The Draw window moves to follow the object. The program must zoom in to a portion of the page for Auto Scroll to work.

To drag an object beyond the edge of the page, drag it to the edge of the displayed part of the page and then just continue dragging the object in the same direction. When you bump the image against the side of the window, the window moves to follow the object.

You also can move a zoomed-in window by placing the pointer at the edge of the displayed area of the page, clicking the mouse button, and dragging in the direction you want the window to move. When the pointer reaches the edge of the displayed area, the window re-adjusts to follow the pointer.

Selecting Page Dimensions and Margins

The size and shape of the page that appears when you start a new file is determined by the settings on the Page dialog box. To see or change these settings, follow these steps:

1. In the **Preferences** menu, choose **P**age. The Page dialog box appears (see fig. 2.19).

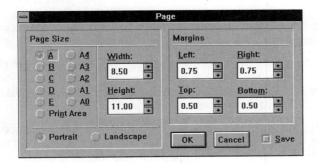

Fig. 2.19

The Page dialog box.

2. Click one of the preset page sizes.

   When you click each page size, the page width and height appear. A standard letter size page (8 1/2" x 11") is A. If you want an irregular page size, enter custom width and height measurements by using the up and down arrows next to each measurement to increase or decrease the numbers that appear in the boxes. You also can click the current measurements and type in new ones.

The following table lists the Page Size settings and their corresponding page sizes.

Table 2.2 Page Size Settings for Various Page Sizes

Page Size Setting	Portrait Page Size	Landscape Page Size
A	8 1/2 x 11 in.	11 x 8 1/2 in.
B	11 x 17 in.	17 x 11 in.
C	17 x 22 in.	22 x 17 in.
D	22 x 34 in.	34 x 22 in.
E	34 x 44 in.	44 x 34 in.
A4	21 x 29.7 cm.	29.7 x 21 cm.
A3	29.7 x 42 cm.	42 x 29.7 cm.
A2	42 x 59.4 cm.	59.4 x 42 cm.
A1	59.4 x 84.1 cm.	84.1 x 59.4 cm.
A0	84.1 x 118.9 cm.	118.9 x 84.1 cm.

3. Choose the orientation by clicking Portrait (vertical) or Landscape (horizontal).

4. Change the margins by clicking the margin measurement numbers and typing in replacement numbers. You also can click the up or down arrows next to each number to increase or decrease the numbers.

   The margin settings are the space from the edge of the physical page to the edge of the active area on the page within which you will work. The default margins for a laser printer are .75 inches left and right, and .50 inches top and bottom.

   If you click the Print Area button, however, Draw reduces the margins to give you the largest possible active area on the page on which your printer can print. If you use a Hewlett-Packard LaserJet Series II laser printer, for example, the margins change to these settings: Left: .20 inches; Right: .30 inches; Top: .25 inches; and Bottom: .22 inches. A Hewlett-Packard LaserJet Series II cannot print any closer to the edges of the paper than the preceding margins. If you use a Hewlett-Packard LaserJet Series III, the margins are .25 inches all around.

5. If you want the current settings to become the new default settings, choose **S**ave in the Page dialog box. Each time you start a new drawing, Draw uses the same settings until you change the settings and choose **S**ave again. If you don't choose **S**ave, the current settings apply only to the current drawing.

6. After you check the Page settings, choose OK.

The appearance of the page readjusts to conform to the new Page settings. Examine the rulers to confirm that the page re-adjusted correctly.

Customizing the Ruler

In addition to customizing the page size, you can customize the appearance of the rulers. You may want to work in centimeters rather than in inches. You also may want to work in tenths of an inch rather than in sixteenths of an inch.

To change the rulers, follow these steps:

1. From the **P**references menu, choose **R**ulers. The Rulers dialog box appears (see fig. 2.20).

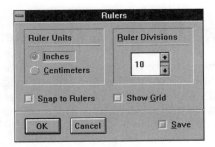

Fig. 2.20

The Rulers dialog box.

2. Choose **I**nches or **C**entimeters as the Ruler Units by clicking the appropriate option.

3. Increase or decrease the number of **R**uler Divisions between each measurement by clicking the up or down arrow next to the current number or by double-clicking the current number and typing in a new number.

   If you choose **I**nches for the Ruler Units, for example, and 10 as the number of **R**uler Divisions, you will see 10 small marker lines between each inch marker on the ruler. This type of ruler division is sometimes referred to as *decimal inches*.

If you choose **C**entimeters for the rulers, Draw displays measurements in the status bar in centimeters, too.

4. If you want the pointer to jump to the nearest ruler increment as you draw symbols, choose **Sn**ap to Rulers. If you set the Ruler Units to **I**nches and the **R**uler Divisions to 4, for example, the pointer jumps to the nearest quarter inch across or down the page.

5. If you want a grid displayed, choose Show **G**rid. This option causes a pattern of dots to appear on the page at the same intervals as you have selected for Ruler Units and Ruler Divisions. If you chose **I**nches for Ruler Units and 10 for **R**uler Divisions, for example, Draw spaces the dots of the grid 1/10 inch apart.

6. Click OK to use the current settings. If you click **S**ave in the Rulers dialog box before you click OK, the changes you make to the settings become the default until you change them again and click **S**ave again.

The grid serves two purposes: It shows where the pointer snaps to if you have turned on **Sn**ap to Ruler, and it gives you a visual system for precisely placing objects on-screen by eye.

Saving and Retrieving Drawings

As you create drawings, try to become accustomed to saving your work-in-progress often. That way, should something go wrong with your computer, you retain a copy of your work on disk that you can retrieve if necessary.

Saving a Drawing

To save your work, choose **S**ave from the **F**ile menu. The Save File dialog box appears (see fig. 2.21). The cursor is flashing in the **S**ave file as text box. Type a name for the file in the text box. This name can be up to eight characters. Click the Save button.

If you have already saved your work and you want to save a copy with a different name, choose Save **A**s from the **F**ile menu. Type a new name for the file in the **S**ave file as text box and then click the Save button. You can use up to eight characters in the file name, but you need not supply a three-letter file extension because Draw supplies the file extension DRW.

Fig. 2.21

The Save File
dialog box.

> **CAUTION:** If you type a file extension other than DRW, Draw
> saves the file with the extension you entered, but the file does not
> display on the list of drawings you see when you select **O**pen on
> the **F**ile menu. To open the file, you must supply its full name,
> including the file extension you gave it.

To save a file to another drive or to a floppy disk, click the drive name
that appears on the list in the Save File dialog box. Draw displays a list
of drawings on the drive you choose. Double-click the **S**ave File As text
box, and type the name of the file you want saved on that drive. To
save a file to a disk in drive A, for example, select [-A-] in the list of
drives below the **S**ave File As text box, and type the name of the file you
want to save on the diskette in the text box. Then click the Save button.

To save the file into a specific directory, double-click the current drive
name in the path name that is displayed just above the Save button.
Then double-click the directory you want on the list of directories that
appears in the dialog box. If you usually save files to a directory called
DRWWORK on drive C, for example, but you want to save a file to
C:\PROJECTX, double-click C in the path name C: \DRWWORK, and then
double-click [projectx] on the list of directories.

Opening a Drawing

To open a drawing you created earlier, choose **O**pen from the **F**ile
menu. The Open File dialog box appears (see fig. 2.22). The **F**iles list

box, near the bottom right of the dialog box, displays a list of files in the current directory. If the file you need is in a different directory, use the **D**irectories control to change directories. To go up one directory in the directory structure (to the parent directory), double-click the double dot at the top of the list ([. .]). To enter a specific directory, double-click its name. To set the current directory as the default directory, click the **S**ave check box before clicking the OK button.

Fig. 2.22

The Open File
dialog box.

TIP

You also can double-click the path name displayed near the bottom left of the Open File dialog box, just above the OK button, to change the current directory. To save a file to the directory just above the current directory in the directory structure, double-click that directory name within the path name.

To open a selected file, double-click the file name, or click the file name and then click OK.

Exiting Windows Draw

After you finish using Windows Draw, choose E**x**it from the **F**ile menu, or double-click the Window Control button at the upper left corner of the Draw window, to close the Draw window. You also can press Alt-F4 to close the Draw window, but make sure that the Draw window is the active window by clicking it before pressing Alt-F4, because Alt-F4 closes only the active window.

Summary

This chapter discussed the Windows Draw window and covered some of the basic concepts to keep in mind when you start using the program. In the next chapter, you learn to use the extensive catalog of ClipArt that comes with Draw.

Using ClipArt

One of Draw's greatest attractions is its extensive selection of predrawn pictures called ClipArt. You can use these ClipArt selections to adorn your work, or you can use them as the centerpiece of a drawing and add text and other symbols to complete the work. For example, you may add a personalized message to a ClipArt selection of a Christmas tree to create your own Christmas cards. Or, you might add your company logo, created in Draw and saved in the ClipArt catalog, to one of the ClipArt business forms for use in your office.

Draw's 2,600 selections of ClipArt are so varied that you will probably find selections to enhance just about any graphic you create. Draw's ClipArt includes people, places, and everyday home and office items. Selections also include borders, signs, maps, graphs, and far too many other topics to list. Figure 3.1 shows a few sample ClipArt selections.

In this chapter, you learn how to browse through the visual catalog of ClipArt and how to use the ClipArt catalog to search for a selection by name. You learn to place selections on the page and ungroup them to modify individual components. You also learn to save your drawings in the ClipArt catalog.

Browsing the ClipArt Catalog

The ClipArt catalog contains the entire library of ClipArt images. The catalog is a clever, visual database of images with some of the capabilities of a standard database program. You can browse through the catalog until you find the image you want, or you can search the catalog to find an image by type or by name.

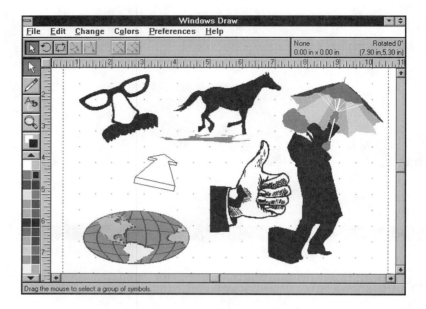

Fig. 3.1

Sample ClipArt
selections.

ClipArt selections are grouped into Draw files that reside on your
system's hard disk. The Draw files are organized in the catalog by subject. Files that contain images relating to holidays, for example, are
grouped together under Holidays. This hierarchical structure makes
the catalog easy to use because you can select a subject and then examine only the files that contain images that relate to the subject.

Finding clip art in the Draw ClipArt catalog is easy. Even if you don't
know the exact image you want, you can start by examining all the images under a particular subject. By starting in the general category of
images that might be suitable, you can scan through the names of individual ClipArt selections until one strikes you. Then you can preview
the image to see whether it fits your needs.

To find a ClipArt selection, follow these steps:

1. From the File menu, select ClipArt. The Find ClipArt dialog box
   appears (see fig. 3.2).

   The Find ClipArt dialog box provides controls that you can use to
   search by name through the ClipArt catalog. This dialog box also
   provides a Catalog button that enables you to browse for a
   selection.

Fig. 3.2

The Find ClipArt dialog box.

2. Click Catalog. The ClipArt Catalog dialog box appears (see fig. 3.3).

    The ClipArt Catalog dialog box shows three fields. The first field contains a subject name. The second field contains a list of files that are related to the subject in the first field. The third field shows the ClipArt symbols that are in the selected file.

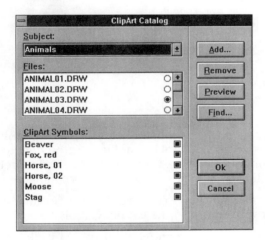

Fig. 3.3

The ClipArt Catalog dialog box.

3. Click the down arrow at the right end of the Subject box to pull down the subject name list.

4. Click the subject you want. For this example, click Cartoons.

    The second field shows a list of files that pertain to the subject.

5. Click a file on the list so that you can examine the ClipArt symbols inside. In this case, click the file CRTOON13.DRW.

Figure 3.4 shows the symbols list. The file contains cartoons of male heads. One of these heads is perfect for the drawing you will create.

CAUTION: If you have not installed this ClipArt file, Draw displays the message Could not find the file CRTOON13.DRW. Use the install program to install the ClipArt subject cartoons.

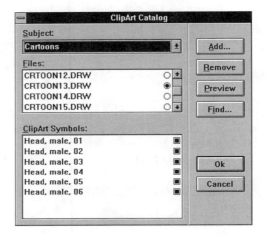

Fig. 3.4

The ClipArt
symbol list.

Previewing ClipArt

When you first select a ClipArt symbol file, all the symbols on the list are selected. A selected symbol has a filled button next to it. To see all the selected symbols, click the **P**review button. The selected symbols appear in the ClipArt Catalog window, as shown in figure 3.5.

The message Press any key to return at the bottom of the window reminds you how to return to the list of symbols.

You also can select a single symbol to preview by clicking it and then clicking the **P**review button. Or, you can compare more than one symbol selection side-by-side. In fact, you can preview as many symbols as are in a ClipArt file by following this procedure:

1. In the list of symbols, click the first symbol to display.

2. Hold down the Ctrl key while clicking the next symbol to display. Continue clicking the other symbols you want to preview.

3. Click the **P**review button.

The preview shows only those symbols that you have selected.

The previewed images appear across the window in rows so you can compare the symbols you have selected. If you see a symbol you like, press a key and then preview individual symbols until you find it.

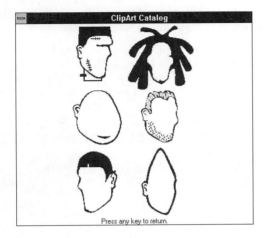

Fig. 3.5

Symbols pre-
viewed in the
ClipArt Catalog
window.

From the list, choose the symbol named Head, male, 04 and then click OK. The ClipArt symbol appears on the Draw page, as shown in figure 3.6. The symbol appears centered on the page at the size it was originally drawn.

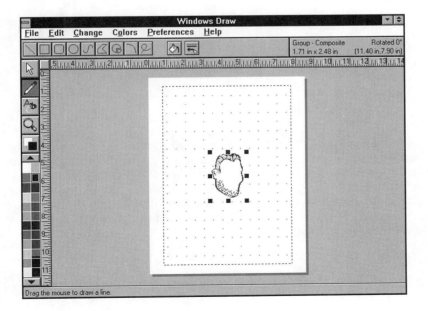

Fig. 3.6

The ClipArt
symbol as it
appears on the
page.

Moving and Resizing ClipArt

Because ClipArt symbols first appear at the center of your page, you almost always need to move them to a different position to fit with the rest of the drawing. You also may need to resize the ClipArt symbols.

You can resize a symbol by dragging any of the eight handles surrounding that symbol. When you drag a corner handle, the image changes size but maintains its proportions (see fig. 3.7). When you drag one of the side handles, the image changes shape, becoming wider or narrower, taller or shorter, as shown in figure 3.8.

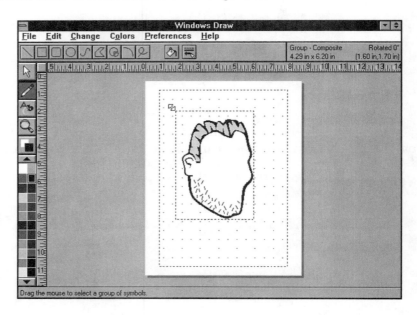

Fig. 3.7

Resizing a symbol proportionately by dragging a corner handle.

To try one example of resizing a ClipArt symbol, put the cursor on the handle at the upper left corner of the symbol. The pointer changes to a double arrow when it is directly on the handle. Drag diagonally toward the upper left corner of the page. Stop when the handle is just within the blue margin line and release the mouse button. Then do the same with the lower right corner handle, but drag that handle to the lower right corner. The symbol now fills the area of the page within the margins, as shown in figure 3.9.

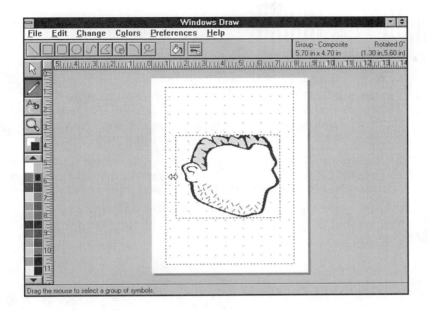

Fig. 3.8

Stretching a
symbol by
dragging a top
or side handle.

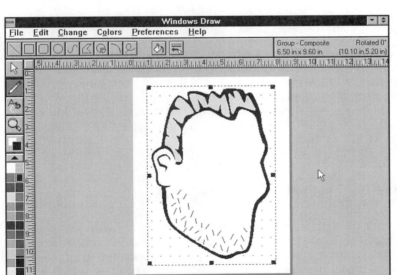

Fig. 3.9

The symbol
stretched to fill
the page.

To try another example of moving and resizing a symbol, drag the lower right corner handle back up and to the left. See if you can reduce the symbol to its former size.

To move a symbol, follow these steps:

1. Put the pointer in the middle of the symbol. Notice that the pointer now shows a four-way arrow to indicate that you can move the symbol under the pointer. The hint line tells you to `Drag the mouse to move the selected symbol`.

2. Click and hold the mouse button and drag the entire symbol. For the example, drag the symbol to the upper right so that its upper right corner aligns with the upper right margin corner.

3. Release the mouse button to drop the symbol in the new location. The symbol is now positioned at the upper right corner of the page.

TIP If you hold the mouse button a moment (without moving the mouse) after you select a symbol, an outline of the symbol appears. You can use this outline to help position the symbol.

Now you have had a chance to try resizing and repositioning a symbol. Before continuing, take a moment to resize the symbol so it fills the page. In the following sections, you will place additional symbols on this symbol to complete a picture of a face. To resize the symbol so it fills the page, position the pointer on the symbol's lower left corner handle and drag it to the lower left margin corner. The image fills the page within its margins.

Searching the Catalog

To come up with the ClipArt symbol of the male head, you browsed through the ClipArt catalog. You can use a search procedure to find ClipArt symbols when you know which symbols you need. For the current example, you need a mouth, nose, and pair of eyes to finish the head. (This guy already looks like he will have a few scars, too.)

Searching For Specific Pieces of ClipArt

When you know what kinds of symbols you need for your drawing, use Draw's search capabilities. These capabilities enable you to search for symbols by name.

To search for ClipArt symbols, follow these steps:

1. From the **File** menu, select ClipArt. The Find ClipArt dialog box appears.

2. Type a name for a symbol into the second text box (next to Enter ClipArt symbol name). For this example, type **mouth**.

   Before clicking OK, you can change the options in the Find ClipArt dialog box to define the search.

3. Choose between the two options that determine which symbols (or files) will be found:

   ■ Choose **C**omplete Match if you want to find only those ClipArt symbols that have the name you have entered—in this case "mouth."

   ■ Choose **P**artial Match if you want to find every ClipArt symbol name that contains the name you have entered. The search might find symbols named Smiling mouth, Grinning mouth, and Mouthwash. By selecting **P**artial Match, you can be sure to find every ClipArt symbol that has the word "mouth" in its name. Partial Match is the default setting; do not change the setting for this example.

4. Select between the following two options in the dialog box that enable you to distinguish between searching for a symbol and searching for a file:

   ■ Choose ClipArt **F**ile to search for a file. For example, you might be aware of a file called Noses. After the search finds that file, you can browse through it for the symbol you need.

   ■ Choose ClipArt **S**ymbol to search for a symbol. ClipArt **S**ymbol is the default setting; do not change it for this example.

The dialog box should now look like figure 3.10.

Fig. 3.10

The Find ClipArt
dialog box.

5. Click OK to begin the search.

    If only one symbol matches the search criteria you have entered,
    the symbol is placed on the page. If Draw finds more than one
    symbol, it tells you with a message box that it has found multiple
    files that match the search criteria, in this case "mouth" (see
    fig. 3.11). Draw asks whether you want to view the list of files it
    has found. You can click OK to view the list or click Cancel to
    enter different search criteria.

Fig. 3.11

The multiple
matches message
box.

6. Click OK to see the search results.

    Draw creates a temporary subject called Search Results. You see
    it in the **S**ubject field. In the **F**iles field, Draw lists all the files that
    contain a symbol that has "mouth" in its name (see fig. 3.12).

7. Click the files until you find the one you want. When you click a
    file, its symbols appear in the ClipArt Symbols list. As you encoun-
    ter symbols that may meet your needs, you can select them and
    then click **P**review to see the symbols.

    For this example, click GROCER02.DRW. Notice that the symbol
    "Mouthwash" matches the search because it contains "mouth,"
    but that's not the kind of mouth you need. Look in the ClipArt file
    CRTOON16.DRW by clicking its file name and then clicking the
    Preview button.

    Because all the symbols in CRTOON16.DRW are selected, you see
    all the symbols in the preview, as shown in figure 3.13.

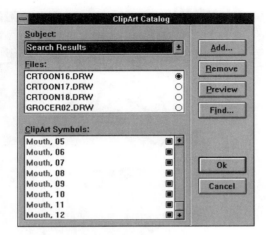

Fig. 3.12

Files found under
the Search
Results subject.

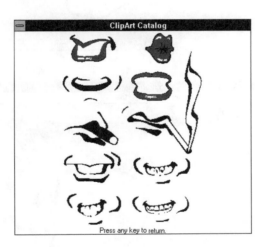

Fig. 3.13

The preview of
the symbols in
CRTOON16.DRW.

8. Press any key to return to the list of symbols.

9. Select the symbol you want from the list. If necessary, use the scroll
   bar at the right side of the list to move to the desired symbol.

   In this case, select Mouth, 16. Then click **P**review again just to be
   sure you have selected the correct file. Press a key after you have
   seen the preview.

10. Click OK to place the symbol on the page, as shown in figure 3.14.

11. Move and resize the symbol to the proper position. The drawing
    should look like figure 3.15.

Clicking on the page away from the symbol deselects it.

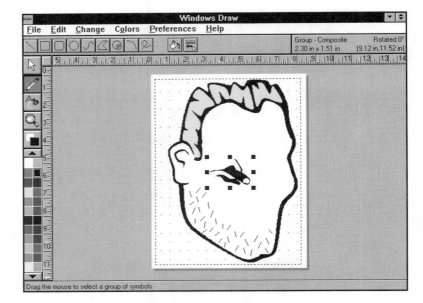

Fig. 3.14

The drawing with the mouth added.

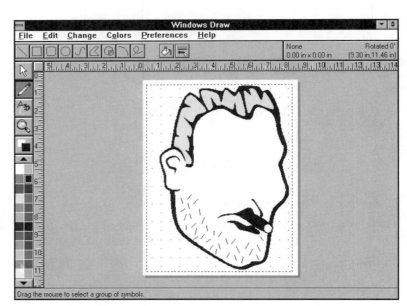

Fig. 3.15

The drawing with the mouth properly positioned.

Adding More ClipArt Symbols

You can add an indefinite number of symbols to a drawing. ClipArt provides many files from which you can select symbols to incorporate into your work. As you browse through a subject to find a symbol, you may want to narrow the number of possibilities by using the Find button. The following example demonstrates this procedure while adding another symbol to the example.

The next step in the example is to add a ClipArt symbol of a nose. To add the nose, select ClipArt from the File menu. Then click the current subject and select Cartoons from the pull-down list. Click the Catalog button at the lower right corner of the dialog box to browse for the proper nose symbol.

As you scroll through the list, you see that it contains 25 cartoon files. You can click each file sequentially and examine the file names on the list until you find files named "nose." That process is tedious, however, and you're a busy person. If you discover many symbol files under a ClipArt subject, you can click the Find button to use the catalog's searching facility to search through them. After you click the Find button, type **nose** in the Enter ClipArt symbol name text box. Click OK.

The ClipArt Catalog dialog box now shows only files that contain symbols with "nose" in their names. Notice that the file CRTOON23.DRW is highlighted. Click **P**review to see the symbols in the file. Before selecting from among these symbols, you may want to preview the other symbol file. Press a key to return to the list and select the next symbol file, CRTOON24.DRW. This file contains Clown nose, which is not the type of nose you need. Instead, click CRTOON23.DRW again and click **P**review. Figure 3.16 shows the symbols you will see.

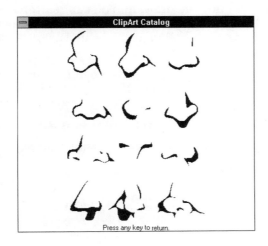

Fig. 3.16

The preview of CRTOON23.DRW.

The first nose looks the most interesting, so scroll to the top of the list by using the scroll bar to the right of the list. Click the first symbol name, Nose, 01 and then click OK to place the symbol on the page. The drawing should look like figure 3.17.

The drawing with the nose added.

Modifying ClipArt

Something is wrong with this picture. Either this guy needs a nose job, or you had better modify the drawing. You can rearrange the mouth so that it faces in the same direction as the nose, or rearrange the nose so that it faces in the same direction as the head. For this example, rearrange the nose.

To accomplish this task, use the **F**lip command on the **C**hange menu. When you flip the nose horizontally, it faces toward the right instead of toward the left.

To use the **F**lip command, follow this procedure:

1. Click the symbol to select it. Frame handles appear around the symbol.

2. From the **Change** menu, choose **Flip**.

The right arrow next to the Flip command tells you that an additional menu appears when you choose **Flip**. The pop-out menu gives you the choice between flipping the image horizontally or vertically. A horizontal flip changes the right side for the left (or the left side for the right, depending on how you look at it). Figure 3.18 depicts a horizontal flip. A vertical flip turns the picture upside down. Figure 3.19 shows a vertical flip.

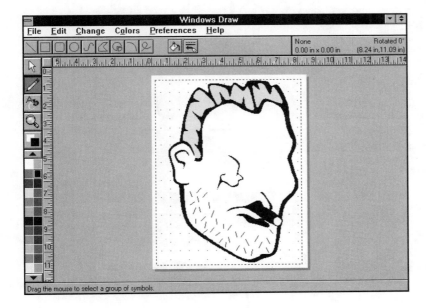

Fig. 3.18

Flipping the symbol horizontally.

3. Choose the direction in which you want to flip the symbol. For this example, choose **Horizontally** from the Flip pop-out menu to turn the nose symbol so it faces toward the right.

4. Move and resize the nose to fit the face, as shown in figure 3.20.

Adding Multiple ClipArt Symbols

So far, you have pulled one ClipArt symbol at a time from a ClipArt file. You can pull more than one symbol at at time from a file, though. This capability will be helpful in the example to add two eye symbols to create a pair of eyes for the face.

Fig. 3.19

Flipping the symbol vertically.

Fig. 3.20

The nose properly positioned on the face.

To find the eyes, follow these steps:

1. From the File menu, choose ClipArt.

2. Scroll through the list of subjects in the Find ClipArt dialog box and select the subject you want. In this case, select Cartoons.

3. Into the Enter ClipArt symbol name text box, type a term to match. In this case, type **eye**.

4. Be sure to choose the appropriate Match setting—**P**artial or **Com**plete. In this case, make sure **P**artial Match is chosen so that the catalog finds all symbols that contain the term "eye." **P**artial Match finds symbols that contain "eyes" as well as "eye."

5. Choose ClipArt **S**ymbol or ClipArt **F**ile, as is appropriate. For this example, make sure that ClipArt **S**ymbol is chosen to search for symbol names that contain the term "eye."

6. Click OK to begin the search and then click it again when Draw asks whether you want to view the multiple search results.

   The ClipArt Catalog dialog box appears. You see that CRTOON19.DRW is selected and that it contains a number of symbols with the word "Eye" (see fig. 3.21).

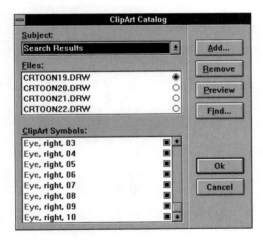

Fig. 3.21

The list of symbols in CRTOON19.DRW.

7. Click the **P**review button to see all the symbols that are selected (all the symbols in the file are selected).

   The preview shows ten pairs of eyes arranged in five rows. The face we're putting together deserves none other than the first pair of eyes in the third row because they're so clearly shifty and mean, and they coordinate perfectly with the hook nose you have already selected (not to mention the unshaven face).

Press any key to return to the symbol list. Scrolling through the list, you see 20 separate symbols in the file: 10 left eyes and 10 right eyes. You have to choose both a left eye symbol and a right eye symbol to create a matching pair.

The pair of eyes you want consists of two symbols: Eye, left, 05 and Eye, right, 05. Both symbols are on the list, but not next to each other. To choose two symbols from the list, follow these steps:

1. Click one symbol. In this case, click Eye, left, 05.

2. Hold down the Ctrl key while scrolling down the list and clicking the other symbol. In this case, click Eye, right, 05.

3. Click **Preview** to confirm that you have the correct two symbols. If you're following the example, your preview should look like figure 3.22. You always can delete an incorrect symbol and start again. When you finish previewing, press any key to return to the list.

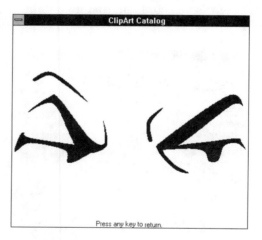

Fig. 3.22

The correct pair of eye symbols.

4. Click OK to place the symbols on the page.

The two eyes are separate symbols; but because you have pulled them from the catalog together, they are surrounded by one set of handles. Therefore, you can click and hold the mouse button anywhere within the handles and drag both eye symbols to the correct position.

Grouping ClipArt

Draw comes with a special command called **G**roup that can combine two or more symbols into a single object. The objects still retain their individual identities and can be separated later, but while they are grouped, they can be acted on with the commands of Draw as though they are a single object.

The symbols are part of a group, so you cannot make changes to any one symbol. Any change you attempt affects the entire group. One advantage is that after you have grouped a symbol, you can make a change to the entire set of symbols at once. When you select a group and change its color, for instance, all the component symbols change color. Another advantage is that the objects stay arranged just as they were when you grouped them, even if you resize or move the group. After you have grouped a number of objects to form a logo, for example, you can use the **G**roup command to create a single object that you can easily move and resize to fit wherever you need it on the page.

To confirm that the eyes in the example are two separate symbols, try clicking the nose and then one of the eyes. Just as promised, only the selected eye is surrounded by frame handles. If you group the two eye symbols, you can resize them and reposition them together. Both eyes resize to the same degree so that neither eye is larger than the other.

To group two symbols, follow these steps:

1. Click one of the symbols to select it.

2. Hold down the Shift key while clicking the other symbol to select it. Notice that the handles now surround the two objects.

3. From the **C**hange menu, select **A**rrange and then select **G**roup from the pop-out menu.

Group the eyes following the above steps. Now, you can resize and reposition them as a single unit. Take a moment to move and resize the mouth, nose, and eyes so that they fit properly on the face. Use figure 3.23 as a guide.

For further practice, try deleting the mouth symbol by clicking it and then pressing Del. Then, select different mouths from the catalog and see the result. Figure 3.24 shows a few samples you might create.

Now that you have completed the face, you may want to take a moment to group all of the symbols that it contains. When all the symbols are grouped into a single object, you can more easily move and resize the object. To select all the symbols for grouping, choose **S**elect All from the **E**dit menu. This action selects every symbol in the drawing. Then, use the **G**roup command.

Fig. 3.23

The correctly positioned mouth, nose, and eye symbols.

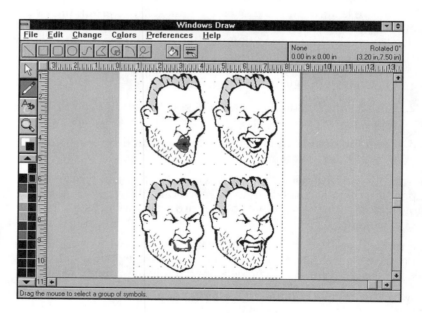

Fig. 3.24

Sample faces with different mouth symbols.

The shortcut key for **S**elect All is F2. Press F2 to select all the symbols in the drawing. You will see a single set of handles surrounding all the symbols.

TIP

Ungrouping ClipArt

When none of the ClipArt images in the catalog seems to fit your needs just right, keep in mind that many of the 2,600 selections are actually composites of several symbols. These selections consist of several individual objects, any one of which can be used. One of the buildings in a cityscape ClipArt symbol might be just what you need, or three of the people in a ClipArt symbol that shows a meeting of four people might be just the ticket.

Depending on how the ClipArt selection was created, you may be able to take it apart and delete everything you do not need. Taking some of the symbols apart is possible because their individual components were drawn as separate objects. After the separate objects were drawn and arranged together, the artist grouped the symbols into a single object with the **G**roup command. Think of a group as a family portrait. You squeeze together all the aunts and uncles for a single picture, but they still retain their separate identities. After the shot, they go about their business as separate and unique entities. In a similar fashion, the **G**roup command retains the individual identity of each of the components while they are grouped in an object.

Just as the **G**roup command groups symbols into a single object, the **U**ngroup command separates those symbols into individual objects. By ungrouping a ClipArt symbol that is composed of several symbols, you can select a single symbol and discard the rest. Or, after a composite group has been ungrouped, you can select and modify each of its individual symbols separately. Perhaps the symbol would be more fitting if it showed your company's colors. By ungrouping the symbol, you can change the colors of each of the component symbols individually.

To try ungrouping a symbol, start a new file by choosing **N**ew on the **F**ile menu. Then, perform the following steps:

1. Choose ClipArt from the **F**ile menu, and then choose a subject from the **S**ubject list. For this example, choose Holidays.

2. In the Enter ClipArt symbol name text box, type a symbol name, and then press Enter. In this case, type **father's day**. Because only one Holiday symbol has the words "father's day" in its name, the symbol appears on the page (see fig. 3.25).

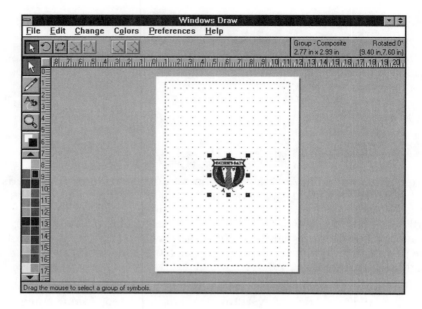

Fig. 3.25

The Father's Day
Sale symbol.

3. Click the View button in the Toolbox, and then choose the Zoom tool (the far left tool on the pop-out menu).

4. Draw a rubber band box around the symbol with the Zoom tool. Draw zooms in on the symbol, as shown in figure 3.26.

Fig. 3.26

A zoomed view
of the symbol.

5. To confirm that the symbol is a group of separate objects, click it. Notice that the status bar at the upper right identifies the symbol as a `Group - Composite`.

6. Ungroup the composite group by choosing **A**rrange from the **C**hange menu and then selecting **U**ngroup from the pop-out menu.

The symbol does not appear to change, but the status bar now should read `Multiple Symbols`. You can now click one of the symbol's components and modify it. In fact, what you want to do is to remove the words "Father's Day" so that you have a symbol with a blank placard. Now you can use the symbol for any holiday by simply entering the holiday name on the placard with the Text tool.

To modify and then regroup a composite symbol, follow these steps:

1. Click the words Father's Day. Frame handles surround the text, as shown in fig. 3.27.

2. Press Del to remove the text and make space for other text.

3. To regroup the drawing, choose **S**elect All from the **E**dit menu.

4. From the **C**hange menu, choose **A**rrange. Then choose **G**roup from the pop-out menu. The status bar should now read `Group - Composite` again. This message confirms that you have successfully regrouped the objects.

Because you need this drawing for the examples in following sections, save it with the name "Menssale."

Saving a Drawing in the Catalog

After creating any drawing, you can store it in the ClipArt catalog for later use. Your company's logo is an ideal candidate for the ClipArt catalog, for example. You can then put your company's logo on any drawing that you create simply by retrieving the logo from the ClipArt catalog.

Saving a Drawing As a ClipArt Symbol

To add a drawing to the catalog as a symbol, you must give the drawing a name and save it in a standard DRW file. Then you can add the drawing to one of the existing subjects in the catalog or create your own subject.

In the preceding section, you altered the Father's Day Sale symbol to make it more generic. You might want to store the new drawing in the catalog to use whenever your store wants to run a sale. But before you can save the drawing in the ClipArt catalog, you must name it. First, open the file containing the drawing that you want to save, unless that file is already open. For this example, open the MENSSALE file. Then follow these steps to name the drawing:

1. Select the drawing that you want to save.

2. From the Change menu, choose Name.

3. In the Symbol Name text box, type a name of up to 80 characters. Then press Enter or click OK. For this example, type **Generic Men's Sale Logo**.

4. Save the file again by choosing Save from the File menu.

Saving the Symbol in the Catalog

Before you can add the new symbol to the catalog, you will need to take one more step. Close the file that contains the symbol by choosing New from the File menu. When Draw starts a new file, as you have instructed it to do, it closes the current file. Now you can add the symbol to the catalog without causing an error message that informs you of a Sharing Violation in Windows.

Having named and saved a symbol in a file, you can now save it to the ClipArt catalog. To save the symbol to the catalog, perform the following steps:

1. From the **F**ile menu, select ClipArt.

2. In the Find ClipArt dialog box, click the C**a**talog button.

3. In the ClipArt Catalog dialog box, click the **A**dd button. The Add ClipArt dialog box appears, as shown in figure 3.28.

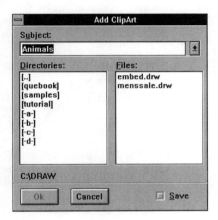

Fig. 3.28

The Add ClipArt dialog box.

4. To create a new subject, type the name of the subject—**Ads**, for instance—in the S**u**bject field.

   If you want to add the symbol to an existing subject, click the existing subject name.

5. Use the **D**irectories and **F**iles controls to navigate to the file you want—in this case, MENSSALE. Then double-click the file name.

You can add more than one file to a subject by selecting all the files before clicking OK. Hold down Ctrl while selecting each file. If the files that you need are in a list one after another, you can select the first file, hold down Shift, and then click the last file on the list.

TIP

6. When the ClipArt Subject Directory dialog box opens, which enables you to select a directory for the subject file, accept the directory in the text box by pressing Enter or clicking OK.

In the example, you have now created a new subject called Ads that contains the Men's Sale symbol. To confirm that the file exists, press Esc to cancel out of the dialog box and then choose ClipArt from the File menu. Select Ads from the list of subjects and click the Catalog button. You see the file MENSSALE.DRW on the list of files and the symbol name on the list of ClipArt symbols, as shown in figure 3.29.

Adding a Symbol to an Existing ClipArt File

Each ClipArt file can contain as many symbols as you want, although you probably want no more than a dozen in any one file. Keeping the number of symbols to a dozen or less lets you easily preview all the symbols in the file simultaneously.

When you add the ClipArt file to a subject in the catalog with the Add button, as described in the previous section, all the named symbols in the file appear on the list of ClipArt symbols in the file. To add more symbols to the same ClipArt file, create the symbols or composite groups of symbols. You can create the symbols within the file (on a different part of the page) or create the symbols in their own files and then copy them into the ClipArt file. Then give the new symbols their own names with the Name command on the Change menu and save the ClipArt file.

After you have closed the ClipArt file by starting a new file, you must add the ClipArt file to the subject again. Click the **A**dd button in the catalog, and then select the ClipArt file even though it is already in the catalog. Draw tells you that the file is already cataloged and asks whether you want to update the subject. Click **Y**es, and Draw adds the symbols to the ClipArt file in the catalog. Press Esc or click Cancel to leave the ClipArt Catalog dialog box.

Following is a step-by-step procedure you can follow to try adding an additional symbol to the MENSSALE.DRW ClipArt file. First, you add a second symbol to the file by following these steps:

1. Start a new file by choosing **N**ew from the **F**ile menu.

2. Create a symbol on the page. For this example, use the ClipArt catalog to select the symbol called "Sale, marquee," 04 in the ClipArt file named SIGNS11.DRW. (We can pretend that you created this ClipArt image.)

3. Choose Name from the **C**hange menu. You see the current name of the symbol.

4. Replace the current name with the new name. In this case, type **Sale** for the new name and click OK.

5. Select the symbol and then choose **C**opy from the **E**dit menu to copy the symbol to the Windows clipboard. You also can press the Ctrl-Ins key combination rather than choosing **C**opy.

6. From the **F**ile menu, select **O**pen. When Draw asks whether to Save changes in drawing?, click **N**o.

7. Select the file to which you want to copy the ClipArt symbol. In this case, select MENSSALE.DRW from the list of files.

You can choose **R**ecall from the **F**ile menu and then choose the file you want from the pop-out list of previously saved files. The pop-out menu lists the last nine files you have saved.

TIP

8. Select **P**aste from the **E**dit menu to paste the symbol from the Windows clipboard onto the page. You also can press Shift-Ins to paste the symbol.

9. Select the symbol that you pasted and drag it above or below the symbol that is already on the page. To see the entire page, click the View tool and then click the View Page button (see fig. 3.30).

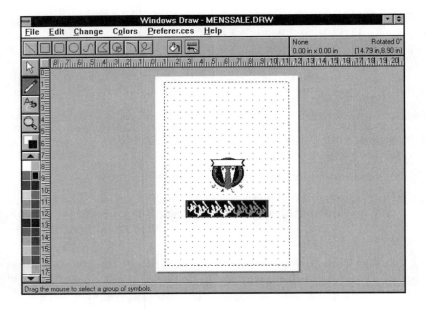

10. From the **File** menu, choose **S**ave to resave the file with the same name.

11. From the **File** menu, choose **N**ew to clear the current file from the screen.

Now, you're ready to add MENSSALE.DRW to the catalog again. When you do, the new symbol will appear on the symbol list. To add MENSSALE.DRW, follow these steps:

1. From the **F**ile menu, choose **C**lipArt.

2. Click the C**a**talog button.

3. Select a subject. In this case, click the subject text box to highlight the current entry, and then press the A key to see the first entry that begins with *A*. The subject "Ads" appears.

4. Click the **A**dd button to bring up the Add ClipArt dialog box.

5. Select the file that you want to add to the subject. In this case, double-click MENSSALE.DRW.

6. Click **Y**es when Draw informs you that the file has already been cataloged and asks whether to update the subject.

Now you see the new symbol join the existing symbols. In this case, the symbol named "Sale" joins the Generic Men's Sale Logo symbol on the list. If you click the **P**review button, you see the two symbols just as they're arranged on the page in the file.

Removing ClipArt from the Catalog

You probably will not want to remove any of the ClipArt selections that come with Draw; however, you may want to remove ClipArt selections that you have created, but no longer need. For example, you may want to remove the logos of clients with whom you no longer do business. You may even want to remove ClipArt that somebody else has left on your system.

When you remove ClipArt from Draw, you remove it from the ClipArt catalog. You do not delete the ClipArt files from your hard disk; however, they no longer show up in the catalog.

You can delete a ClipArt subject or a ClipArt file, but you cannot remove individual ClipArt symbol names from the catalog. Instead, you must manually delete the symbol from the file, remove the file from the catalog, and then add the file back into the catalog without the symbol. The file name reappears in the catalog, and only the names of the symbols that are actually in the file reappear on the symbols list.

To remove a ClipArt symbol file or subject, follow these steps:

1. From the **File** menu, select **ClipArt**.

2. Use the controls of the ClipArt Catalog dialog box to find the ClipArt file or subject that you want to remove.

3. Click the **R**emove button. Draw displays a small menu with two choices: Selected **F**ile and Selected **S**ubject. If you want to remove a file, make sure that the file name is selected on the list.

4. Choose Selected **F**ile or Selected **S**ubject. Draw removes the ClipArt file or subject from the list.

If you remove a ClipArt file, you can modify the contents of the file— add new symbols, delete symbols, or change the names of existing symbols—and then add the ClipArt file back into the catalog, assigned to the same or a different subject.

Using the ClipArt Maps

Draw's ClipArt maps give you the flexibility to select a single country or geographic location, or to select several countries in a geographic area and display them in correct proximity to one another. Your selections can even be displayed against a black shadow of the entire geographic region.

Draw comes with eight geographic maps that include the countries or regions in Africa, Antarctica, Asia, Australia, Europe, North America, South America, and Southeast Asia. Each map consists of individual ClipArt symbols that are arranged according to their actual locations on the globe.

These symbols are arranged on top of a single object in the shape of the entire continent or geographic region. By selecting only the shadow symbol, you get a solid black object in the shape of the entire continent, as shown in figure 3.31.

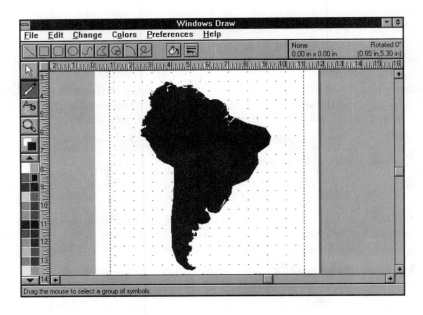

A shadow symbol.

By selecting individual countries, you get only those countries in their proper arrangement, as shown in figure 3.32.

By choosing certain countries and also choosing the shadow, you get the chosen countries highlighted against a black shadow of the entire continent, as illustrated in figure 3.33.

The three following series of steps provide practice exercises that enable you to see how Draw's maps work. To create a shadow area, perform the following steps:

1. If you have any other symbols on-screen, select New from the File menu to start a new file.

2. From the File menu, select ClipArt.

3. From the list of subjects in the ClipArt Catalog dialog box, select Maps.

4. Click the Catalog button.

5. Click MAP04.DRW in the list of ClipArt files.

6. From the list of ClipArt symbols, select Europe, shadow.

7. Click the **P**review button. The shape of Europe appears in the preview window, as shown in figure 3.34.

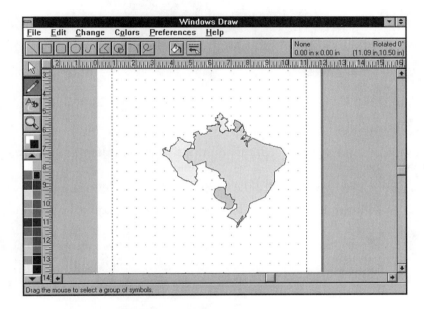

Fig. 3.32

Countries arranged in proper proximity to one another.

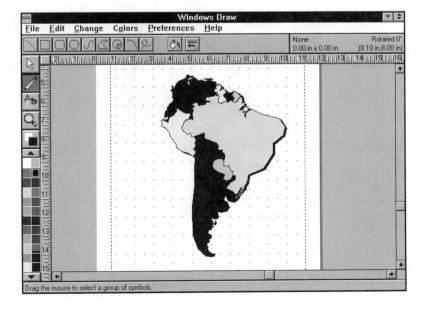

Fig. 3.33

Country symbols and the shadow symbol of the region.

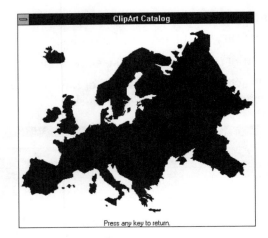

Press any key to return.

Fig. 3.34

The Europe
shadow symbol.

Now to add specific highlighted countries to the continent's shadow, follow these steps:

1. Press any key to return to the ClipArt Catalog dialog box.

2. Hold down the Ctrl key and select Austria, Finland, Spain, and the United Kingdom from the list of symbols.

3. Click the **Pr**eview button. Notice that Draw superimposed these countries on the shadow of Europe to show their respective locations (see fig. 3.35).

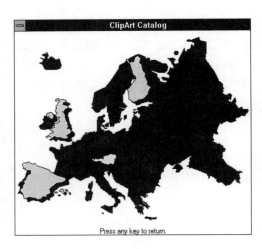

ClipArt Catalog

Press any key to return.

Fig. 3.35

European country
symbols super-
imposed on the
Europe shadow
symbol.

After previewing a map drawing, you may decide to deselect one or more of the included symbols. To deselect symbols, follow these steps:

1. Press any key to return to the ClipArt Catalog dialog box.

2. Hold down the Ctrl key and click Europe, shadow in the symbol list to deselect it.

3. Click the **P**review button to see that Draw has removed the shadow. Now you see only the countries, arranged in proper proximity to one another, as illustrated in figure 3.36.

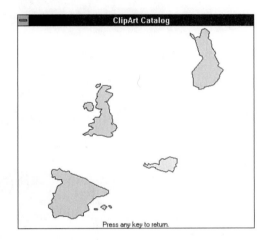

Fig. 3.36

The country symbols previewed.

You can select any one country or several countries that are in the same regions, place them on a page, and then use the **G**roup command to be sure that they don't change position relative to one another even when you move or resize the composite group.

When you're finished previewing the ClipArt, press any key to return to the ClipArt Catalog dialog box and then click Cancel to remove the dialog box. To use what you saw in the preview, you could have clicked OK at any time.

NOTE To find landmarks that are identified with certain countries and cities, such as the Eiffel Tower of Paris, be sure to examine the symbols in the files under the Landmarks subject. You also can find globes of the world in the file LANDMK09.DRW.

Summary

In this chapter, you learned how to use the vast catalog of drawings created by professional artists that is included with Draw. For many projects, you may be able to create the designs you need simply by using ClipArt selections and text. You may never actually need to draw.

In the next chapter, you learn to create and modify text that you can incorporate into drawings.

Working with Text

Windows Draw gives you extensive control over the text that you want to incorporate in a drawing. Entering text is easy, as is changing its font, character styling, and size. You can even convert text characters to curves that can be reshaped, repositioned individually, and filled with colors and color gradients. And if a plain, straight line of text is too tame for the design you need, you can have text follow the curve of a symbol. Figure 4.1 provides a sampling of some of the text effects you can create.

In this chapter, you learn how to enter and edit text, how to change its character and paragraph formatting, and how to create special text effects by using some of Draw's advanced text handling capabilities.

Entering Text

To enter and edit text in a drawing, use the Text tool from the Toolbox. When you click the Text tool, the Ribbon area at the top of the screen becomes filled with special text controls that enable you to vary the font, size, and character styling of text that you're about to create or that already exists on the drawing (see fig. 4.2).

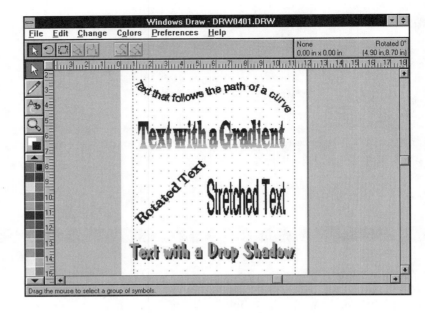

Fig. 4.1

Sample text effects.

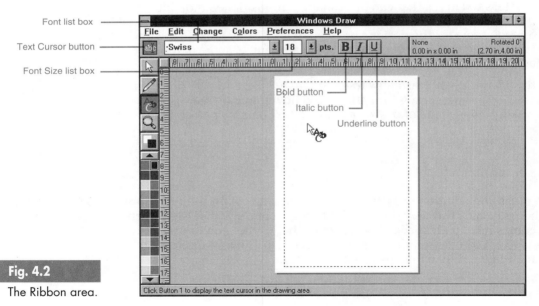

Font list box

Text Cursor button

Font Size list box

Bold button

Italic button

Underline button

Fig. 4.2

The Ribbon area.

To enter text, select the Text tool and then click the page at the spot where the text should begin. Before you begin typing text, you can change the settings in the Ribbon area to affect how the text will appear. You may want to choose a font and size for the text and determine whether the text is boldfaced, italicized, or underlined. Or, you can simply type the text and modify its appearance after it is on-screen.

Before you try entering text, save any work you have been doing in Draw and then choose **New** from the **File** menu to start a new drawing. Click the Text tool after the new blank page appears. When you move the mouse pointer onto the page, you see that the pointer is accompanied by the *Abc* design of the Text tool, which signifies that a text cursor will appear when you click the mouse (see fig. 4.3).

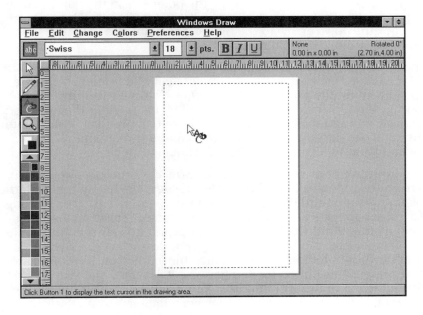

Fig. 4.3

The pointer in text mode.

In the Ribbon area near the top of the page, you see a control for choosing a font and a font point size. When you click the down arrow to the right of the font name or click the font name field, a pull-down menu of font choices appears (see fig. 4.4). Use the scroll bar to move up and down the list. The fonts that appear on the list are those that have been installed in your copy of Windows. If a type manager is installed, such as Adobe Type Manager (ATM) or Bitstream Facelift for Windows, you

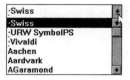

Fig. 4.4

The font list box.

may see a substantial list of font names. Even if you don't have a type manager installed, you still see the fonts that come with Windows (Arial, Times New Roman, and others) and the fonts that come with Draw. See Appendix B for a list of the fonts that come with Draw.

For practice, choose Vivaldi from the list of fonts. Then, from the list of point sizes, choose 60. You can type the point size in the point-size field or choose the size from the pull-down list. To pull down the point size list, click the down arrow to the right of the point-size field. Use the scroll bar to move down the list.

A point is the unit of measurement of type. Most printed text in books and magazines is between 9 and 11 points tall. Old-fashioned electric typewriters usually produce 12-point type. You can enter text into a drawing at any size, from 4 points up to 144 points. After the text is on the page, you can stretch it still larger, even to more than 2,000 points when you use the largest page size available. For reference, 72 points equals 1 inch, so 60 points is a little less than 7/8 inch.

After you have chosen a font and point size, click the page where you want the text to begin. Try this by clicking near the left margin with the pointer, about a third of the way down the page. Notice that a flashing text cursor appears on the page. The text cursor (called an insertion point in other Windows applications) appears because the Text Cursor button is selected automatically every time you select the Text tool. The Text Cursor button is the button at the left end of the Ribbon area. Draw presses this button for you because it assumes that you intend to add text to the drawing or edit existing text every time you select the Text tool. In the next section, you see what happens when the Text Cursor button is not pressed.

To try entering text, type **Water Mill** and press Enter. Then type **Symphony** to create two lines of text, as shown in figure 4.5.

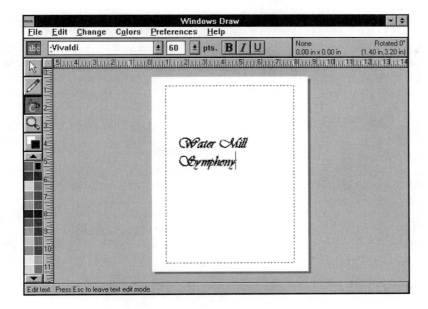

Fig. 4.5

Two lines of text
added to the
Draw page.

Editing Text

Because the Text Cursor button is still activated, you can click anywhere within the text to move the text cursor to where you need to
make changes. To move the cursor within the text, click where you
need the cursor positioned or press the arrow keys on the keyboard.
The Home key moves the text cursor to the beginning of a line and the
End key moves the cursor to the end of a line. To delete text to the
right of the cursor, press the Delete (Del) key. To delete text to the left
of the cursor, press the Backspace key.

To enter text on the page at another location, press Esc and then click
the Text Cursor button with the mouse. Now you can click somewhere
else on the page and get a text cursor. Or, you can click existing text
and insert a text cursor for editing. Rather than press Esc and then
click the Text Cursor button, you can double-click with the mouse.

Try using the double-click method by double-clicking the mouse button, moving the mouse lower on the page, and clicking once to place a
text cursor. Now type **Gala Benefit** and press Esc. Everything looks
fine, but the benefit coordinator who happens to be looking over your
shoulder informs you that the benefit will be called "The Gala."

To make this correction, click *Gala Benefit* to select it and then click the Text Cursor button. This procedure places a text cursor at the beginning of the text block. Type **The** followed by a space. Then move the cursor just after the word Gala and hold down the Shift key while pressing the right-arrow key to highlight the word *Benefit*. Press the Delete key. Now you can press Esc, double-click the mouse, or go to the Toolbox and select a different tool for a different task. For now, press Esc to leave text editing mode.

Typed text is automatically inserted because Draw is always in Insert mode unless you press the Insert key to toggle to Overwrite mode, which causes new text to overwrite existing text. When you press the Ins key to toggle to Overwrite mode, the cursor becomes a block on top of the text that will be overwritten when you type new text.

Understanding Text Blocks

After you leave text editing mode, the mouse pointer is a standard pointer that you can use to select an entire block of text, move it, or stretch its size. The words *Water Mill Symphony* comprise a single text block even though the text appears on two lines. To confirm this, make sure the Text Cursor button in the Ribbon area is no longer activated (if it is active, click the button once to deactivate it) and then click the text block. You see a single set of handles that surround the entire block, as shown in figure 4.6.

You have always learned that, when using a word processor, pressing Enter at the end of a line starts a separate paragraph. In Draw, however, pressing Enter starts a new line but keeps the text in the same text block. The advantage of a single text block is that it can be manipulated as one object. The disadvantage is that the lines of text remain locked in position relative to one another. Draw provides no control for changing the distance between successive lines of text to bring them closer together or spread them a little farther apart. Many word processors and desktop publishing programs that work only with text provide a line-spacing control.

Another technique for entering text solves this problem. Press Shift-Enter to start a new line instead of Enter. This key combination places each line you type into its own text block. Then, after you have entered the blocks, you can move them closer together or farther apart by dragging them. You can still move the lines as a group by selecting them all. Remember that when you select several objects, Draw puts handles around the temporary group just as though you had used the **G**roup command to combine the objects into a group. You can always use the **G**roup command to lock the objects into position relative to one another.

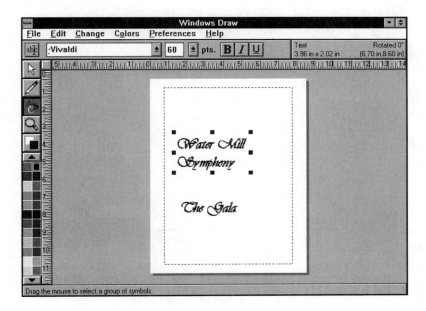

To use the Shift-Enter technique for entering text as separate blocks, follow this procedure:

1. Click somewhere on the page background to deselect any selected text.

2. Click the Text Cursor button.

3. Click once in a blank area of the page to place the text cursor.

4. Type **Water Mill**.

5. Press Shift-Enter.

6. Type **Symphony**.

7. Press Esc to leave text editing mode.

Now try clicking the lines of text you just entered. Notice that each line is a separate block. You can drag the second line up so that it is closer to the first block, as shown in figure 4.7. You can even draw a box around both lines with the pointer and use the handles to manipulate both lines as a temporary group. You learn about manipulating text blocks with the handles in the following section.

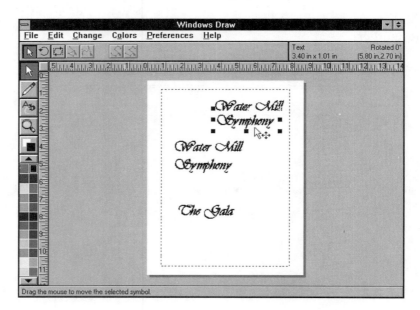

Fig. 4.7

Dragging text blocks close together.

Working with Text Blocks

You can move and stretch text blocks just as easily as you can move and stretch symbols. When you click a text block or select several text blocks, a set of handles appears around the block. To move the block, place the pointer within the block, click and hold the mouse button, and then drag the block. When the pointer is within the block, a four-way arrow appears. To stretch the text block, click and hold one of the handles and drag it. When you place the pointer on a handle, the pointer becomes a double-headed arrow.

When you stretch a text block, the text inside stretches to fill the block. If you drag a corner handle, the text changes size but stays proportionate to its original shape. By dragging a top or side handle, on the other hand, you can create stretched text that looks very different from normal text. Such stretching can create the illusion of different text typefaces even when you stretch text only a small amount.

Unfortunately, Draw does not indicate the degree to which you have stretched a block of text, so you do not have an automatic way to stretch multiple text blocks uniformly. But you can create several text blocks that have the same stretch factor by duplicating one block and editing it.

To create a text block with the same stretch factor as another block, perform the following steps:

1. Add a block of text and press Esc.

2. Click the block and then stretch it to the size that you want. Figure 4.8 shows a stretched text block example.

Fig. 4.8

A sample stretched text block.

3. Hold down the Shift key and click the text block. Then, while holding the mouse button, move the mouse pointer to another part of the screen.

    This procedure drags a copy of the text block to the new position (see fig. 4.9).

4. Release the mouse button.

5. Click the Text Cursor button at the left end of the Ribbon area to place a cursor within the text block.

6. Press Shift-End to select the text in the second block, as shown in figure 4.10.

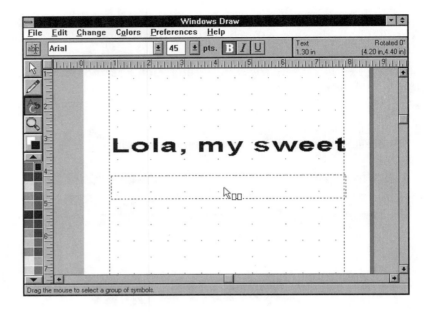

Fig. 4.9

Duplicating a text block.

Fig. 4.10

Highlighting the entire text block.

7. Type the text for the second block. The new text replaces the highlighted text, but the block retains the same stretch factor.

Figure 4.11 shows the two blocks of text stretched to the same degree.

Fig. 4.11

Two text blocks with the same stretch factor.

You can use this same technique to duplicate a text block any time you want a second block that has the same text formatting as the first, including the same font, text styling, and paragraph formatting. Then you can simply edit the text in the duplicate.

TIP

Using the Text Editor

To edit text, you click the Text Cursor button and then click within a text block to place a text editing cursor. But if you press Shift while clicking a text block, a window called the Text Editor opens at the top of the screen, as shown in figure 4.12.

The Text Editor displays the contents of the text block in the easy-to-read Windows system font. After you finish editing text in the Text Editor, press the Esc key or click somewhere on the page to close the window and place the revisions on the page.

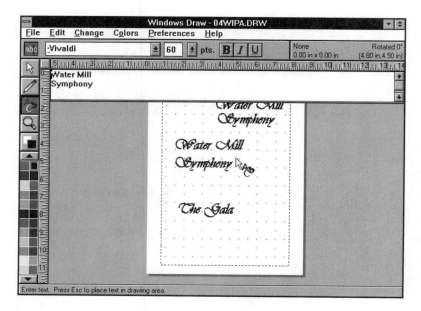

Fig. 4.12

The Text Editor
window.

While editing in the Text Editor window, you can use the Delete and
Backspace keys to delete text and the mouse cursor to select text to
revise. You also can select text and use controls from the Ribbon area
to alter the text's appearance. The Text Editor does not show these
type-style changes but does underline any text that has been changed.

The Text Editor opens automatically when you click text that is too
small to read or text that has been rotated. As a general rule, text
smaller than eight points in a full page view is displayed in the Editor.

Changing Character Formatting

When you know how text should be formatted, you can select the type
style and text attributes before you enter the text. But to change the
appearance of characters that you have already placed into a text
block, click the Text Cursor button and then select only those characters that you want to change. After selecting the characters, you
can use the controls in the Ribbon area to modify the characters'
appearance.

Changing the Font

The font list box in the Ribbon area enables you to choose from among the fonts available for use in Draw. Windows 3.1 provides a starter set of fonts. These fonts include Arial (a version of the old favorite Helvetica) and Times New Roman (a version of the popular Times Roman). Draw adds another 32 TrueType fonts to the Windows 3.1 collection. Because these fonts are installed into Windows, they become available to all of your Windows applications. If you use Microsoft Word for Windows to create documents, for example, you will see the same new TrueType fonts on Word's font list.

Draw provides two types of fonts. The fonts that are preceded by a dot on the font list are Bitstream fonts. You can use these fonts with either Windows 3.0 or Windows 3.1. The other fonts are TrueType fonts that you can use only with Windows 3.1. Both Bitstream and TrueType fonts can be stretched to any extent and rotated on-screen, which makes them ideal for use in drawings with text characters that you want to compress, rotate, or stretch.

You can choose a font for text before you enter the text or after the text is already on the page. To choose a font for text you are about to enter, follow these steps:

1. Select the Text tool from the Toolbox.

2. To pull down the font list, click the down arrow next to the font name field in the Ribbon area bar.

3. Scroll to the font you want by using the scroll bar.

4. Click the font name.

Draw uses the font that appears in the Ribbon area to format text that you then put on the page with the Text tool.

To change the font of text that is already on the page, you can click a text block to change the font of an entire block, or select specific characters from within a text block to change only those characters.

To change an entire text block, click the text block to select it. To select only certain characters, click the Text Cursor button and then click a text block to move the cursor to it. Select the desired characters within the text block, as shown in a magnified view in figure 4.13. After the characters are selected, choose a font from the font list in the Ribbon area.

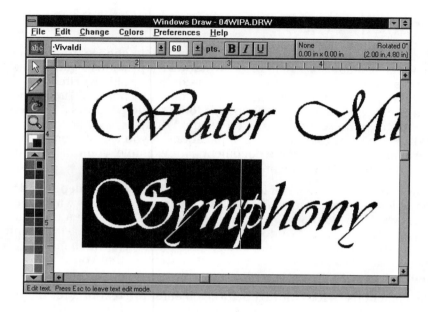

Fig. 4.13

Selecting
characters with
the text cursor.

Changing the Point Size

While a text block or individual text characters are selected, you can
choose a point size for them from the font size list box in the Ribbon
area. Click the down-arrow button to the right of the point-size field to
see a list of even-numbered point sizes. On the odd chance that you
need a point size that is not even, you can click the point-size field, type
a new size, and press Enter.

You can type any point size up to 144 points, but you must use a whole
number. Draw does not accept decimal values such as 10.5 points. To
create text that is larger than 144 points, you must manually stretch the
text to a larger size. After you stretch the text, the point-size control in
the Ribbon area displays the new text height. If you create text that is
larger than 999 points, the point-size control displays only the last
three digits of the number. 1,500 points displays as 500 points.

Adding Character Styling

You use the three buttons in the Ribbon area labeled B, I, and U to apply boldface, italics, and underlines to text, respectively. You can use
any combination of these styling attributes by clicking the buttons that
you need. Clicking any of the buttons a second time toggles off the text

styling effect. You can style an entire selected text block or individual characters that you have selected with the text cursor.

Kerning Character Pairs

Professional typographers know that some character pairs look better when the characters are brought a little closer to one another. Changing the space between a pair of characters is called *kerning*. Draw enables you to kern character pairs by placing the text cursor between the pair and then pressing the Ctrl-left arrow and Ctrl-right arrow key combinations.

Take a look at the *Water Mill Symphony* text that you previously put on-screen. Notice that the uppercase *W* and lowercase *a* in *Water* seem to be farther apart than the rest of the characters. The extra space occurs because the fancy swirl at the top of the *W* extends so far to the right. You can improve the appearance of the word by moving the lowercase *a* to the left, tucking it under the swirl.

Try kerning this character pair by following these steps:

1. Click the Text Cursor button.

2. Click just after the *W* in *Water*. The text cursor should appear between the *W* and the *a*, as shown in figure 4.14.

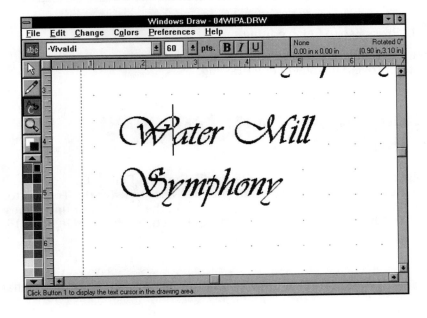

Fig. 4.14

Kerning a character pair.

3. Hold down the Ctrl key and press the left-arrow key about ten times. (The amount of kerning you apply to character pairs is up to you.) The character pair kerns together, as shown in figure 4.15.

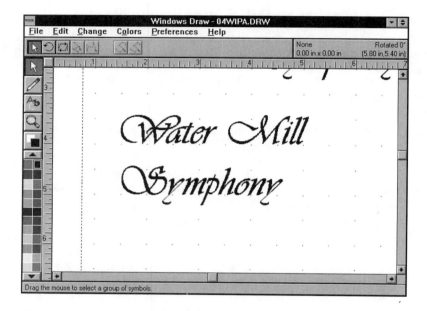

Fig. 4.15

The kerned characters.

4. Press Esc to finish editing.

Remain vigilant for pairs of letters that need kerning. Properly kerned text improves the look of any drawing.

Changing Character Formatting in the Text Editor

You can change character formatting in the Text Editor, but you do not see the effect of the change until you press Esc to leave the Text Editor and place the changes on the page. Instead, the Text Editor underlines text that has had character formatting applied, as shown in figure 4.16.

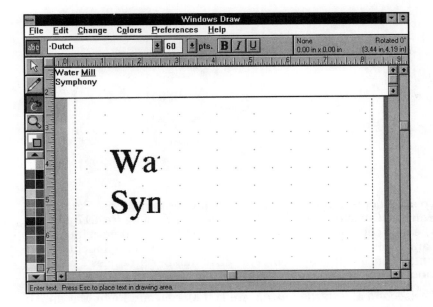

Fig. 4.16

Formatted text in
the Text Editor
window.

Changing Paragraph Formatting

Draw includes controls for modifying the appearance of paragraphs
placed in a drawing. With these controls, you can change the first line
indent of the paragraph and the right and left margins; activate Draw's
word wrap capability; and determine whether the paragraph is left
aligned, centered, or right aligned. This section describes the format
procedures available for paragraph formatting in Draw.

Setting Indents and Margins

Before you enter a paragraph, choose **P**aragraph from the **C**hange
menu and then type exact indent and margin settings into the Paragraph dialog box (see fig. 4.17). After entering a paragraph, you can
place the text cursor in the paragraph and then use the triangular controls within the ruler at the top of the screen to change the paragraph's
indent and margin settings.

Draw enables you to specify indents and margins for paragraphs that
you enter while using the program. You can set specific indents and
margins before entering a paragraph, or you can change the indent and
margin settings for existing paragraphs.

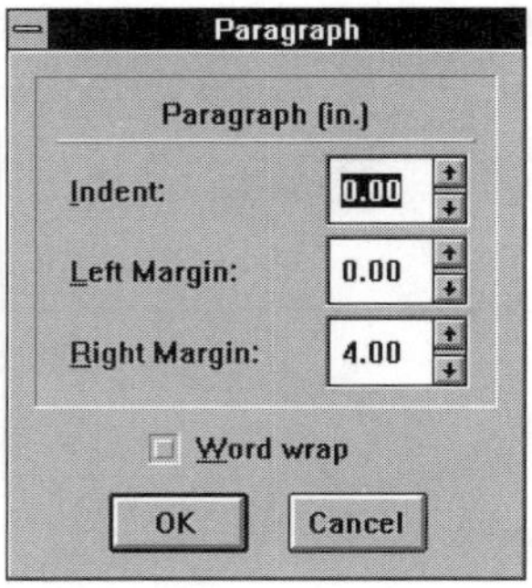

Fig. 4.17

The Paragraph
dialog box.

To set indents and margins for a new paragraph, choose Paragraph
from the Change menu. The dialog box shown in figure 4.17 appears.
The first control in the dialog box is Indent, which determines the
paragraph's first-line indent. A positive number in the Indent field results in normal indentation. A negative number produces a hanging
indent.

The second and third controls are Left Margin and Right Margin. The
Left Margin setting applies to the left margin of all the paragraph lines
except the first line. The Right Margin setting determines the right margin of all the paragraph's lines.

Type exact indent and margin settings in the appropriate fields, or use
the increment arrows to the right of each field to increase or decrease
the settings. For the margin settings to take effect, you also need to
activate Word wrap by clicking the Word wrap button just below the
indent and margin controls. When you have the desired settings entered, click OK.

To change indent and margin settings in an existing paragraph, put the
text cursor within the paragraph and use the same procedures as for
new paragraphs. Or, click within the paragraph to select it, which acti-
vates indent and margin controls on the ruler (see fig. 4.19 for an example of a ruler with these triangular controls). Use these controls to
adjust the paragraph's indent and margin settings.

When you choose Paragraph from the Change menu, the Paragraph
dialog box appears. The first control, Indent, changes the first line indent of the selected paragraph. The Left Margin control sets the left
margin of the rest of the lines of the paragraph. The Right Margin control affects every line of the paragraph. Double-click the number you
want to change or use the up and down arrow buttons next to the numbers to increment or decrement them, respectively.

Turning On Word Wrap

The margin controls have no effect unless the **W**ord wrap button is selected. If **W**ord wrap is not selected, a paragraph of text runs in a single line out to the right edge of the screen. If **W**ord wrap is selected, the paragraph reforms into several lines that stay within the margins you have chosen.

Justifying Paragraphs

The **J**ustification command on the **C**hange menu produces a pop-out menu with three choices for a selected paragraph of text. You can left justify, center, or right justify the paragraph. Left-justified text is aligned with the left edge of the text block. Right-justified text is aligned with the right edge of the text block. And centered text is horizontally centered within the text block. Figure 4.18 shows the effects of the three justification settings.

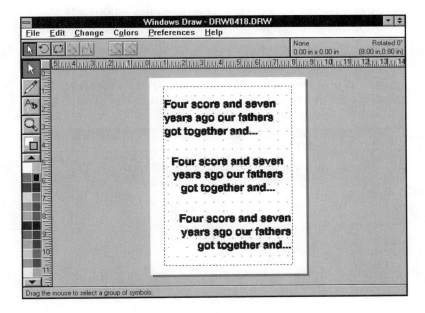

Fig. 4.18

Left-justified, centered, and right-justified text.

Formatting a Paragraph

To try using the Paragraph controls to format a paragraph, follow these steps:

1. Select the Text tool from the Toolbox.

2. From the **C**hange menu, choose **P**aragraph.

3. Use the arrows to the right of the **I**ndent setting to change the Indent to 1.00 inch.

4. Use the arrows to the right of the **L**eft Margin setting to change the left margin to .500 inches.

5. Use the arrows to the right of the **R**ight Margin setting to change the right margin to 7.00 inches.

6. Click the **W**ord wrap button to select it. Make sure the button next to **W**ord wrap is filled.

7. Click OK to apply the paragraph settings.

8. Click the Text Cursor button, and then click near the left margin at the bottom of the page.

9. Change the font to Swiss, 24 point, boldface by using the controls in the Ribbon area.

10. Type **All proceeds from The Gala benefit the Water Mill Symphony and the Water Mill Conservation Society** (see fig. 4.19).

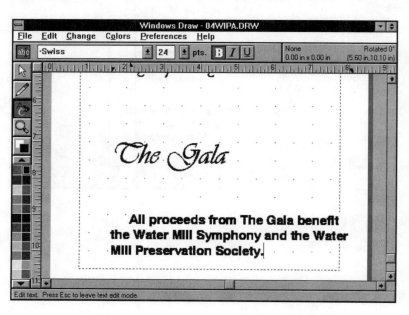

Fig. 4.19

Entering a paragraph of text.

11. Press Esc when you are finished entering text.

Notice that triangular controls have appeared on the ruler at the top of the drawing area (see fig. 4.20). The two triangles toward the left side of the ruler align with the left side of the paragraph. The top triangle aligns with the first-line indent. The bottom triangle aligns with the left margin. A third triangle, toward the right of the ruler, aligns with the paragraph's right margin. You can drag these triangles to change the indent and margin settings. Try dragging the right triangle to the left to increase the right margin. These controls only appear when Word wrap is on.

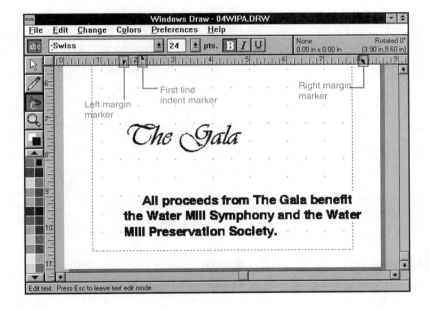

Fig. 4.20

Paragraph alignment markers on the ruler.

Special Text Effects

So far, you've learned in this chapter how to enter and edit text characters, lines, and paragraphs. Draw provides special capabilities for working with text that enable you to create unusual and interesting effects. In this section, you'll learn to convert text to curves so you can manipulate the text as a series of graphics objects. You will learn how to make text follow the curve of a symbol. You also learn to rotate text and to create drop shadows to give text a three-dimensional appearance.

Working with Text as Graphic Objects

The text that you place on a page with the Text tool can be stretched, moved, rotated, and styled with the controls in the Ribbon area. Because it is a text object, however, and not a graphic object, such as a rectangle or circle, you cannot use the full array of Draw controls to change the text's appearance. You can change the color of text, for example, but you cannot fill a text block with a color gradient. You can kern individual character pairs to move them closer together or farther apart, but you cannot drag individual characters up or down and rotate them to create a jaunty, playful look.

Draw's Convert to Curves command, however, transforms a block of text into individual graphic objects that you can modify as you would any other graphic shape. After you have converted a text block to curves, you can select each text character in the block and change its color, fill it with a color gradient, change its outline width, move and rotate it, and even fill it with a bit-map texture.

After converting a text block to curves, you can no longer edit the text with the Text tool. In fact, none of the Text controls will affect the characters because they are no longer treated as text. Just as you cannot use the Text tool to change the appearance of a rectangle, you cannot use the Text tool to change the appearance of a word that has been converted to curves. Draw provides no method to reconvert curves back to text, so be sure to make all the modifications that you want before converting text to curves.

Converting a Text Block to Curves

To convert a text block to curves, simply select the block and then choose Convert to Curves on the Change menu. Figure 4.21 shows the Change menu. A block's appearance does not change when the block is converted to curves, but you can click each character separately with the pointer tool and use all the symbol editing features of Draw on that one character. The text block becomes a set of graphic objects that you can manipulate just as you would any other graphic object.

To create a text block to convert to curves, follow these steps:

1. Select the Text tool from the Toolbox.

2. Choose Latin Wide from the font list.

3. Choose 60 from the point-size list.

4. Click the page near the left margin.

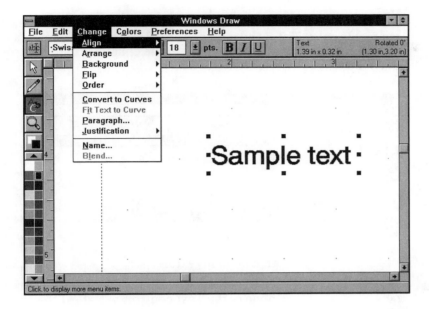

Fig. 4.21
The Change menu.

5. Type **The Gala**.

6. Press Esc when you finish entering text. The text should look like the text shown in figure 4.22.

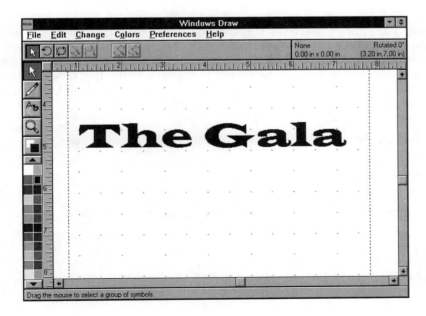

Fig. 4.22
The text on the page.

Before converting the text to curves, you may want to kern the character pairs. The *h* and *e* of the word *The* are too far apart, as are the *G* and *a* of the word *Gala*. Kern the character pairs to produce the text block shown in fig. 4.23.

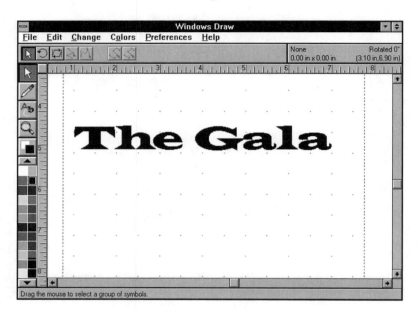

Fig. 4.23

The text after kerning.

You don't have to kern the text before converting it to curves. You can always drag the individual characters closer together after they have become discrete objects. But using the kerning key combination slides the characters left and right along the baseline of the text block without moving them up or down. The baseline is the invisible straight line that runs along the bottoms of the characters in a text block. Figure 4.24 shows the baseline of a text block.

Now convert the text block to curves by following these steps:

1. Select the text block. Notice that the Status bar tells you that the selected object is Text.

2. Choose **C**onvert to Curves from the **C**hange menu. The Status bar now tells you that the selected objects are Multiple Symbols.

Now, try clicking each of the characters with the Pointer tool. You see that you can select each character separately, such as the *G* in figure 4.25. When you select a character, the Status bar tells you what kind of symbol you have selected. Notice that the Status bar in figure 4.25 reads Closed Bézier. A *Bézier* is a type of curve that you can reshape with the Reshape Points and Reshape Bézier buttons. You learn about reshaping curves in Chapter 6, "Changing the Appearance of Symbols."

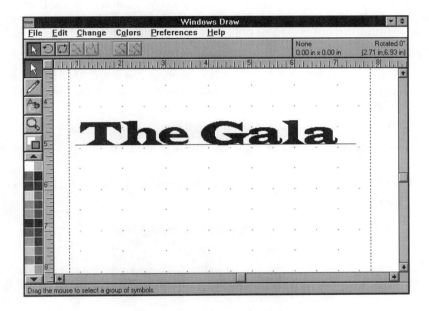

Fig. 4.24

The baseline of a text block.

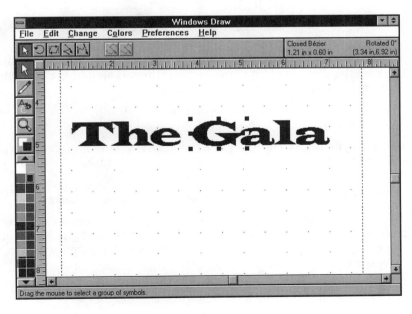

Fig. 4.25

A single curve selected.

Changing the Text Fill

When you work with text that has been converted to curves, you can select a single character to change, or you can select more than one character and change them all simultaneously. To select more than one character, hold down the Shift key as you click each object or draw a box around the collection of objects with the Pointer tool.

To change the fill in converted text objects, follow this procedure:

1. With the Pointer tool, draw a box around the word *The*. Remember, *The* is composed of individual curves in the shapes of the letters *T*, *h*, and *e*.

2. Select the Draw tool from the Toolbox.

3. Click the Fill Style button in the Ribbon area. (It shows a bucket pouring.)

4. From the pop-out menu, choose **B**itmap. The Bitmap dialog box appears (see fig. 4.26).

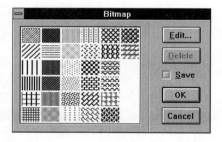

Fig. 4.26

The Bitmap dialog box.

5. From the display of bit maps in the Bitmap dialog box, choose the bit map at the right end of the first row.

6. Choose OK. The text curves you selected fill with the bit map, as shown in fig. 4.27.

Another fill you may want to try is a *gradient*. A gradient is a color wash that starts at one color and gradually changes to another. To fill the word *Gala* with a gradient, follow these steps:

1. With the Pointer tool, draw a box around the word *Gala*.

2. Drag the upper right corner handle diagonally, up and to the right, to increase the size of the word so you can see the gradient more clearly. When you drag the handle, you are changing the size of all of the curves simultaneously.

Fig. 4.27

Text curves filled
with a bit map.

3. Select the Draw tool and then click the Fill Style button in the Ribbon area.

4. Choose **G**radient from the pop-out menu. The Gradient dialog box appears (see fig. 4.28).

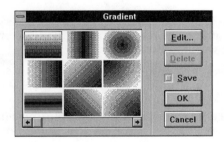

Fig. 4.28

The Gradient
dialog box.

5. Click the diagonal gradient at the center of the Gradient dialog box's display.

6. Choose OK. The diagonal gradient appears in each of the selected characters, as shown in figure 4.29.

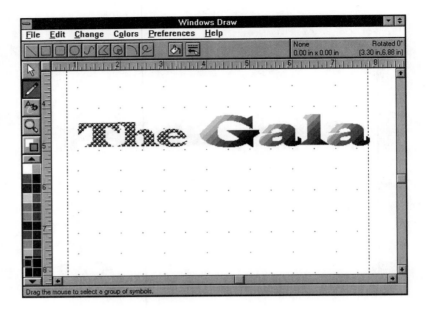

Fig. 4.29

Gradients filling
the characters of
Gala.

In Chapter 8, "Working with Color Palettes," you learn how to select
starting and ending colors for the gradient.

Changing the Text Outline Width

Because the words *The Gala* are now graphic symbols rather than a
text symbol, you can change the outline width of the characters. To
change the outline width, follow these steps:

1. Select a character or group of characters.

2. Click the Draw tool.

3. In the Ribbon area, click the Line Style button (next to the Fill
   Style button) and choose a line style from the pop-out menu. Try
   selecting a dotted line style.

4. Click the Line Style button again and choose a width of five points.
   The text should look like the text in figure 4.30.

For additional practice, return to the Line Style menu and choose the
solid line and Hairline as the width.

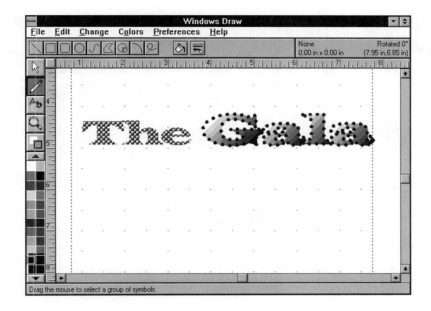

Fig. 4.30

Text with a 5-point-wide dotted line.

Reshaping Characters

After converting text characters to curves, you can change the shape of the curves to change the shape of the characters. This technique gives you the freedom to bend characters and stretch them in ways that make text fit a logo or graphic design.

To reshape a character that you have converted to a curve, you must use the Reshape Points tool to drag the points that the curve passes through. By moving the points, you cause the curve to take on a new shape. To reshape a curve, follow this procedure:

1. Select the character by clicking it with the Pointer tool.

2. Select the Reshape Points tool from the Ribbon area.

3. Click any of the points along the outline of the character and drag the point to a new position. Continue clicking and moving points until you have the shape you want.

4. Click the Select button in the Ribbon area (it shows the pointer) when you are finished moving points.

After selecting the Pointer tool from the toolbox and clicking the character, you also can use the Reshape Bézier button to move the points and change the angles at which the curve approaches the points. You learn all about the Reshape Bézier button in Chapter 6, "Changing the Appearance of Symbols."

Figure 4.31 shows text that has been reshaped character-by-character to fit a particular need.

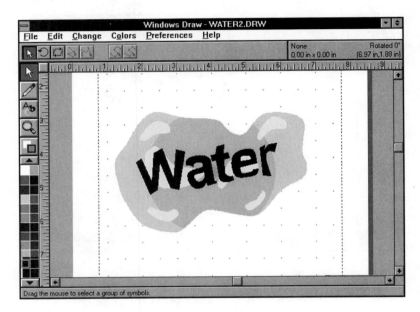

Fig. 4.31

Reshaped text.

Placing Text on a Curve

With Draw's Fit Text to Curve command, you can place text along an arc, circle, or curved line. You'll appreciate this feature any time you need to curve text to fit a special logo or other design.

Here's the general procedure you follow. You must enter a line of text and create a symbol. Select both the text and the symbol, and choose Fit Text to Curve from the Change menu. Then, if necessary, you can delete the symbol and leave behind only the text that has been wrapped along the curve.

You can fit text to an individual graphic symbol but not a composite symbol composed of multiple symbols, such as most ClipArt symbols. You also cannot fit one text symbol to another text symbol. After text has been fit to a curve, you can resize and edit the text, but you cannot stretch its shape. Therefore, you should stretch text before fitting it to a curve.

Fitting Text to a Symbol

To fit a line of text to a symbol, open a new file with **New** on the **File** menu and then perform the procedure outlined in the following steps. As an example, you create the logo of Worldwide Enterprises by fitting text to the boundaries of a ClipArt symbol of a globe.

1. Create a line of text. For this example, type **Worldwide Enterprises**, using the Swiss font at 24 points.

2. Stretch the text to the proper shape. In this case, stretch up the top of the text block to exaggerate the height of the text to approximately 60 points.

3. Create the symbol to which you want to fit text. In this example, fit text to the outline of a globe. Use the ClipArt command from the **File** menu, and select the symbol World, 01 from the file LANDMK09.DRW. The text and symbol appear in figure 4.32.

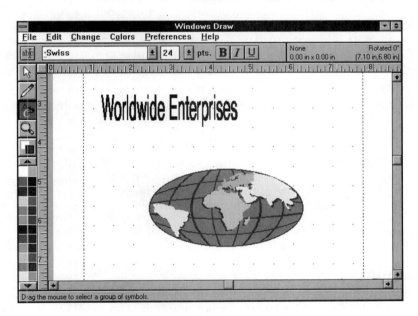

Fig. 4.32

The text and ClipArt symbol.

As you select the Fit Text to Curve command, you can place the text along the inside of the curve by pressing Shift. Otherwise, the text appears along the outside of the curve.

TIP

Unfortunately, you cannot fit text directly to the World symbol because the symbol is a grouped collection of several symbols. What you can do instead is temporarily ungroup the World symbol, select the ellipse that forms the outline of the globe and the text, and then fit the text to the ellipse.

TIP

When you are about to make a dramatic change to a symbol, such as ungrouping the World symbol, you may want to drag a duplicate of the symbol to an unused part of the drawing. If you make a mistake that you cannot undo, you can always resort to the intact duplicate. To drag a duplicate away, press Shift, click the symbol, and then drag off the copy.

To work with only the world symbol's ellipse, select Arrange from the Change menu and then choose Ungroup from the Arrange pop-out menu. Click the world symbol repeatedly until `ellipse` appears in the Status bar. This message confirms that you have properly selected the globe outline and not one of the other components of the world ClipArt symbol.

4. Press Shift, select the text, and then select the symbol. In this case, you have already selected the ellipse, so press Shift and select the text block.

5. Select Fit Text to Curve from the Change menu.

The text jumps to the outline of the globe (see fig. 4.33). Unfortunately, the text does not center itself across the top of the globe. Instead, the text starts at the left side of the globe. To fix this, you need to change the starting point of the text. This procedure is covered in the next section.

Changing the Starting Point for the Text

The first letter of text that you fit to a curve is aligned with one of the anchor points along the curve. *Anchor points* are the small black handles along the curve. You can drag the anchor points after choosing the Reshape Points button. By dragging the anchor points, you can change the shape of the curve. You may want the text to start at a different anchor point, or you may want the text to start between two existing anchor points. For the logo that you began creating in the previous section, you want the text to start at a point between the anchor point at the left side of the ellipse and the anchor point at the top of the ellipse.

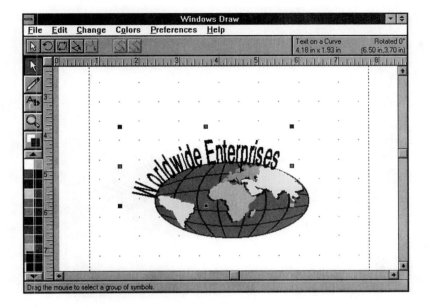

Fig. 4.33

The text fit to the
ellipse of the
globe.

To start the text at a different anchor point along the curve, you must make sure that the text symbol is still selected and then click one of the anchor points along the symbol with the Reshape Points tool. When you click an anchor point, the first letter of the text jumps immediately to the starting point you select. Figure 4.46 shows what happens if you click the anchor point at the top of the ellipse.

To start the text between two existing points, you must add a new anchor point along the outline of the symbol. To accomplish this task, follow these steps:

1. Choose the Reshape Points button.

2. Press Ctrl-D or choose Duplicate from the Edit menu. The cursor changes its appearance to show that the duplicate function is selected.

3. Click the outline of the symbol where you want the new anchor point to appear. For the Worldwide Enterprises logo, click where the letter *r* of *World* touches the globe. A new anchor point appears, and the text now starts at the new anchor point. Figure 4.35 shows the new location of the text.

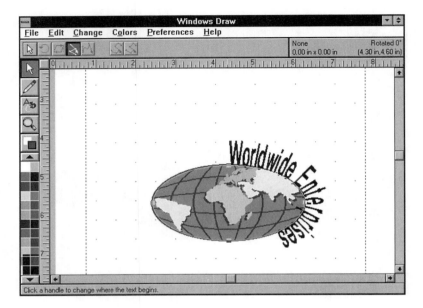

Fig. 4.34

Changing the
starting point of
the text.

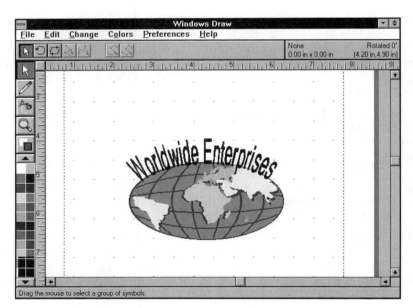

Fig. 4.35

The revised logo.

4. From the Ribbon area, choose the Select button (which looks just like the Pointer tool) to finish using the Reshape Points button.

The text is now surrounded by a set of frame handles, but only the corner frame handles are black. The top, bottom, left, and right side handles are "grayed out" to indicate that they are unusable. After you fit text to a curve, you only can resize the text block proportionately by dragging a corner handle. You cannot stretch the block by dragging a side handle.

If you select the text with the Text tool while the Text Cursor button is pressed, you can edit text that has been fit to a curve. Rather than place a text cursor in the curved text, Draw opens the Text Editor window at the top of the drawing area and places the curved text inside the window. Press Esc when you finish editing the text in the Text Editor.

Rotating Text

You can rotate text on the page just as easily as you can rotate any object. After text has been rotated, you can resize its text block proportionately, but you cannot stretch the text block to make it taller or wider.

To rotate text, follow these steps:

1. Select the text with the Pointer tool.

2. Choose the Rotate button in the Ribbon area. A pivot point appears at the center of the selected text block.

3. Drag the pointer around the pivot point to rotate the text.

4. Release the mouse button when the text block is rotated properly.

5. Choose the Select tool in the Ribbon area to finish rotating the text.

After you rotate text, you will notice that only the corner handles surrounding the text block are black, as shown in figure 4.36. The side frame handles are grayed out to indicate that they are unavailable. You can resize rotated text proportionately by dragging a corner frame handle, but you cannot stretch rotated text by dragging a side handle.

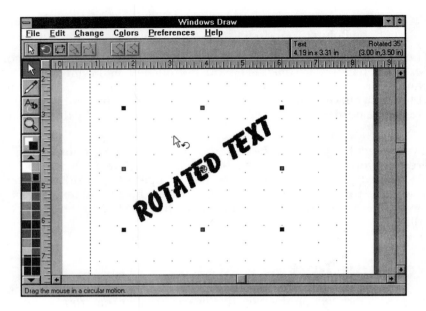

Fig. 4.36

Rotated text and
its frame handles

To edit rotated text, choose the Text tool and then select the text. The
Text Editor opens, and the text appears inside. Edit the text in the Text
Editor and press Esc. The rotated text redraws and displays your cor-
rections

Creating Drop Shadows

You can give text a three-dimensional appearance by adding a drop
shadow. A *drop shadow* is a duplicate of the text, slightly offset from the
original, colored black or gray, and moved behind the original text.

The duplicate of the text should be offset from the original only
slightly. Make sure that Snap to Rulers is off so you can move the
pointer freely (select Rulers from the **P**references menu and then turn
off S**n**ap to Rulers on the Rulers dialog box). Also, make sure that the
original text is a medium to light color so it contrasts well with the dark
shadow. You can change the color of the text by selecting the text and
then choosing a color from the Color palette, or you can convert the
text to curves and fill the text with a light colored gradient.

After you add a drop shadow, you need to group the original text
symbol and the shadow so you can move and resize them as a single
symbol.

To add a drop shadow to existing text, follow these steps:

1. Select the text with the Pointer tool.

2. Press Shift and drag a copy of the text down and to the right only slightly.

3. Select black or a dark gray from the Color palette.

4. From the **C**hange menu, choose **O**rder and then choose Move to **B**ack from the Order pop-out menu.

To try adding a drop shadow to a line of text, follow these steps:

1. Type **Drop Shadow** on the page.

2. Choose a font with thick characters, such as Latin Wide, and a large point size, such as 48.

3. Choose a light color for the text, such as light blue.

4. Press Shift, select the text, and drag a copy down and a little to the right.

5. Choose black from the Color palette.

6. Choose **O**rder from the **C**hange menu.

7. Choose Move to **B**ack from the Order pop-out menu. The drop shadow appears in figure 4.37.

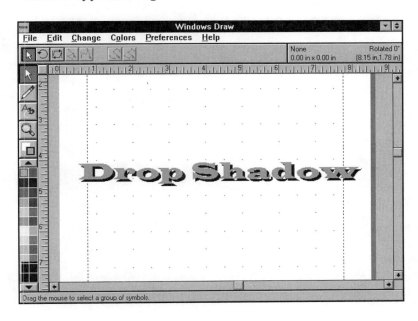

Fig. 4.37

A completed drop shadow.

NOTE In the example above, you positioned the drop shadow just below and to the right of the original to give the effect of light coming from the upper left. You may want to try moving the drop shadow, changing its relative position and distance from the original, to change the apparent position of the light source.

Importing a Text File

If you need a block of text and it is in a plain ASCII text file, you can import the file into Draw. This process prevents you from having to retype the text.

You must import an entire file of text; you cannot select only a portion of a file to import. When the text is imported, it appears on-screen in the font and size that is currently selected. You may want to change the current font and size settings before you import text so it appears correctly on the page.

To import text in an ASCII text file, choose Import from the File menu. From the Import File dialog box, choose TXT ANSI Text as the file type. The Import File dialog box appears in figure 4.38. Draw will display a list of all the files with the extension TXT. Select the file you need and choose OK.

```
┌─────────────────────────────────────────┐
│ ▬             Import File                 │
├─────────────────────────────────────────┤
│ Filename:                                 │
│ ┌───────────────────────────────────────┐│
│ │ *.TXT                                  ││
│ └───────────────────────────────────────┘│
│ File Type:                                │
│ ┌─────────────────────────────────────┬─┐│
│ │ TXT   ANSI  Text                    │±││
│ └─────────────────────────────────────┴─┘│
│ Directories:          Files:             │
│ ┌──────────────────┐ ┌──────────────────┐│
│ │ [..]             │ │ logotxt1.txt     ││
│ │ [-a-]            │ │                  ││
│ │ [-b-]            │ │                  ││
│ │ [-c-]            │ │                  ││
│ │ [-d-]            │ │                  ││
│ └──────────────────┘ └──────────────────┘│
│ c:\draw\tutorial                          │
│ ┌──────┐   ┌────────┐      ┌─┐           │
│ │  OK  │   │ Cancel │      │ │ Save      │
│ └──────┘   └────────┘      └─┘           │
└─────────────────────────────────────────┘
```

Fig. 4.38

The Import File dialog box.

If the text size setting is too small to make the text readable on-screen, the text will appear in the Text Editor. This process enables you to check the accuracy of the text before pressing Esc and placing the text on the page. If the current text size is large enough, the text is placed directly on the Draw page in a single text block. Use the **P**aragraph and **J**ustification settings on the **C**hange menu to change the appearance of the text.

Draw's text import recognizes carriage returns in imported text but does not recognize tabs. Each carriage return in the file starts a new line in the text block; tabs are ignored.

If you plan to import several text files from a directory on your hard disk, choose **S**ave from the Import File dialog box before choosing OK. This action saves the current directory selection. The next time you select **I**mport from the File menu, the dialog box displays the files in that directory.

TIP

If the text you need is in another Windows application, you can select the text, copy it to the Windows clipboard, switch to Draw, and then paste the text from the Windows clipboard to the Draw page.

Creating Word Charts for Presentations

It's easy to create bulleted lists of text items with Draw. These lists are ideal word charts for presentations. Figure 4.39 shows a sample word chart.

To create a word chart, use the Text tool and type a list of text items. Press Enter two or three times, respectively, after each item to double or triple space the list. Select a font and point size for the list that fills the page properly and select appropriate margins and other settings from the Paragraph dialog box (from the **C**hange menu, select **P**aragraph to display the dialog box).

After the list is on the page, use the Draw tool to draw a bullet point to the left of the first item of text. For round bullet points, select the Draw tool and then choose the Circle button in the Ribbon area. Draw a small circle and then fill it with a solid color. Press and hold Shift and Ctrl and drag a copy of the first bullet straight down the page. Align the second bullet next to the second item of text. Continue until you have bullets next to each text item. By pressing Shift and Ctrl, you constrain the movement of the duplicate bullet to directly up and down.

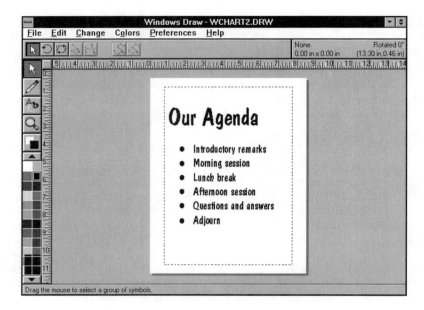

Fig. 4.39

A sample word
chart.

After entering the bullet points, you can enter a title at the top of the
page as a separate text item.

Understanding Draw's Fonts

Windows Draw comes with six text fonts and 13 display/decorative
TrueType fonts. TrueType fonts are the fonts that all Windows programs running under Windows 3.1 can use.

The text fonts that come with Draw are classic fonts that are frequently
used for the body text of books, magazines, and reports. Draw's dis-
play/decorative fonts are distinctive, attention-grabbing fonts that are
best used for titles, logos, signs, and headlines.

In addition to the TrueType fonts, Draw includes three Bitstream
Fontware typefaces and three URW Nimbus-Q typefaces (see Appendix B).

What Is TrueType?

TrueType is a font management system that is built into Windows 3.1.
When you install a TrueType font into Windows 3.1, the font becomes
available to every Windows application you use.

When you select a TrueType font from the font list in any Windows application, Windows 3.1 displays the same font on-screen that it sends to the printer. You see on-screen an accurate representation of how your printed work will look.

TrueType is built into Windows so it is always available and it works with any output device you can use with Windows. TrueType fonts even work with PostScript printers. The TrueType system sends PostScript font information to a PostScript printer when you use a Windows PostScript printer driver.

Adding TrueType Fonts

Windows 3.1 comes with five TrueType fonts: Arial, Times New Roman, Courier, Symbol, and Wingdings. Windows Draw adds another 19 fonts. Other Windows applications on your system may have installed still more TrueType fonts into your copy of Windows 3.1. But if the fonts you see when you examine Draw's font list are not enough, you can acquire new TrueType fonts from a variety of sources.

Microsoft sells a TrueType Font Pack that adds a handful of additional fonts to Windows. Other companies sell inexpensive collections of TrueType fonts, too. If your local computer store doesn't carry an adequate selection of TrueType font packages, you may want to check the mail-order ads in computer magazines. Remember, TrueType fonts that you add to Windows become available to Draw and to every other Windows program in your system; therefore, you'll get plenty of value for your money.

The *Microsoft Windows User's Guide* describes the simple procedures for installing TrueType fonts into Windows 3.1.

Using Type Managers with Draw

Another font management system for Windows is the Adobe Type Manager for Windows from Adobe Systems, Inc. Referred to as ATM 2.0, Adobe Type Manager performs the same sort of magic as TrueType, displaying fonts on-screen exactly as they will be printed. However, ATM requires Adobe PostScript Type 1 fonts.

The Adobe Type Library of PostScript Type 1 fonts is an industry standard typeface family. Fonts from the Adobe Type Library are found in everything from inexpensive desktop PostScript printers to high-resolution imagesetting equipment for professional publishing. PostScript Type 1 fonts have been around far longer than TrueType fonts. Adobe Type Manager made them usable in the previous version of Windows (Windows 3.0). You or your company, therefore, may have already accumulated a sizable collection of PostScript Type 1 fonts.

The good news is that you can use ATM side-by-side with Windows 3.1's TrueType so you can have both TrueType fonts and PostScript Type 1 fonts installed and active in your system. In fact, you can mix TrueType and PostScript fonts on one Draw page. Both font types display on the font menu in every Windows application. The appropriate font manager, TrueType or ATM, takes care of displaying and printing the fonts you have selected.

Adobe Type Manager is available as an inexpensive add-on for Windows 3.0 or 3.1. If you already have PostScript fonts, ATM enables you to use them in Draw. If you're planning on using OS/2 2.0 applications, you will find that OS/2 has ATM built in, so you also can use your PostScript fonts in OS/2. But if you're just starting your font collection for Windows, you may want to buy TrueType fonts because they generally are less expensive.

Creating a Text Logo

Now is your chance to try the basic techniques you have learned for working with text. In this exercise, you will create a text logo with the words "Water Mill Symphony." You will also borrow a simple graphic from one of the ClipArt symbols to complete the logo.

Setting Preferences

Begin by starting a new drawing. Follow these steps:

1. From the **F**ile menu, select **N**ew. If Draw asks whether to save the current drawing, click **N**o.

2. From the Preferences menu, select **P**age....

3. Make sure that Page Size A and Portrait are selected.

4. Choose OK

5. From the Preferences menu, select **R**ulers....

6. Change the setting for **R**uler Divisions to 10 and uncheck **S**nap to Rulers to turn it off.

7. Choose OK.

With the basic page and Draw controls set up, you're ready to begin entering the text.

Entering the Logo Text

Although you planned to use the Vivaldi font to create the official Water Mill Symphony logo, the director of the Symphony, who has trend-setting plans for the organization, wants something contemporary to draw a more youthful audience. That rules out Vivaldi.

1. Select the Text tool in the Toolbox.

2. From the font list box in the Ribbon area, select Swiss to start with a clean, simple font.

3. From the font size list box in the Ribbon area, select 60 pts.

4. Click near the left margin of the page and type **water mill** with a lower case *w* and *m*. If the director wants trendy, that's what he'll get.

5. Press Esc to finish entering the text. Your page should look like the page shown in figure 4.40.

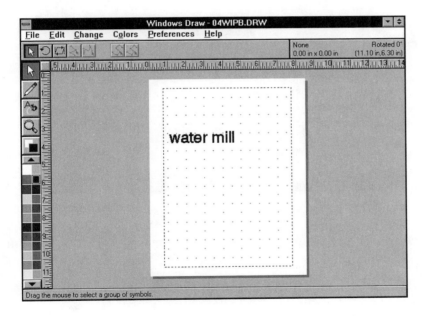

Fig. 4.40

The page with text added.

Adding Effects

The trendiness of the design you create depends in part on what you do with the text. You may want to try these steps:

1. Select the Draw tool from the toolbox (choose the button that shows a pencil).

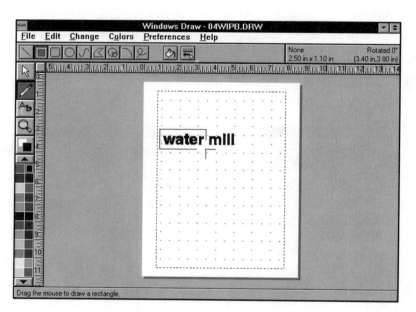

2. In the Ribbon area, choose the Rectangle button.

3. In the Ribbon area, choose the Fill Style button.

4. On the Fill Style menu, choose **S**olid.

5. On the Color palette at the left, choose the color black.

6. Draw a rectangle around the word "water," as shown in figure 4.41. Do not cover the word "mill."

Fig. 4.41

Drawing the rectangle.

The black rectangle covers the word "water." You need to move the rectangle behind "water" and then change the color of "water" to white. Follow these steps:

1. Select the Pointer tool from the toolbox.

2. Click the rectangle to select it.

3. On the **C**hange menu, select **O**rder, and then choose Move to **B**ack from the pop-out menu. Nothing appears to change because the black rectangle is now behind the black text.

4. From the Toolbox, select the Text tool again and select the text block. The word "water" now appears in reverse video as shown in figure 4.42. (The reverse of black is white, so the letters appear against a white background.)

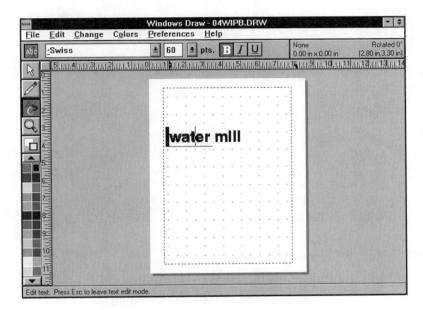

Fig. 4.42

The selected text in reverse video.

5. Drag across the word "water" with the mouse pointer to select the word.

6. Choose White in the Color palette.

7. Press Esc to finish making the change. The newly revised text appears in figure 4.43.

Adding ClipArt

You have already created a very interesting and contemporary effect, so you're on the right track. Now, you will use a piece of ClipArt to adorn the logo.

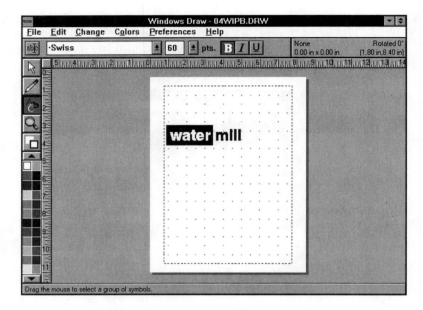

Fig. 4.43

The revised text
design.

1. From the **F**ile menu, choose **C**lipArt....

2. From the list of subjects, select People.

3. Choose the C**a**talog button to inspect the catalog.

4. Select PEOPLE42.DRW from the list of files and then choose the **P**review button. You will use the very stylish water from the ClipArt symbol at the upper right.

5. Press any key to return to the ClipArt Catalog dialog box.

6. Select "Woman, ball" from the list.

7. Choose OK. The ClipArt selection appears on the page as shown in figure 4.44.

Now, you need to ungroup the symbol so you can select and use only the water.

1. With the symbol still selected, choose **A**rrange from the **C**hange menu, and then select **U**ngroup from the pop-out menu.

2. Select the water and drag it away from the rest of the symbol, as shown in figure 4.45.

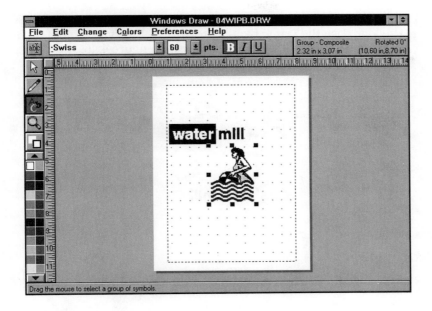

Fig. 4.44

The ClipArt
selection added
to the drawing.

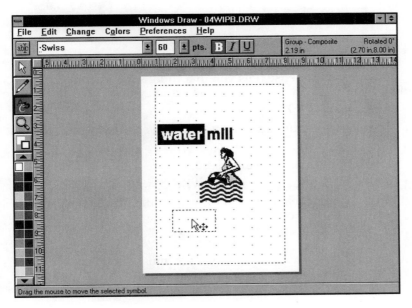

Fig. 4.45

Selecting only the
water from the
ClipArt symbol.

3. Draw a box around the unnecessary woman and ball symbols to
   select them and press Del.

4. Drag the water symbol up and just under the black rectangle in the logo. Use the frame handles to stretch the symbol so it is the same length as the rectangle, as shown in figure 4.46.

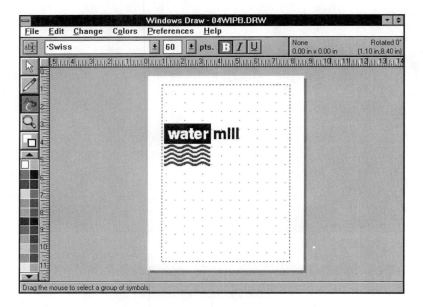

Fig. 4.46

The water symbol positioned properly.

Your innate artistic sense tells you that there's just too much water under "water mill." By ungrouping the water symbol, you can remove one or two of the wavy blue lines.

1. Make sure that the water symbol is still selected. If not, select it.

2. From the **C**hange menu, choose **A**rrange, and then choose **U**ngroup from the pop-out menu.

3. Select the bottom wavy blue line to select it, as shown in figure 4.47, and then press Del to remove the line. You will probably want to remove one more line.

4. Select one more blue wavy line at the bottom and then delete it.

Your logo is taking shape nicely. Now you must find a place for the word "symphony."

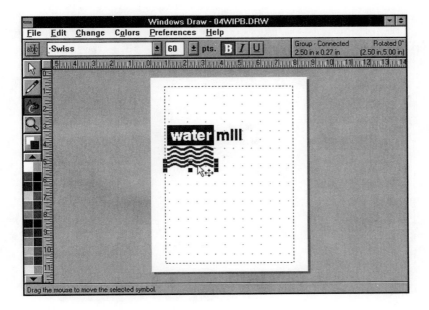

Fig. 4.47

Selecting a part
of a symbol to
delete.

Finalizing the Text

To complete the logo, you'll place the word "symphony" to the right of
the water symbol.

1. Select the Text tool from the Toolbox and then make sure that the
   Text Cursor button is pressed so you can place more text on the
   page.

2. Click to the right of the wavy blue lines and type **symphony**. Use a
   lowercase *s* for consistency. Figure 4.48 shows the text added to
   the logo.

3. Press Esc to finish entering the text.

You need to drastically reduce the size of the word "symphony" and
apply some additional styling to it. Follow these steps:

1. Drag the lower right corner handle of the "symphony" text block
   up and to the left to reduce the size of the word by about half.

2. Choose the Italicize button in the Ribbon area to italicize "symphony."

3. Choose a medium gray in the Color palette for the finishing stylis-
   tic touch.

Fig. 4.48

The additional
text added to the
logo.

4. Drag the word "symphony" so its left edge is aligned with the word "mill" and its top edge is aligned with the top edge of the water symbol.

Only one last change is required to professionalize your work. The words "water mill" need to be kerned to bring their letter pairs closer together. You may want to use the Zoom button to zoom in so you can better see the logo.

1. Choose the Text Cursor button and then select "water mill."

2. Position the cursor between the *w* and *a* of "water" and press and hold Ctrl while pressing the left arrow key three times.

3. Move the cursor between the *a* and *t* and press Ctrl-left arrow once.

4. Repeat the actions for the rest of the letters in the word "water."

You would like to perform the same kerning on the word "mill," but the black characters are invisible against the black highlight. You can work with the characters and temporarily change their color to white by following these steps:

1. Select the word "mill" and then choose white from the Color Palette.

2. Place the cursor between each of the letters in "mill" and press Ctrl-left arrow to kern the letters closer together.

3. Select the word "mill" again and choose Black from the Color Palette.

4. Press Esc to finish changing the text. Figure 4.49 shows the kerned text.

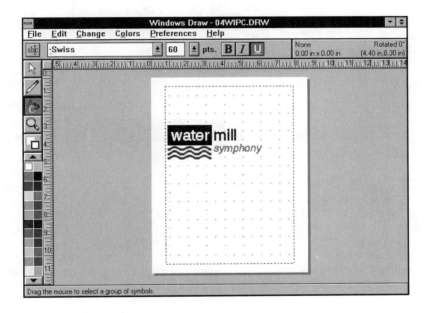

Fig. 4.49

The kerned logo text.

Because you have kerned the characters, the words "water mill" take up a little less space. You can use the right handle of the text block to widen the block a bit so "water" properly fills the black rectangle.

1. Select the "water mill" text block.

2. Drag the handle on the right side of the block to the right to stretch the text, as shown in figure 4.50. Stop when "water" fills the rectangle.

3. Drag the text block if necessary to properly position the text.

Fig. 4.50

Stretching the
text block.

The Final Product

You have now created a logo that conveys the chic stylishness the director of the Water Mill Symphony envisions. Before you save the file, you may want to group the text and graphics into a single object by drawing a box around the entire logo with the pointer, choosing **Ar**range from the **Change** menu, and then choosing **G**roup on the pop-out menu. Figure 4.51 shows the completed logo.

Save the completed logo as WMLOGO.DRW. You will need it for exercises later in this book.

Fig. 4.51

The completed
Water Mill
Symphony logo.

Summary

In this chapter, you learned to enter, edit, and manipulate text blocks.
Combining ClipArt and text is often enough to create stylish logos and
other graphic designs, but you may need to add other graphic shapes
to a drawing. In the next chapter, you will learn to draw your own
symbols.

Adding Symbols

I n the previous chapters, you learned to place ClipArt and text symbols on the page. In this chapter, you learn to add graphic objects such as lines, boxes, and curves to your work.

Understanding the Drawing Buttons

Creating a drawing in Windows Draw is much like creating a drawing on paper. As you form each shape, you add to the drawing until you have a completed picture. Just as an artist uses a variety of pencils and brushes to create the shapes needed for a drawing, you use a variety of buttons in Draw to create the shapes you need. All the buttons appear in the *Ribbon area* when you select the *Draw tool* from the toolbox.

When you're ready to add graphic objects to a drawing, click the Draw tool. Immediately, the Ribbon area changes to show a selection of *buttons*. The first nine buttons enable you to create different graphic shapes as the pictures on the buttons indicate. The last two buttons, separated from the rest, lead to pop-out menus that enable you to choose a fill style and a line style for a symbol. Figure 5.1 shows the Ribbon area. Table 5.1 shows the function of each button.

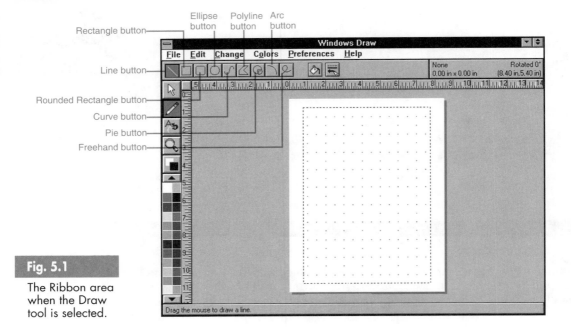

Fig. 5.1

The Ribbon area when the Draw tool is selected.

Table 5.1 The Drawing Buttons

Button	Function
The Line button	Draws a straight line between two points.
The Rectangle button	Draws a rectangle or a square.
The Rounded Rectangle button	Draws a rectangle or square with rounded corners.
The Ellipse button	Draws ellipses and circles.
The Curve button	Draws a Bézier curve.
The Polyline button	Draws a multisegmented line or a polygon.
The Pie button	Draws a pie chart.
The Arc button	Draws an arc or segment of a circle.
The Freehand button	Draws a continuous line.

When the Draw tool is selected, you can pass the pointer over each button in the Ribbon area and inspect the Hint line to learn the button's purpose.

TIP

Setting Up Draw's Positioning Aids

Before you begin drawing, take a moment to check the settings on the **P**references menu. These settings determine how the screen will act, how the rulers and page will look, and how large the handles will be around selected objects.

Setting the Rulers

To change the settings for the horizontal and vertical rulers on the screen, choose **R**ulers from the **P**references menu. The Rulers dialog box appears, as shown in figure 5.2.

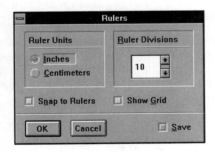

Fig. 5.2

The Rulers dialog box.

Choose **I**nches or **C**entimeters as the **R**uler Units by clicking the button next to the units you want to use. The **R**uler Divisions setting determines the number of increments that appear between each whole number measurement along the ruler. Enter a number from 1 to 100 for Ruler Divisions or use the up and down arrows next to the number to increment or decrement the number, respectively. Then, click the OK button. If you are using inches as the ruler unit, for example, and want a ruler that shows sixteenths of an inch, type **16** as the number of Ruler Divisions. For quarters of an inch, type **4**.

The number of Ruler Divisions is important for two reasons. First, the setting determines how many markings appear along the ruler. The divisions also affect the results you achieve when you turn on Snap to Rulers. (The Snap to Rulers control is described in the next section.) Figure 5.3 displays two examples of settings for Ruler Divisions and the rulers that result.

Turning On Snap to Rulers

Snap to Rulers is another setting on the Rulers dialog box. You can get to it by selecting **R**ulers from the **P**references menu.

When Snap to Rulers is turned on, the object that you draw or move automatically aligns with the horizontal and vertical division mark nearest the pointer. This option restricts the freedom with which you can move or place objects on the page by forcing the lines, rectangles, and other symbols you draw to jump to the nearest division.

On the other hand, Snap to Rulers helps you align objects. You may not be able to align the left edges of two objects by sight as you draw or move them, but you get a little help when Snap to Rulers is turned on— the left edges of the objects snap to the same division on the horizontal ruler. Figure 5.4 demonstrates the value of using Snap to Rulers. The top pattern of rectangles was positioned without Snap to Rulers, so the alignment of the rectangles is not precise. The bottom pattern of rect- angles was positioned after Snap to Rulers was turned on.

 NOTE The more divisions you choose for the rulers, the more snap points you have along the ruler, so the insertion point does not jump as far when you draw or move symbols. Having many divisions allows for detail work but still provides alignment assistance.

Turning On the Grid

When the Show **G**rid option is chosen from the Rulers dialog box, a pattern of very small dots appears across the page to display the snap points. If the number of divisions is high, Draw does not display every snap point. Instead, every other snap point or every third snap point appears so the grid is not too dense.

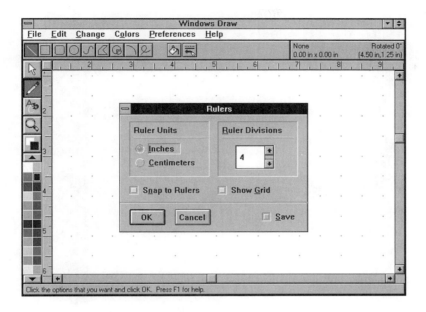

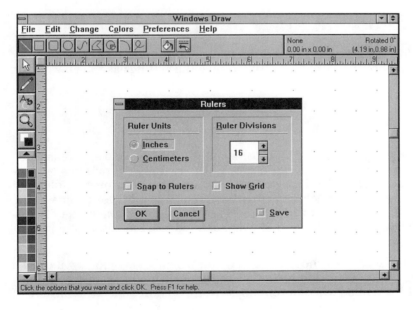

Fig. 5.3

Sample settings for Ruler Divisions and the resulting rulers.

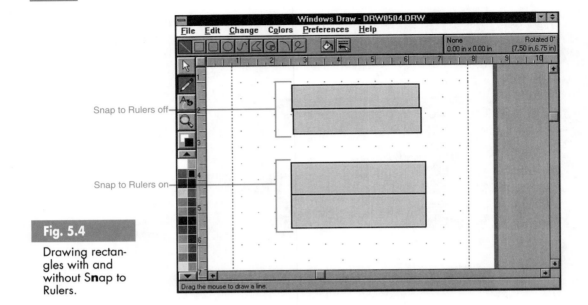

Snap to Rulers off

Snap to Rulers on

Saving the Ruler Settings

Before you click the OK button to accept the settings on the Rulers dialog box, you can click Save to save the settings as the new default.

Choosing a Fill Style

Until you choose a fill style for symbols that have closed areas, such as rectangles, circles, or polygons, you see only the outlines of symbols you draw. A rectangle looks like a hollow box, for example. Draw enables you to easily select patterns, colors, and color blends for the interiors of objects you create. Figure 5.5 shows some of the fill possibilities next to the kind of plain, unfilled box that Draw otherwise creates.

The best time to choose a fill style for a symbol is before you draw it. The fill style you choose will be used within every symbol you draw until you choose a different fill style. If you don't choose a fill style first, you can create the symbol with the Draw tool, select the symbol with the Pointer tool, and then choose a fill style for it. This method requires an extra step and a few extra mouse clicks. You can choose line styles the same way, as described in the next section.

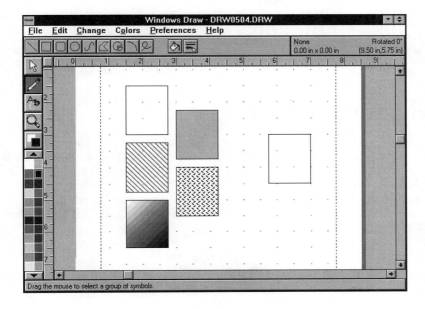

Fig. 5.5

Sample fill styles
and unfilled
boxes.

In this section, you learn about choosing a fill style before you draw a
symbol. In the next chapter, you learn about changing the fill styles of
objects you already have drawn.

Draw's four fill styles encompass a variety of different looks. Among
your choices for filling a symbol are a hatch, a bitmap, a gradient, and a
solid color.

- A *hatch* is a pattern of straight lines that run vertically, horizontally, or diagonally.

- A *bitmap* is a pattern of dots that is repeated to fill a symbol.

- A *gradient* is an area of color that gradually changes from one hue
to another. The color transition can flow in a variety of directions,
such as left to right, top to bottom, or center to edge.

- A *solid* color, chosen from any of the colors in the Color palette,
can fill a symbol.

- *Unfilled*, the fifth choice, leaves the symbol hollow.

To choose a fill style before you create a symbol, follow these steps:

1. After selecting the Draw tool, click the Fill Style button. The Fill
Style menu appears, as shown in figure 5.6.

2. Choose **H**atch, **B**itmap, or **G**radient, and then choose one of the
selections on the dialog box that appears or choose **S**olid to fill
the symbol with the currently selected fill color.

Fig. 5.6

The Fill Style
menu.

Choosing a Hatch

A hatch is a pattern of straight lines that run vertically, horizontally, or
diagonally. The lines, which appear in the current fill color, are opaque
against a transparent background. Other objects behind the symbol
filled with a hatch show through the symbol. To apply a hatch pattern,
choose **Hatch** from the Fill Style menu. Then choose OK to open the
Hatch dialog box (see fig. 5.7). Choose one of the Hatch patterns listed,
then choose OK.

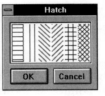

Fig. 5.7

The Hatch dialog
box.

Choosing a Bitmap

A bitmap is a dot pattern that represents various textures, from a
smooth gray to a basketweave. The bitmap is repeated so it fills the
object you draw.

To apply a bitmap, choose **Bitmap** from the Fill Style menu. The Bitmap
dialog box appears (see fig. 5.8). Draw comes with 32 predefined
bitmap fills, but you can create your own by clicking the **Edit** button on
the Bitmap dialog box. Editing a bitmap is described in Chapter 6,
"Changing the Appearance of Symbols."

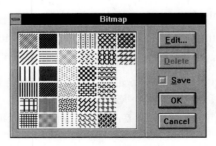

Fig. 5.8

The Bitmap
dialog box.

The colors displayed in the bitmap are the fill and outline colors selected with the Color Tool. You learn how to use the Color tool in Chapter 6, "Changing the Appearance of Symbols."

Choosing a Gradient

A *gradient* is an area of color that gradually changes from one hue to another. Draw comes with 18 predefined gradients from which to choose. After you choose **G**radient on the Fill Style menu, Draw displays the Gradient dialog box (see fig. 5.9). You can choose one of the existing gradients or edit a gradient to create your own. You'll learn about editing a gradient in Chapter 6, "Changing the Appearance of Symbols."

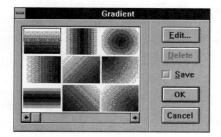

Fig. 5.9

The Gradient dialog box.

The starting and ending colors of the gradient are determined by the buttons that appear when you select the Color tool. After you click the Background color button, you can choose the starting color of the gradient from the Color palette. After you click the Fill Color button, you can choose the ending color of the gradient from the Color palette.

To choose one of the preexisting gradients from the dialog box, click one of the nine selections, then choose OK.

Choosing a Solid Fill Color

If you choose **S**olid from the Fill Style menu, the symbol fills with the fill color currently selected on the Color palette. To change the fill color, click the Color tool, then click the Fill Color button. Then choose a color in the color palette.

TIP   The appearance of the Color tool changes to display the currently selected colors. The front rectangle displays the fill color you choose. The back rectangle displays the current background color. The lines around the front rectangle indicate the current Line color setting.

NOTE   When you choose Unfilled from the Fill Style menu, symbols you draw will be hollow.

Choosing a Line Style

The line style for a symbol determines how the outline surrounding the symbol will look. If the symbol is a line or a polyline (a line composed of many line segments), the line style determines the appearance of the line.

Just as you can choose a default fill style before you draw symbols (rather than apply a style to a symbol you already have drawn), you can do the same with line styles.

You can control three primary aspects of how lines and outlines look: their line type, line width, and line endings. The line width option enables you to indicate whether the ends of lines have a rounded, square, or flat cap. This option also enables you to determine how the lines in multiline segments are joined.

To choose a line style before you create a symbol, follow these steps:

1. After selecting the Draw tool, click the Line Style button. The Line Style menu appears (see fig. 5.10).

2. Change the three settings on the Line Style menu to match the line or outline style you want to create. The previous three settings you chose for line width and line endings appear on the Line Style menu so you can readily access the same settings again.

Choosing a Line Type

After you click the Line Style button, a menu displays six line styles plus some other options. You can see the first five line styles, but the

sixth, Invisible, is described with text ("invisible" is hard to show).
Figure 5.11 displays the five line styles. The first line style, a solid line,
is the default when you start Draw. A check mark appears on the menu
next to the current default line style.

Fig. 5.10

The Line Style
menu.

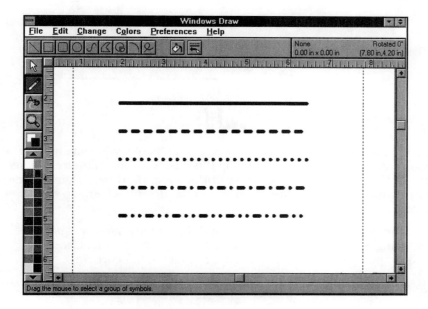

Fig. 5.11

The available
line styles.

Choose the line style you want to use. By choosing Invisible, you can
create objects that are composed entirely of a fill and have no outline.
To create the appearance of a shadow, for example, you want a gray
area slightly offset behind a symbol. To create a gray area without
an outline, set line style to Invisible before drawing the gray area.
Figure 5.12 shows a shadow behind a symbol.

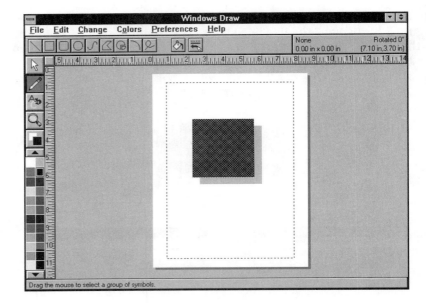

A shadow using a filled gray area without an outline.

Choosing a Line Width

If you have chosen a line style other than **I**nvisible, you can change the line width by choosing from among the three options in the center section of the Line Style menu. These options are: **H**airline, 5 Points Wide, and **W**idth. The first option, **H**airline, is the default when you start Draw.

Hairline creates an extremely thin line that is only a *hair's width* wide. Choosing 5 Points Wide creates a medium thickness line. Choosing **W**idth opens the Line Width dialog box, shown in figure 5.13.

The Line Width dialog box.

The Line Width dialog box has settings for Line Cap, Line Join, and Width. The dialog box also displays a preview of the current settings for all three controls.

The Line Cap setting determines how the ends of wide lines look.

- **Round** places a semicircle at both ends of a line you draw. The center of the semicircle is at the end point of the line.

- **Flat** ends the line at the end point.

- **Square** places a square at the end of the line. The square's center is at the end point of the line.

NOTE If you choose a line ending for a line, described in the next section, the line ending will cover the line cap.

The Line Join settings, also in the Line Width dialog box, determine how lines meet in a symbol.

- **Round**, the default setting, rounds off the corner of the line so it does not appear so sharp.

- **Mitre** creates a sharp corner.

- **Bevel** shaves off the corner. You can see the results of these settings by choosing a large width, such as 16 points, then watching the preview as you click each setting. Figure 5.14 displays three line joins with round, mitre, and bevel endings.

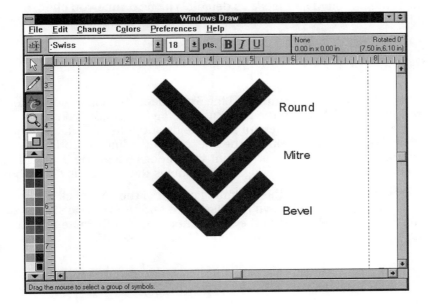

Fig. 5.14

Lines with Round, Mitre, and Bevel joins.

The Width control in the Line Width dialog box enables you to set the width of the line in points. Click the right arrow button to increase the width or the left arrow button to decrease the width.

NOTE When you open the Line Style menu, you may notice three line styles listed between the Hairline and Width options. This list represents the last three line styles you selected; the abbreviations next to the styles indicate the line cap and line join settings. For example, S/R indicates a Square line cap and a Round line join. F/M indicates a Flat line cap and a Mitre line join. Figure 5.15 shows how the Line Style menu looks after you have selected several different line styles.

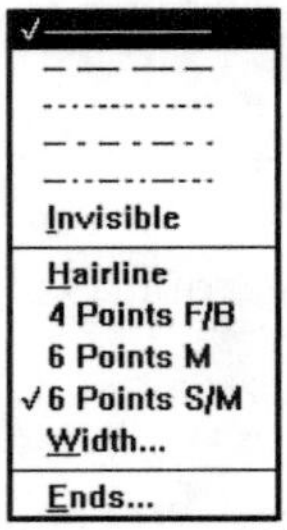

Fig. 5.15

The Line Style menu showing selected line styles.

After you have chosen a combination of Line Cap, Line Join, and Width settings, you can choose the **S**ave button and then OK to save the current combination of settings as a default. The next time you choose Width from the Line Style menu, you will see the same combination.

Choosing Line Endings

When you choose **E**nds from the Line Style menu, the Line Ends dialog box appears. Controls on the Line Ends dialog box enable you to choose from among a variety of arrowheads and other graphic symbols that appear at the beginning of the line, end of the line, or both. The beginning of the line is the first point you choose when you draw a line; the end is the second point. Figure 5.16 shows the Line Ends dialog box.

To choose an ending for the beginning or end of the line, click the current setting, then scroll down the display to find the graphic shape you want. To make both endings the same, choose the **B**oth Same button, then change the setting for either end. Then choose OK.

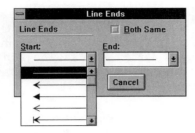

Fig. 5.16

The Line Ends
dialog box.

To create a line without arrowheads or other graphic symbols at the
end, choose the plain line on the Line Ends dialog box. This line is the
first entry on the pull-down menu.

Drawing Symbols

To add a graphic shape to a drawing, select the Draw tool, then select
the appropriate Draw button. If you already have selected a fill style
and line style, as described in the previous section, the symbol you
create will have the fill and line attributes you selected. Otherwise, the
symbol appears with the default fill and line styles. You can always
select the symbol after it's drawn and change its fill and line style
settings.

NOTE   Don't worry if the symbol you draw is not positioned precisely. You can always move it later. You can even move
individual points along the borders of symbols to change
their shape. Chapter 6, "Changing the Appearance of Symbols," describes how to move the points of a symbol to
change the shape after it is drawn.

Adding Lines

To draw a line, you position the pointer at the starting point of the line,
click and hold the mouse button, and drag to the ending point of the
line. When you release the mouse button, the line appears.

TIP
As you draw the line, the Status bar displays the line's length. You can use the readout as a guide to draw a line with an exact measurement. To start the line at an exact spot, use the pointer position display in the Status bar to precisely place the pointer.

If **Sn**ap to Rulers is on, the line's beginning and ending points automatically align with the nearest division on the ruler.

Follow these steps to draw a line:

1. Select the Draw tool from the toolbox.

2. Click the Line button.

> **NOTE** Now would be an appropriate time to click the Line Style button in the Ribbon area and select a line style for the line. You can select both a fill style and a line style for a symbol before you draw it.

3. Position the pointer at the beginning of the line.

4. Click and hold the mouse button.

5. Drag the pointer to the end of the line.

6. Release the mouse button.

Figure 5.17 shows the steps in creating a line.

The line you have created appears in the current line style settings. The color of the line is determined by the current line color setting. To change the line color setting, follow this procedure:

1. Click the Color tool.

2. Click the Line Color button.

3. Choose a color from the color palette.

While the Line button in the Ribbon area is still activated, you can draw additional lines. To remove the last line you have drawn, choose **U**ndo from the **E**dit menu or press Alt-Backspace.

TIP
To constrain the line to an exact horizontal, vertical, or diagonal direction, press and hold the Ctrl key while you draw the line.

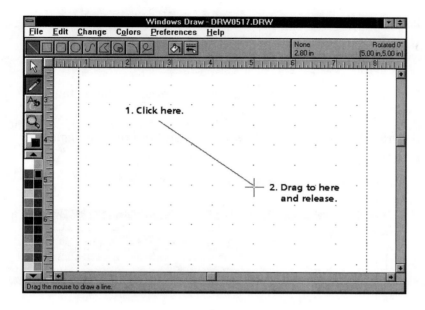

Fig. 5.17

Drawing a line.

Adding Rectangles

Drawing rectangles is similar to drawing lines. You click the upper left corner of the rectangle, then hold the mouse while dragging the pointer to the lower right corner. When you release the mouse, the rectangle forms between the two points. The rectangle's center color or pattern is determined by the current fill style setting. The rectangle's outline is determined by the current line style and line color settings.

To constrain the rectangle to a perfect square, press and hold the Ctrl key while you draw.

As you draw a rectangle, the Status bar indicates the horizontal and vertical distance the pointer has moved. The Status bar also tells you the width and height of the rectangle you're drawing.

If Snap to Rulers is on, the side of the rectangle aligns exactly with the nearest division on the ruler.

To draw a rectangle, follow these steps:

1. Select the Draw tool from the toolbox.

2. Click the Rectangle button.

   You may want to choose line and fill styles for the rectangle ellipse at this point. You also may assign them after the ellipse is drawn.

3. Position the pointer at the upper left corner of the rectangle.

4. Click and hold the mouse button.

5. Drag the pointer to the lower right corner of the rectangle.

6. Release the mouse button.

Figure 5.18 shows the steps in drawing a rectangle.

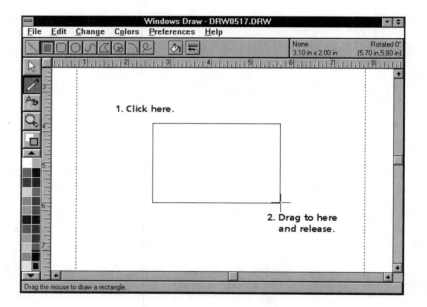

Fig. 5.18

Drawing a rectangle.

While the rectangle button is still activated, you can continue to draw rectangles. To remove the last rectangle you have drawn, choose **U**ndo from the **E**dit menu or press Alt-Backspace.

You can align several rectangles using the **Sn**ap to Rulers feature and the Ruler Divisions setting to create a business form. Try this exercise by following these steps:

1. Start a new drawing by choosing **N**ew from the **F**ile menu.

2. Choose **R**ulers from the **P**references menu.

3. In the Rulers dialog box, type **4** for **R**uler Divisions and make sure **Sn**ap to Rulers is on.

4. Click the Draw tool in the toolbox.

5. Click the Rectangle button.

6. Use the rulers and the Status bar readout to position the pointer 4 inches from the left side of the page and 2 inches from the top.

7. Draw a rectangle that extends to 7 1/2 inches across the page and 2 1/2 inches down, as shown in figure 5.19.

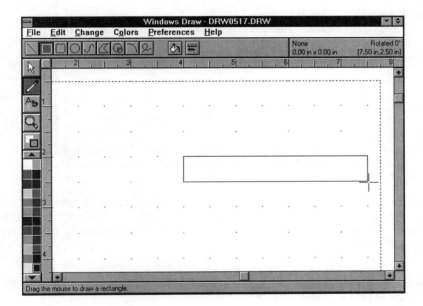

Fig. 5.19

Drawing the first rectangle on a business form.

8. Position the pointer on the lower left corner of the rectangle and draw a second rectangle just below the first. Make the second rectangle the same dimensions as the first. Notice that the rectangles align perfectly because Snap to Rulers is on.

9. Create a third rectangle below the other two.

Now, with the text tool, you can add text to the left of the rectangles. Type **Name**, **Address**, and **Phone number** to create a fill-in-the-blanks form, as shown in figure 5.20.

Creating Rounded Rectangles

To draw a rectangle with rounded corners, follow the same procedure you used to draw a rectangle, but select the Rounded Rectangle button instead.

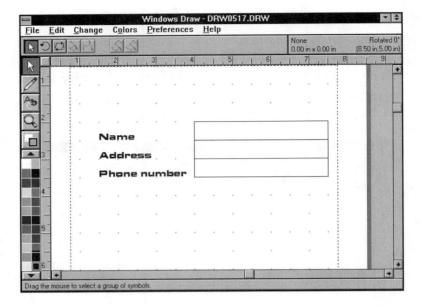

Fig. 5.20

A fill-in-the-blanks
form.

To create a rounded square, press and hold the Ctrl key while dragging
the pointer. To control the roundness of the corners of a rounded rectangle, use the Reshape Points button, covered in Chapter 6, "Changing
the Appearance of Symbols."

Creating Ellipses

Clicking the Ellipse button enables you to draw both ellipses and
circles. To draw an ellipse, click the Ellipse button, then position the
pointer on the page. Click and hold the mouse, then drag diagonally
away from the starting point. An ellipse forms between the starting
point and the current pointer position. Release the mouse to place the
ellipse on the page.

TIP

To restrain the shape of the ellipse to a perfect circle, press and hold
the Ctrl key as you draw the ellipse.

The Status bar indicates the horizontal and vertical dimensions of the
ellipse. The fill color of the ellipse is determined by the current fill
color. The width and color of the outline is determined by the line
style setting and the line color setting.

To draw an ellipse, follow these steps:

1. Select the Draw tool from the toolbox.

2. Click the Ellipse button.

   You may want to choose line and fill styles for the ellipse at this point. You also can assign them after the ellipse is drawn.

3. Position the pointer at the upper left corner of the ellipse.

4. Click and hold the mouse button.

5. Drag the pointer to the lower right corner of the ellipse.

6. Release the mouse button.

Figure 5.21 shows the steps in drawing an ellipse.

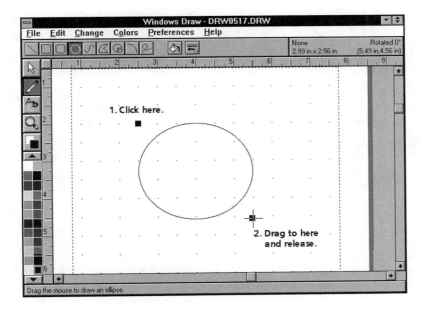

Fig. 5.21

Drawing an ellipse.

Drawing Curves

Draw offers three methods for adding a curved line to your drawing. First, you can draw the curved line with the Freehand Drawing button, which enables you to freely draw across the screen. Unless you're an accomplished artist or have superb hand-eye coordination, this curve is not likely to be very smooth. You also can draw curves by using the Arc button. But arcs curve in only one direction, bending to the right or to the left. You can connect several arcs to form a curved line, but a better method is to use the Curve button.

The curves that you draw with the Curve button are individual segments that pass through anchor points at very specific angles. As you draw a curve, you can control the location of the anchor points and the angles at which the curves pass through the points. Because Draw generates the curve that passes from one point to the next, the curve is continuous and smooth.

You can change the shape of a curve after it is drawn by moving the anchor points or changing the angles at which the curves pass through the points. The next chapter describes an easy method to accomplish both these tasks.

To draw a curve, follow these steps:

1. Click the Curve button in the Ribbon area.

2. Click and hold the mouse button at the starting point of the curve.

3. Drag the pointer a short length in the direction the curve should continue from the starting point and release the mouse.

4. Move the pointer to the next point the curve should pass through, click and hold the mouse button, and drag a short length in the direction the curve should continue.

5. Repeat this process until you have drawn the entire curve. When you have added the last point, finish the curve in one of three ways: select another drawing tool, click the Pointer tool in the toolbox, or double-click the mouse.

TIP

As you draw the curve, you can make any line segment a straight line that connects two points by holding the Shift key as you draw the segment. You can hold the Shift key as needed when you draw a curve to achieve a combination of straight and curved segments. To add a line segment that is exactly horizontal, vertical, or diagonal, hold the Ctrl key as you draw a segment.

The color and thickness of the curve is determined by the current line color setting and line style setting. As you draw the curve, though, you see only a black hairline representation. When you finish the curve by selecting another drawing button, by clicking the Pointer tool, or by double-clicking the mouse, the curve redraws with the current line color and line style settings.

Follow these steps to draw a curve:

1. Select the Draw tool from the toolbox.

2. Click the Curve button.

3. Click and hold the mouse button at the first point for the curve.

4. Drag to the next point and then release the mouse button.

5. Click and drag to the next point and then release the mouse button.

6. Repeat step 5 until the entire curve is drawn.

7. Finish the curve by selecting a different drawing button, by clicking the Pointer tool, or by double-clicking the mouse. The curve takes on the current line style and line color settings.

Figure 5.22 shows the steps in drawing a curve.

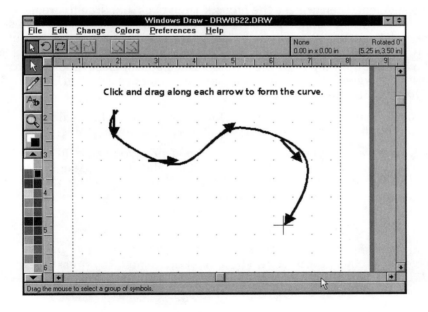

Fig. 5.22

Drawing a curve.

Try drawing a curve by using the Curve button to create a pair of Mickey Mouse ears. Another exercise is to try using the Curve button to sign your name on the page. Remember, you can hold the Shift key when necessary to make a line segment straight rather than curved.

You can remove the last segment of the curve you have drawn by choosing Undo from the Edit menu or pressing Alt+Backspace. Each time you choose Undo, Draw removes another segment from last to first.

Drawing Polylines

Polylines are multisegmented lines that go from point to point. When you join the first and last points of a polyline, you create a closed object called a *polygon*. Polygons have centers you can fill with the Fill Style button and outlines you can style with the Line Style button.

To create a polyline or polygon, click and drag the mouse to create a line segment, then release the mouse. Then click and drag to create a second segment connected to the first and release the mouse. To finish the polyline, click somewhere on the page, select another drawing button, or click the Pointer tool in the toolbox. To finish the polygon, place the last point on top of the first point. You also can close a polyline to form a polygon by using the Connect command, described in Chapter 6, "Changing the Appearance of Symbols."

If you're drawing a polyline, the color and style of the line is determined by the current line color and line style settings.

As you draw a polyline segment or polygon side, you can hold the Shift key to draw a freehand line that connects to the other line segments. You also can hold the Ctrl key to draw a line segment or side that is exactly horizontal, vertical, or diagonal.

You can remove the last segment of the polyline or polygon you have drawn by choosing Undo from the Edit menu or by pressing Alt-Backspace. Each time you choose Undo, Draw removes a line segment in reverse order.

If Snap to Rulers is on, the points of the polyline or polygon jump to the nearest ruler division. As you draw the polyline or polygon, the Status bar tells you the length of each line segment you draw.

Follow these steps to draw a polyline or polygon:

1. Select the Draw tool from the toolbox.

2. Click the Polyline button.

   You can select both line and fill styles for the polyline at this point. You also can draw the polyline and select line and fill styles later.

3. Click and hold the mouse at the first point for the polyline or polygon.

4. Drag to the next point and release the mouse.

5. Repeat steps 3 and 4 until you have drawn all the line segments you need. Place the last point on the first point to form a polygon.

6. Finish the polyline or polygon by selecting a different drawing button, by clicking the Pointer tool, or by clicking somewhere else on the page. The line redraws with the current line style and line color settings.

Figure 5.23 shows the steps in drawing a polyline. Figure 5.24 shows the steps in drawing a polygon.

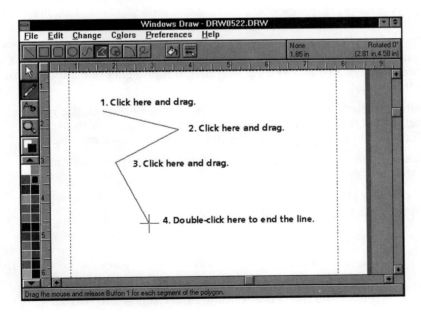

Fig. 5.23

Drawing a polyline.

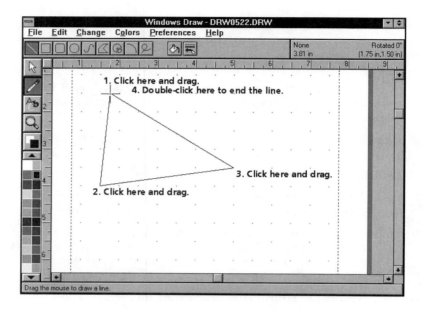

Fig. 5.24

Drawing a
polygon.

Drawing Pies

The pie button enables you to create pie charts quickly and easily. Pie charts often are used in presentations and printed material to show the breakdown of a total. Each slice of the pie represents one contribution to the total.

Using the Pie button, you can draw the outline of the pie, then create each of the pie slices to the exact size you need. As you create each slice, the Status bar indicates the percentage the slice represents.

After you have created the slices, you can change the colors and fill patterns of each of the slices.

To create a pie chart, follow these steps:

1. Select the Draw tool from the toolbox.

2. Click the Pie button.

3. Click and hold the mouse button where you want the center of the pie chart.

4. Drag out from the center until the pie circle is the correct size, as shown in figure 5.25.

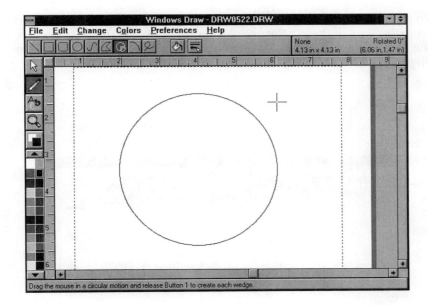

File   Edit   Change   Colors   Preferences   Help

Drag the mouse in a circular motion and release Button 1 to create each wedge.

Fig. 5.25

Dragging out from the center to create the pie outline.

5. Release the mouse.

6. Position the pointer on the circumference of the circle where you want the first slice to start.

7. Click and hold the mouse button, then drag clockwise along the circumference, checking the Status bar as you move. The circle disappears while you drag out slices. The Status bar tells you the percentage the slice represents.

8. Release the mouse to finish creating the slice, as shown in figure 5.26.

9. Click and hold the mouse on the circumference, then drag clockwise to create another slice. Release the mouse when the slice is the size you need.

10. Repeat step 9 as many times as necessary to finish the pie.

All the slices have the current fill style and line style, but you can select any slice with the Pointer tool and choose a different fill and line style for it. Chapter 6, "Changing the Appearance of Symbols," describes how to accomplish this step.

To try this technique, you can create a pie chart that shows the sales contributions of three salespeople: Sarah, Andy, and Lola. All together, the three managed to sell 36 subscriptions in their door-to-door campaign. The breakdown is listed below.

Sarah	16
Andy	14
Lola	6

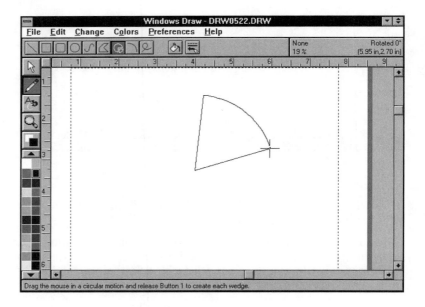

Fig. 5.26

Creating a slice.

Before you create the pie, calculate the percentage of the total that each salesperson's figure represents. You should come up with these figures:

Sarah	44%
Andy	39%
Lola	17%

To create the pie outline, follow these steps:

1. Select the Draw tool from the toolbox.

2. Select the Pie button.

3. Position the pointer at the center of a new page.

4. Click and hold the mouse, then drag to the right until the Status bar indicates you have created a circle with a diameter of 5 inches.

5. Release the mouse button.

Now create the slices by following this procedure:

1. Click and hold the mouse at the top of the circle.

2. Drag clockwise along the circumference of the circle until the Status bar reads 44%.

3. Release the mouse button to create the first slice, as shown in figure 5.27.

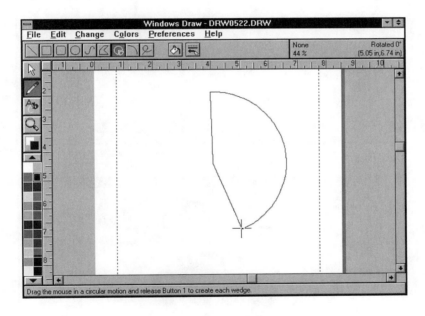

Fig. 5.27

Creating the first slice in the sales chart example.

4. Click and hold the mouse button again and drag along the circumference of the circle until the Status bar reads 39%.

5. Release the mouse to create the second slice, as shown in figure 5.28.

6. Drag along the circumference one last time until you have closed the circle, then release the mouse button.

7. Now you can add text and fill the slices with different colors to finish the pie chart, as shown in figure 5.29. You'll learn about

choosing colors for symbols in Chapter 6, "Changing the Appearance of Symbols."

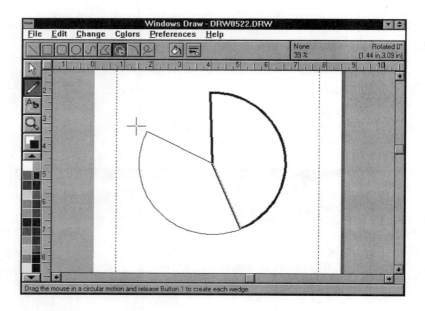

Fig. 5.28

Creating the second slice.

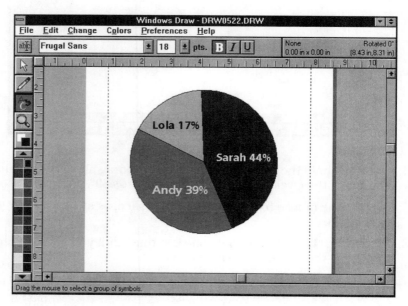

Fig. 5.29

The finished pie chart with text and colors added.

Drawing an Arc

An *arc* is a smoothly curving line that is one quarter the circumference of an ellipse. The Arc button enables you to draw arcs easily.

To create an arc, follow these steps:

1. Select the Draw tool from the toolbox.

2. Click the Arc button.

    You can select a line style for the arc before you draw it.

3. Position the pointer on the spot where you would like the arc to begin and click and hold the mouse button.

4. Drag the pointer to the other end of the arc and release the mouse. The arc appears.

To create an arc that is one quarter of a circle, press and hold the Ctrl key while dragging the mouse. To invert the arc so it curves in the opposite direction, press and hold the Shift key while dragging the mouse.

TIP

Figure 5.30 shows the steps to drawing an arc.

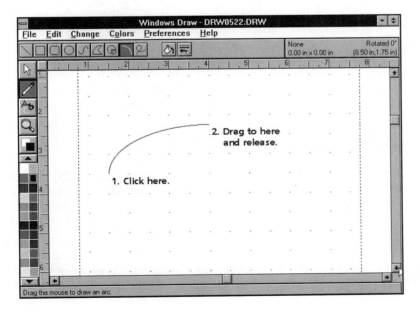

Fig. 5.30

Drawing an arc.

The color and line style of the arc is determined by the current line style and line color settings. If Snap to Rulers is on, the beginning and end points of the arc align with ruler divisions.

Drawing Freehand

The Freehand button enables you to draw as though you were moving a pencil across the page. You click the Freehand button, then click and hold the mouse while dragging the pointer across the page. As you draw with the Freehand button, a black hairline appears. You finish drawing by clicking the mouse once, and a smooth curve replaces the freehand symbol, following the same path with the current line style and line color settings.

If you close the freehand shape you're drawing by joining the beginning and ending of the line, you can fill it with a color or pattern.

You also can edit the curve with the Reshape Bézier button to change the curve's shape. Using the Reshape Bézier button is described in Chapter 6, "Changing the Appearance of Symbols."

To draw a freehand symbol, follow these steps:

1. Select the Draw tool from the toolbox.

2. Click the Freehand button.

   You can select a line style for the freehand symbol now.

3. Click and hold the mouse, then move the pointer to begin drawing.

4. Release the mouse to finish drawing.

5. Click the mouse anywhere to redraw the symbol as a smooth curve with the current line style and line color settings.

Duplicating Objects

After you have drawn an object, you can make a copy of it on the page by using the Duplicate command. You then have an immediate copy to use elsewhere in the drawing. You also can use the Duplicate command to create a design composed of a repeated symbol or group of symbols.

The Duplicate command is easy to use. In fact, the command is so easy that you may want to get in the habit of duplicating a symbol or collection of symbols before attempting any modifications on the original. Then if your modifications fail, you can always delete the modified symbols and use the duplicate.

To duplicate an object, follow these steps:

1. Click the symbol with the Pointer tool to select it.

2. Choose **D**uplicate from the **E**dit menu. The pointer changes to show that you are in duplicate mode. Figure 5.31 shows the duplicate mode pointer.

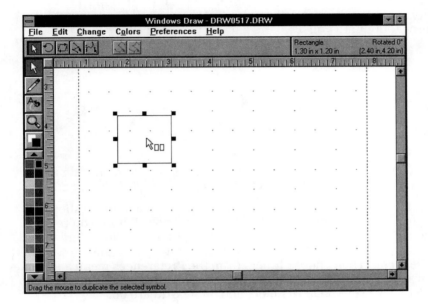

Fig. 5.31

The duplicate mode pointer positioned on an original drawing.

3. Position the pointer on the object and click and hold the mouse button.

4. Drag the mouse to the position for the duplicate.

5. Release the mouse button.

Try this useful shortcut. To duplicate an object, position the pointer on it, press the Shift key, click and hold the mouse, then drag away a copy of an object. Release the mouse to drop the duplicate.

TIP

TIP

To form a pattern of evenly spaced duplicates, press and hold both the Shift and the Ctrl keys when duplicating an object. This technique restrains the movement of the pointer to a horizontal, vertical, or diagonal direction. When the duplicate is positioned properly, check the Status bar before you release the mouse to see how far you moved the pointer. Then release the mouse to duplicate the copy. Move the pointer the same distance as before and repeat the procedure until you have the pattern you need.

Exercise: Building a Drawing by Adding Symbols

Now that you have learned how to add symbols to a drawing using Draw's buttons, you have a chance to practice with some guidance.

In this exercise, you will create the simple, familiar image shown in figure 5.32 by combining several Draw symbols. Before you're done, you will have the chance to use the Line, Polyline, Circle, and Curve buttons. First, though, create a new drawing by choosing New from the File menu. Then choose Rulers from the Preferences menu and make sure the Ruler Units is set to Inches and the Ruler Divisions is set to 10. Also make sure Snap to Rulers and Show Grid are on.

Choosing a Fill Style and Line Style

Begin by creating the fence among the snow drifts. Follow these steps to set the fill style for the fence:

1. Select the Draw tool from the toolbox.

2. Click the Fill Style button.

3. Choose Solid from the Fill Style menu.

4. Click the Color tool in the toolbox.

5. On the Color tool pop-out menu, click the first button, the Fill Color button.

6. Choose a medium brown in the color palette. Notice that the Color tool now shows a medium brown fill in the front rectangle.

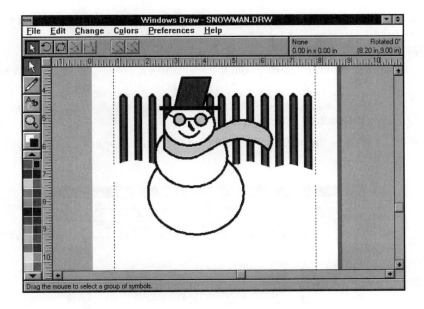

Fig. 5.32

The sample
drawing.

Now follow these steps to set the line style:

1. Click the Line Style button.

2. On the Line Style menu, make sure that the solid line is selected.

3. Choose **W**idth from the Line Style menu.

4. Change the width setting to 6 points by using the Width control in the middle of the Width dialog box.

5. Choose OK to return to the drawing.

Creating a Symbol

Now you can create a single slat of the fence. Then duplicate the slat to create the rest of the fence. Create the first slat by following these steps:

1. Click the Draw tool in the toolbox.

2. Click the Polygon button in the Ribbon area.

3. Use the rulers and the Status bar to position the pointer 1 inch from the left side of the page and 4 inches from the top.

4. Press and hold the Ctrl key.

5. Click and hold the mouse, then drag down 3 inches. (Use the Status bar to see how far you have moved the pointer.)

6. Continue to hold the Ctrl key and mouse, and drag the pointer to the right .20 inches then back up 3 inches.

7. Continue to hold the Ctrl key and mouse, and drag the pointer diagonally up and to the left .14 inches then down to the left another .14 inches.

8. Release the mouse. The first slat of the fence appears, as shown in figure 5.33.

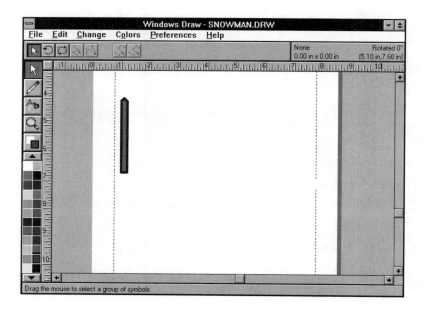

Fig. 5.33

The first polygon of the drawing.

Duplicating the Symbol To Create a Fence

Create the rest of the fence by duplicating the slat to the right in an evenly spaced pattern. Follow these steps:

1. Press and hold the Shift and Ctrl keys.

2. Position the pointer on the first slat and click and hold the mouse.

3. Drag the mouse to the right .50 inches. (Use the Status bar as a guide.)

4. Release the mouse to place the duplicate but keep pressing the Shift and Ctrl keys.

5. Click the copy you have just made and drag another duplicate to the right .50 inches.

6. Continue dragging duplicates until you have a fence that runs most of the way across the page, as shown in figure 5.34.

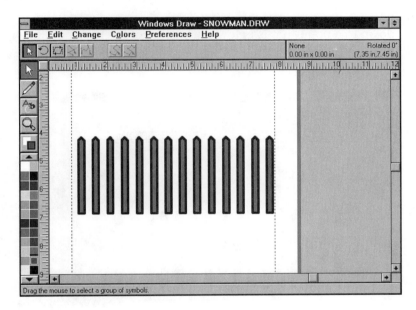

Fig. 5.34

An evenly spaced duplicate pattern of slats.

Creating a Closed Curve To Form a Snow Drift

Now you can use the Curve tool to create a snow drift, adding realism to the scene. Follow these steps:

1. Click the Curve tool in the Ribbon area.

2. Click somewhere on the page background to deselect the last fence slat you duplicated.

3. Choose the color White in the color palette to change the fill color. (You don't need to click the Fill Color button before you choose a color because this button is still selected. The Fill Color button stays selected until you choose a different color.)

4. Click the Line Style button in the Ribbon area.

5. Choose **Invisible** from the Line Style menu.

6. Position the pointer .80 inches from the left of the page and 6 inches from the top.

7. Use the pointer to draw an irregular, wavy curve that extends just to the right of the fence.

8. Press and hold the Ctrl key while dragging the pointer straight down to a point that is below the bottom of the fence, as shown in figure 5.35. You will enclose the bottom of the fence within the curve.

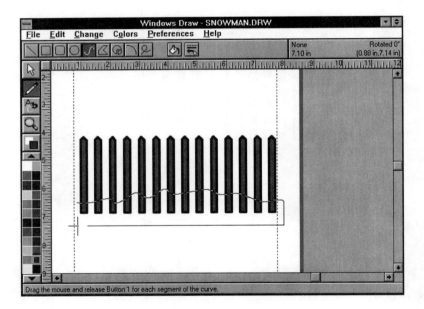

9. Keep pressing the Ctrl key and drag the pointer back to the left to a point directly below the starting point of the curve.

10. Without releasing any of the keys or the mouse, drag the pointer to the exact starting point of the curve.

11. Click the mouse to finish drawing the curve. The closed curve filled with white should now cut off the bottoms of the fence slats at varying heights, as shown in figure 5.36. If the slats are not cut off, click the Pointer tool in the toolbox and click the curve to select it. Choose **Arrange** from the **Change** menu, then choose Connect on the pop-out menu. This command should connect the

first and last points to create a closed curve filled with white with an invisible outline.

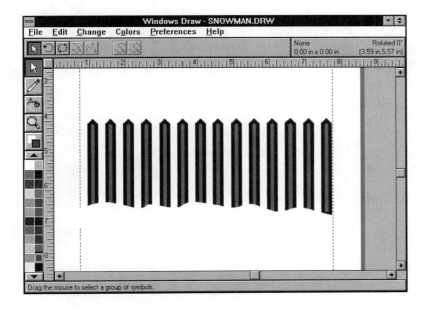

Fig. 5.36

The closed curve filled with white.

Grouping a Set of Symbols To Create a Fence Object

Before you continue, you may want to take a moment to group together the objects you have already created. You can make the fence and snow drift one group, and the snowman you create will be a second group. Then you can easily move the two grouped objects independently of one another.

To group the fence slats and snow drift, select every symbol you have drawn so far. You can use the pointer to draw a rubber band box that surrounds every symbol (remember, every symbol must be entirely within the box), or you can choose **S**elect All from the **E**dit menu. To try using **S**elect All, follow this procedure:

1. Choose **S**elect All from the **E**dit menu or press F2. The Status bar tells you that multiple symbols are selected.

2. Choose **A**rrange from the **C**hange menu.

3. Choose **G**roup from the pop-out menu. The Status bar tells you that a composite group is now selected.

Creating a Circle

You can create the snowman's three snowballs next. Your first task is to change the fill and line style settings. Because the fill style is already set to solid and the Fill Color button was the last Color tool button to be selected, you can choose a different color from the color palette to change the fill color. Choose the color White from the color palette.

Then follow these steps to set the line style:

1. Click the Line Style button.
2. On the Line Style menu, make sure the solid line is selected.
3. Choose OK to return to the drawing.

Now you're ready to begin creating the snowballs. Follow these steps:

1. Click the Ellipse tool in the Ribbon area.
2. Position the pointer 2 inches from the left side of the page and 5 inches from the top. Use the rulers and the Status bar to guide you.
3. Click and hold the mouse, then drag 3.6 inches to the right and 3.2 inches down. Again, use the Status bar to guide you.
4. Release the mouse to form the first snowball. Your drawing should now look like the drawing shown in figure 5.37.

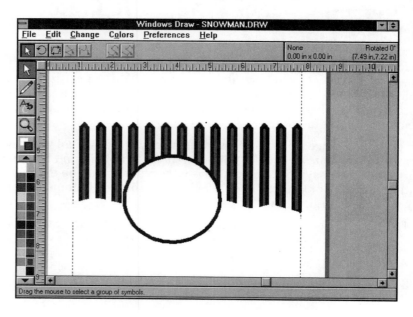

Fig. 5.37

The drawing with a circle (snowball) added.

Duplicating the Circle To Create a Second Snowball

You can draw two other slightly smaller snowballs that appear to be resting on the first, or you can duplicate the first snowball then reduce the size of the duplicate. The second method is the fastest and enables you to create three snowballs of the same shape but different sizes. Try duplicating the symbol by following these steps:

1. Select the Pointer tool from the toolbox.

2. Press and hold the Shift key.

3. Click the snowball.

4. Click and hold the mouse and drag a copy of the snowball above the original but let the top symbol overlap the bottom symbol. This overlap gives the appearance that the snowballs are resting on one another.

5. Drag a corner handle of the top snowball toward its center to make this snowball smaller than the first.

6. Position the pointer in the middle of the top snowball, click and hold the mouse, and drag the snowball to the position shown in figure 5.38.

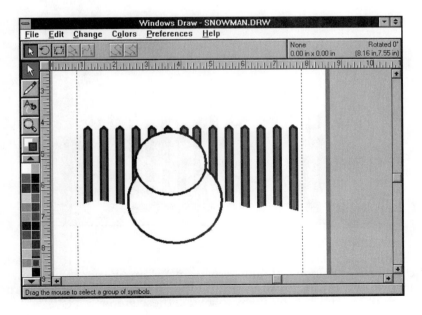

Fig. 5.38

The first circle and its duplicate properly arranged.

Creating the Scarf with a Second Closed Curve

You will create the third snowball after you have created a scarf for the snowman. To make the scarf, you will create a second closed curve with the Curve tool. This curve should be filled with yellow, so choose the color Yellow from the color palette. The fill color changes because the Fill Color button was the last button pressed when you selected the Color tool earlier in this exercise. Follow these steps to begin drawing the curve:

1. Select the Draw tool from the toolbox.

2. Click the Curve button in the Ribbon area.

3. Position the pointer in the upper portion of the page in a clear area. You will draw the scarf in this clear area, then move the completed scarf into position.

4. Draw the curve shown in figure 5.39.

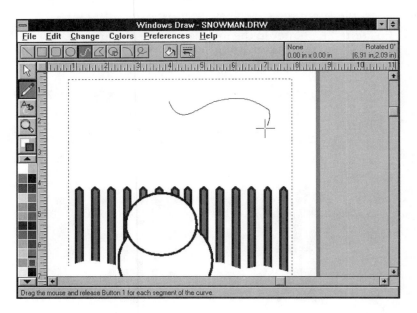

Fig. 5.39

The curve in progress.

You have formed the top edge of the scarf. Now, you need to complete the curve. At this point, though, you want a sharp corner. When you press the Ctrl key as you draw a curve, you can create the sharp corner you need. Try this technique by following these steps:

1. Move the pointer to the left a little, press the Ctrl key, and then release the mouse. A straight line appears between the last point you selected and the current pointer position.

2. Create a second curve under the first that follows the same path.

3. Finish the curve by moving the pointer directly on top of the line's starting point, then clicking the mouse to close the curve. The curve should fill with yellow, as shown in figure 5.40. If not, click the Pointer tool, click the curve, and choose Arrange Connect from the Change menu.

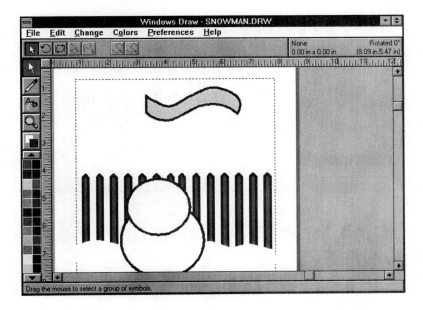

Fig. 5.40

The closed curve.

Now you can use the Pointer tool to resize the scarf and drag it to position on top of the second snowball. Figure 5.41 shows you where the scarf can be placed.

Using Duplicate To Create the Third Snowball

You can create the third snowball by duplicating the second snowball. Press the Shift key and drag a copy above the second snowball, overlapping the scarf and snowball. Notice that the duplicated snowball overlaps the scarf even though the symbol you have duplicated (the second snowball) is underneath the scarf. Remember that every object you add, even if it is a duplication of an existing object, goes on top if it overlaps other objects.

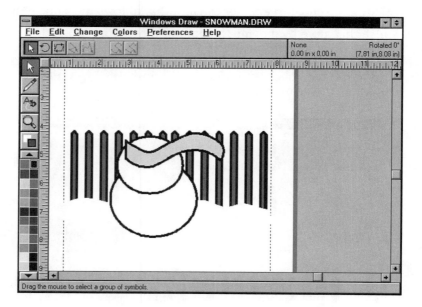

Creating the Hat by Using Line and Polygon Symbols

To form the brim of the snowman's hat, draw a line across the top of the top snowball. Then add a polygon to form the rest of the hat. Follow these steps:

1. Select the Draw tool from the toolbox.

2. Click the Line button in the Ribbon area.

3. Draw a line across the top of the top snowball, as shown in figure 5.42.

Now set the fill color for the polygon and create the polygon that makes up the rest of the hat.

1. Choose the color Red in the color palette to change the current fill color.

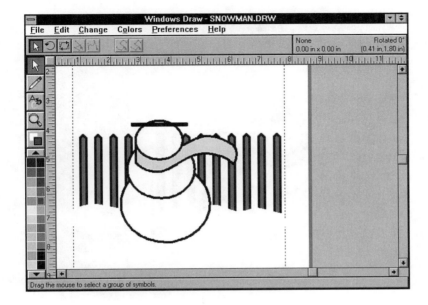

Fig. 5.42

Adding a line to
form the brim of
the hat.

2. Select the Polyline button from the Ribbon area.

3. Position the pointer at about 1 inch above the center of the line.

4. Press Ctrl to restrain the pointer movement, then click and hold
   the mouse. Drag horizontally to the right 1 inch to create the top
   side of the polygon. Use the Status bar to gauge how far you have
   moved the pointer.

5. Release the mouse and Ctrl key.

6. Click and hold the mouse, then drag the pointer down to the brim.
   Move the pointer slightly to the left (to angle the hat) along the
   line, then release the mouse.

7. Press and hold the Ctrl key, then click and hold the mouse. Drag
   the pointer to the left 1 inch. Then release the mouse.

8. Click and hold the mouse again, then drag the pointer up until it is
   exactly on top of the starting point for the polyline. Release the
   mouse.

9. Click the mouse to finish the polygon. The drawing now looks like
   figure 5.43.

Fig. 5.43

Adding a hat to
the drawing.

Creating the Face with Ellipses, Arcs, and a Polygon

Now you can create the face. For the eyes, create a pair of circles filled
with baby blue. For the nose, create a carrot-shaped polygon. For the
smile, you can use a pair of arcs.

For this part of the exercise, you may want to zoom in on the top snowball to make creating the face easier. To zoom in, follow these steps:

1. Select the View tool from the toolbox.

2. Select the Zoom button from the pop-out menu of View tool
   buttons.

3. Draw a rubber band box around the top snowball with the Zoom
   button. The top snowball zooms to fill the screen.

Begin creating the face by making the eyes.

1. Select the Draw tool from the toolbox.

2. Select the Ellipse tool from the Ribbon area.

3. Choose the color Baby Blue from the color palette.

4. Draw a small ellipse at the position for the left eye.

5. Press Shift and drag a copy of the ellipse to the right to get two eyes of the same color and size, as shown in figure 5.44.

Fig. 5.44 .

Ellipses added to create eyes.

6. Select the Polyline tool from the Ribbon area.

7. Choose Orange from the color palette.

8. Draw a closed polyline in the shape of a carrot where the nose should be. Use figure 5.45 as a guide for the shape and positioning of the polygon.

9. Select the Arc tool from the Ribbon area.

10. Position the pointer at the left edge of the smile, click and hold the mouse, then drag diagonally down and to the right. Then release the mouse.

11. Click and hold the mouse, then drag diagonally up and to the right. You will see that the second arc bends in the wrong direction.

12. While still holding the mouse, press the Shift key to invert the arc. Then release the mouse. The face should now look like figure 5.46.

Now all that is left are the glasses. You can draw the glasses using ellipses and lines. Be sure to change the Fill Style to Unfilled before drawing the circles. Follow these steps:

1. Select the Fill Style button in the Ribbon area.

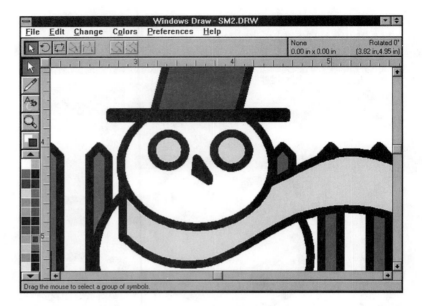

Fig. 5.45

The face with a nose added.

Fig. 5.46

The completed face.

2. Choose **U**nfilled from the Fill Style menu.

3. Select the Ellipse tool from the Ribbon area.

4. Press and hold the Ctrl key and mouse.

5. Draw a circle around the left eye that is slightly larger than the eye.

6. Release the Ctrl button and mouse.

7. Shift-drag a copy of the circle onto the right eye.

8. Select the Line tool from the Ribbon area.

9. Draw a line between the circles to form the bridge of the glasses.

10. Draw two more lines to create the two earpieces for the glasses, as shown in figure 5.47.

Fig. 5.47

The snowman with glasses added.

Finally, you should group the symbols you have drawn to make the snowman a single object. Then you can easily move and resize the snowman. First, zoom out to view the full page by following these steps:

1. Select the View tool from the toolbox.

2. Select the Full Page View button from the pop-out menu of buttons.

Now use the Pointer tool to draw a rubber band box around the snowman. The box can include part of the fence, but make sure all the fence is not within the box. Choose Arrange Group from the Change menu. Figure 5.48 shows the completed drawing.

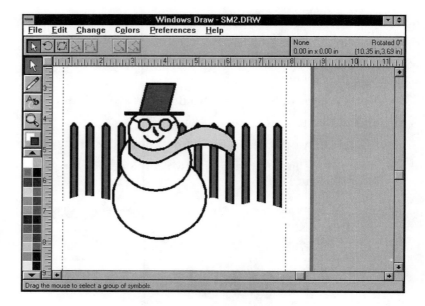

Fig. 5.48

The completed
snowman
drawing.

Summary

In this chapter, you learned how to add to your drawings graphic objects created with the Draw tool. You learned how to set up Draw's positioning aids, such as the ruler and grid. You also learned about choosing a fill and line style before creating symbols such as rectangles, ellipses, curves, polylines and pies.

The next chapter describes how to change the appearance of objects you have already created.

Changing the Appearance of Symbols

The best time to decide what a symbol should look like is before you draw it, but all is not lost if you draw a symbol without specifying all of its characteristics, such as selecting the color with which you want it filled. You easily can change the appearance of symbols after they are on the page.

This chapter explains how to change the appearance of a symbol after you have drawn it. The two-step process requires you to select the symbol and then choose a menu command, color, tool, or button to make a modification. Remember that *Select-Change* are the two steps you always need.

Selecting Symbols

When you click the Pointer tool to select a symbol, the Select button is depressed automatically (see fig. 6.1). The Select button gives the Pointer tool the power to select symbols. You can use the tool to click a symbol you want to select.

Select button ——

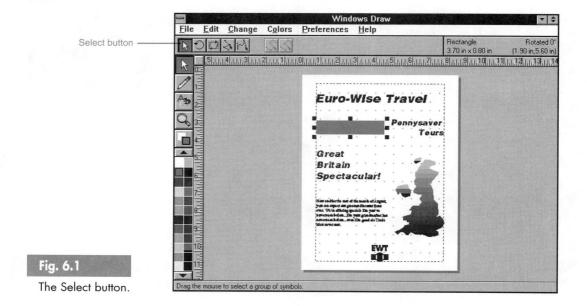

The Select button.

To select more than one symbol, draw a rubber band box around the symbols with the Select button. When you draw a rubber band box, every object you want selected must be enclosed entirely within the box. If part of a symbol extends beyond the box, the symbol will not be part of the selected group. You can exclude symbols by drawing the box carefully. Figure 6.2 shows a rubber band box that includes only the ellipse symbol.

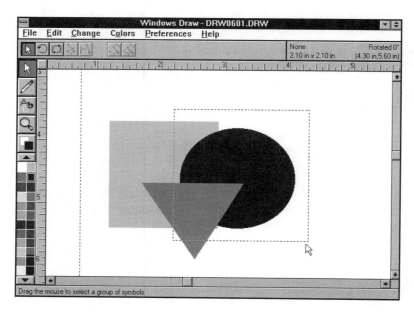

A rubber band box containing only the ellipse symbol.

If the symbols you want to select are scattered about the screen, you can select them by pressing the Shift key and then clicking each one. Each new symbol you select is highlighted and joins the already selected symbols.

If symbols are stacked on top of one another, you can select the symbols one by one from top to bottom by clicking the stack repeatedly. Each time you click, you select the next symbol down. If the symbol you want is underneath another symbol, click twice. The top symbol is selected first, and then the symbol below is selected.

Selecting Colors for Symbols

The three buttons that appear when you select the Color tool enable you to select the color of one of the three parts of a symbol. After you select a Color tool button, select a color from the color palette. Figure 6.3 shows the Color tool buttons.

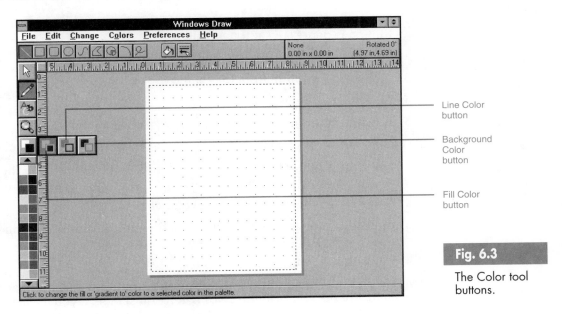

Line Color button

Background Color button

Fill Color button

Fig. 6.3

The Color tool buttons.

The following list describes the Color tool buttons.

- The *Fill Color button* enables you to select a color from the color palette for the fill of symbols. If the symbol is text, the fill color button changes the text color. The fill color also determines the color of a pattern or hatch and the fade-to color of a gradient (see "Filling Symbols with a Gradient," later in this chapter).

- The *Line Color button* enables you to select a color from the palette for lines and the outlines of symbols.

- The *Background Color button* enables you to select a color for the background of a hatch or bitmap pattern or the fade-from color of a gradient. You also can use this button to select a background color for text (a color that fills the text block).

The button you press on the Color tool pop-out menu remains in effect until you click a different button. It also determines the effect of the selections you make from the color palette.

The squares on the face of the Color tool always display the colors that are currently active. The fill and outline of the square in front display the fill and line colors, respectively. The fill of the square behind displays the background color.

A symbol fills with color only if Solid is the currently selected fill style. If Unfilled is selected (the default when you start Draw), no color appears within the symbol. To change the fill style to solid, follow these steps:

1. Select the Pointer tool from the toolbox. The Select button in the Ribbon is depressed automatically.
2. Click the symbol that requires a fill style change.
3. Select the Draw tool from the toolbox.
4. Click the Fill Style button.
5. Select Solid from the Fill Style menu.

To change the color of a symbol, follow these steps:

1. Select the Pointer tool from the toolbox. The Select button in the Ribbon is depressed automatically.
2. Click the symbol that requires a color change.
3. Click the Color tool and select one of the three buttons. You can skip this step if the button you want is already pressed.
4. Click a color in the color palette.

If you use a high-resolution video display and monitor, you may be able to see most of the colors in the color palette on-screen. If you use an IBM PS/2 or another computer that has a standard VGA display, you can see only a part of the color palette. To see the rest of the palette, click the buttons at the top and bottom of the palette. These buttons scroll the palette up or down to reveal more colors. Figure 6.4 shows the color palette scroll buttons.

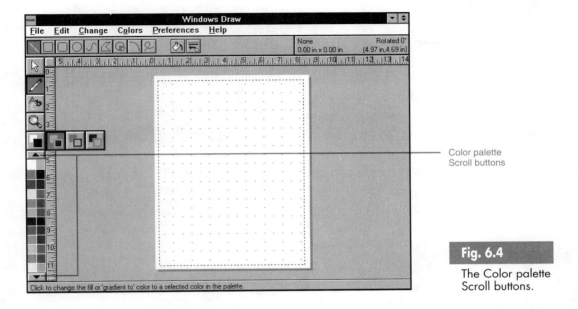

Color palette
Scroll buttons

Fig. 6.4

The Color palette
Scroll buttons.

After a symbol is selected, you can choose a different part of the symbol to color by clicking the appropriate button on the Color tool pop-out menu and then selecting a color from the color palette.

Filling Symbols with a Gradient

You can create an impressive effect by filling symbols with a *gradient*. A gradient starts at one color and ends at a different color. Bright gradients that run from one primary color to another, such as from red to yellow, create a highly colorful effect. Subtle gradients that change only slightly, from one shade of a color to another, can add depth to objects or the illusion of a light source in a drawing.

To fill symbols with a gradient, follow these steps:

1. Select the Pointer tool from the toolbox.

2. Select the symbol or symbols to fill with a gradient.

3. Select the Draw tool from the toolbox.

4. Click the Fill Style button.

5. Select **G**radient from the **Fi**ll Style menu. The Gradient dialog box appears (see fig. 6.5).

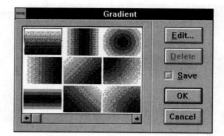

Fig. 6.5

The Gradient
dialog box.

6. Use the scroll bars below the gradient display to view all the current gradients and then click the gradient you want.

7. Click OK to return to the drawing and apply the gradient to the selected symbol(s).

TIP

You also can double-click a gradient on the Gradient dialog box. The gradient immediately fills the selected symbol.

Selecting the Colors for a Gradient

The Fill Color and Background Color buttons on the Color tool pop-out menu determine the starting and ending colors of a gradient.

The following list describes the buttons.

- The *Fill Color button* enables you to select the ending color of the gradient (the *fade-to color*).

- The *Background Color button* enables you to select the starting color of the gradient (the *fade-from color*).

To change the starting or ending color of the gradient, select the Fill Color button or the Background Color button and then click a color in the color palette.

The sample gradients displayed in the Gradient dialog box are drawn in black and white. The fade-from color is represented by white; the fade-to color is represented by black.

Editing a Gradient

When you select **G**radient from the Fill Style menu, the Gradient dialog box shows the current selection of gradients. You can edit any of the existing gradients, add a new gradient, or delete a gradient you no longer want. To edit a gradient, follow these steps:

1. From the toolbox, click the Draw tool.

2. Click the Fill Style button.

3. Select **G**radient from the Fill Style menu.

4. Select a gradient to edit and then click **E**dit. The Edit Gradient dialog box appears (see fig. 6.6).

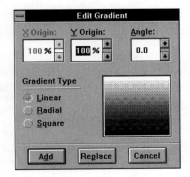

Fig. 6.6

The Edit Gradient dialog box.

5. Use the dialog controls to edit the gradient to suit your needs. (The individual controls are covered in the following sections.)

6. After you are done editing the gradient, choose **A**dd to add the new gradient to the list or Re**p**lace to replace the gradient you are editing.

Selecting a Gradient Type

In the Gradient dialog box, you can choose from among three gradient types: **L**inear, **R**adial, and **S**quare. Figure 6.7 shows an example of each type.

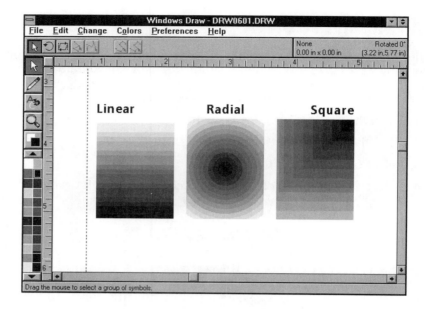

Fig. 6.7

Linear, radial,
and square
gradients.

The following list describes the gradient types.

■ A *linear* gradient fades from one color to another in a straight line across the gradient. The straight line can run from top to bottom, left to right, or at any other angle across the gradient.

■ A *radial* gradient fades from inside out in concentric circles. You can change the center point of the radial.

■ A *square* gradient fades from inside out in concentric squares. You can change the center point of the squares and the angle of the squares.

Select the type of gradient you want by clicking one of the three Gradient Type buttons near the bottom left of the Gradient dialog box, above the A**d**d button.

Setting the X and Y Origins

The **X** Origin and **Y** Origin controls enable you to set the position of the center point of a radial or square gradient. The **X** Origin number is the distance across the gradient from the left; the **Y** Origin is the distance

down the gradient from the top. These distances are measured in percentages. Halfway across or down is 50 percent. All the way across or
down is 100 percent. Figure 6.8 shows three combinations of **X** Origin
and **Y** Origin settings and the effects of these settings on a radial gradient.

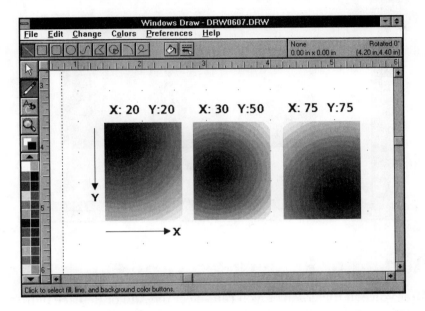

Fig. 6.8

Three sample **X**
Origin and **Y**
Origin settings.

Only the **Y** Origin control is active when you edit a linear gradient. The
Y Origin control determines how far down the gradient the fade-to
color appears. If you select 50% for the **Y** Origin, the fade-to color appears halfway down the gradient. The second half of the gradient fades
back to the fade-from color.

Setting the Angle Control

The **Angle** control determines the angle at which the linear and square
gradients fade. A setting of zero degrees causes a linear gradient to
fade from top to bottom. The angle changes in a counterclockwise direction when you increase the **Angle** setting. A 90-degree angle fades
from left to right. A 270-degree angle fades from right to left. The **Angle**
control has no effect on radial gradients. Figure 6.9 shows three sample
angle settings and the effects of these settings on a linear gradient.

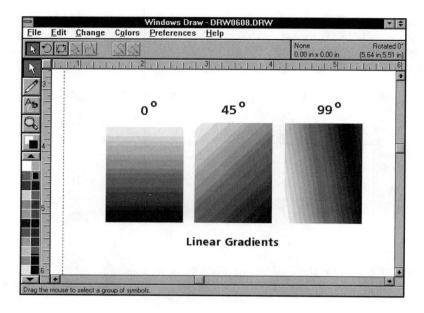

Fig. 6.9

Three sample
Angle settings.

Adding or Replacing a Gradient

After you edit the gradient, you can select the **A**dd or Re**p**lace buttons
to save the edited gradient. If you choose A**d**d, the new gradient is
added to the dialog as a new gradient. If you choose Re**p**lace, the gradient you selected to edit is replaced with the new gradient.

NOTE   The gradient dialog box can display up to 63 gradients.

Deleting a Gradient

If you no longer need one of the gradients displayed in the Gradient
dialog box, you can delete it by clicking the gradient and then clicking
the **D**elete button. Deleting a gradient removes it from the Gradient
dialog box. If you have already used the gradient, the symbols in which
you used that gradient do not change when you delete the gradient.

Saving the Revised Collection of Gradients

Gradients that you add or edit are available in the dialog box until you quit from Windows Draw. To save the gradients permanently so that they are available the next time you use Windows Draw, click the **S**ave button on the Gradients dialog box before you click OK to close the dialog box. You also must click the **S**ave button to save the gradient collection after you delete a gradient. Otherwise, the gradient re-appears the next time you use Windows Draw.

Filling Symbols with a Pattern

Rather than fill symbols with solid colors, you can fill them with colored patterns called *hatches* and *bitmaps*.

Hatches are patterns of straight lines that run horizontally, vertically, diagonally, both horizontally and diagonally, or diagonally in both directions. Hatches often are used to fill the slices of a pie in a pie chart or the bars in a bar chart to distinguish among them when the chart is not printed in color.

A *bitmap* is a pattern of dots that is automatically repeated to fill the symbol. With Windows Draw, you can edit the existing bitmap patterns and create your own permanent additions to the bitmap library.

Selecting a Hatch

To select a hatch for a symbol, follow these steps:

1. Click the Pointer tool in the toolbox. The Select button is depressed automatically.

2. Select the symbol that you want to fill with a hatch.

3. Click the Fill Style button.

4. Select **H**atch from the Fill Style menu. The Hatch dialog box appears (see fig. 6.10).

Fig. 6.10

The Hatch dialog box.

5. Click one of the hatches and then click OK.

TIP

You can save a step by double-clicking the hatch you want on the Hatch dialog box.

You cannot edit the hatches or create new hatches. You also cannot change the spacing between lines in the hatch. To create a pattern of straight lines with more space between them, you must create a bitmap. Bitmaps are covered in the next section.

Choosing a Bitmap

To select a bitmap for a symbol, follow these steps:

1. Click the Pointer tool in the toolbox. The Select button is depressed automatically.

2. Select the symbol that you want to fill with a bitmap.

3. Click the Fill Style button.

4. Select **B**itmap from the Fill Style menu. The Bitmap dialog box appears (see fig. 6.11).

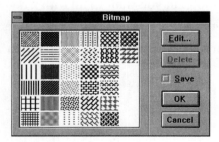

Fig. 6.11

The Bitmap dialog box.

5. Click one of the bitmaps and then click OK.

You can double-click a bitmap on the Bitmap dialog box
to save a step.

The last three hatches and bitmaps you use are saved as the
Fill Style menu selections so that you can easily choose
them again.

Editing a Bitmap

You can edit any of the existing bitmaps or create new bitmaps by
clicking the Edit button in the Bitmap dialog box. The bitmap selected
when you click the Edit button appears in the Edit Bitmap window.
Figure 6.12 shows the Edit Bitmap dialog box.

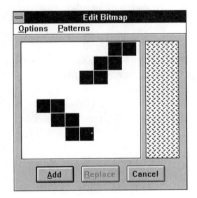

Fig. 6.12

The Edit Bitmap
dialog box.

Most of the Edit Bitmap dialog box is a magnified version of the grid of
dots that compose the bitmap. You can turn these dots on or off by
clicking them. A narrower strip to the right displays the bitmap at normal size so that you can see the result of your changes immediately.

To turn on all the dots in the pattern, click Options in the menu and
then select Black. To turn off all the dots, select White. To choose from
a display of all the current patterns, click Patterns in the menu and
then click the pattern you want to modify.

When you finish editing a pattern, click **Add** to add the edited bitmap to the current selection or **Replace** to replace the selected bitmap with the revised pattern.

Deleting Bitmaps and Saving the New Collection

To delete a bitmap you no longer need, click the bitmap in the Bitmap dialog box and then click the **Delete** button. Make sure to click the **Save** button before you select OK to save the revised collection of bitmaps without the deleted pattern.

To save the new collection of bitmaps permanently, click the **Save** button in the Bitmap dialog box. Otherwise, the bitmaps you have edited will not appear the next time you use Windows Draw.

Choosing Colors for the Pattern

To change the color of the lines or dots in the hatch or bitmap, select the symbol that is filled with the bitmap. Then select the Fill Color button on the Color tool pop-out menu and select a color from the color palette. To change the color of the background on which the lines or dots appear, select the Background Color button before selecting a color.

 NOTE   The Bitmap and Hatch dialog boxes display only black-and-white representations of bitmaps and hatches even though you can select colors for the bitmaps and hatches you use. On the dialog boxes, the black areas represent the fill color and the white areas represent the background color.

Modifying a Line Style

As with selecting a fill style, selecting a line style for a symbol is best done before you draw the symbol, but even after a symbol is drawn, you can experiment with different line style settings until you get just the effect you want.

If the symbol you have drawn is a line, the effect of changing the line style setting is obvious. If the symbol is a graphic shape, however, the line style setting affects the look of the outline surrounding the symbol. You can change the outline's color and thickness, its type (whether the outline is a solid line, dotted, dashed, or a combination of the two), and how the line segments that compose the outline join at corners.

To change the line style of a symbol on the page, follow these steps:

1. From the toolbox, select the Pointer tool.

2. Select the symbol you want to change.

3. From the toolbox, select the Draw tool.

4. In Ribbon, click the Line Style button.

5. Select an appropriate line style setting from the Line Style menu, or choose one of the line style commands that leads to a dialog box where you can change settings. The settings and their effects are covered in the following sections.

Choosing a Line Type

After you initially click the Line Style button, the Line Style menu contains pictures of the available line styles (see fig. 6.13). The first five options show a solid line, a dashed line, a dotted line, and two lines that are a combination of dots and dashes. The sixth option, **Invisible**, removes the outline surrounding filled objects such as rectangles, circles, pies, and polygons. If you filled the objects with colors, removing the outline leaves behind areas of color that are not bounded by lines.

Fig. 6.13

The Line Style menu.

Selecting a Line Width

A group of choices for line width are below the line style choices. The choices include **H**airline (a thin line less than one point wide), and the three most recent width settings you have chosen during the current session with Draw. The fifth option is **W**idth, which leads to the Line Width dialog box (see fig. 6.14).

Chapter 5, "Adding Symbols," covers the options in the Line Width dialog box.

Fig. 6.14

The Line Width dialog box.

Modifying Line Endings

Ends, the option at the bottom of the Line Style menu, enables you to choose the graphic shapes that appear at the beginning and end of lines from a variety of arrowheads and markers. You can choose a point, an arrow, a filled arrowhead, or a round, square, or triangular marker.

To select an ending, click the Ends option in the Line Style menu. The Line Ends dialog box appears (see fig. 6.15). Click the pull-down arrows next to the current Start or End settings to see the available choices. The Start and End points of a line are determined when the line is drawn. To make both endings the same, click Both Same. If you choose an ending for one end of the line after clicking Both Same, the other end gets the same setting automatically. If both Start and End are different when Both Same is checked, the setting for Start is used at both ends. When you finish selecting line endings, click OK.

Fig. 6.15

The Line Ends dialog box.

You can create a line graph by selecting the column chart from the ClipArt library (under the subject Graphs), ungrouping the ClipArt, and removing the bars. Draw lines from one data point to the next and choose the filled circle line ending for the end of each line. Use different line types to differentiate among lines. Figure 6.16 shows such a line chart.

TIP

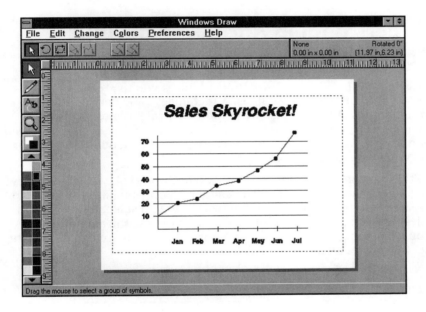

Fig. 6.16

A Windows
Draw line chart.

Changing the Shape of Symbols

After you click a symbol, you can use its handles to change the overall size or shape of the symbol, but you must use another method to change the shape of the lines and curves within the symbol. You must use the Select button, the Reshape button, and the Reshape Bézier button (described in the following paragraph).

Reshaping a Symbol's Points

After you select a symbol by clicking it with the Select button, you can click the Reshape Points button to move *anchor points* or the Reshape Bézier button to move anchor and *control points*. These buttons are in the Ribbon. The following section explains the difference between anchor points and control points.

Understanding Anchor Points and Control Points

Drawing symbols in Windows Draw requires you to create a combination of straight and curved lines. A rectangle, for example, is four straight lines. A polyline is any number of straight lines segments joined end to end. A curve is a number of curving line segments joined end to end. Even freehand symbols are really just a number of small curve segments strung together.

At the starting point of the symbol and at the end of each line or curve segment is an anchor point. The anchor points don't appear while you create the symbol, but they do appear after you select a symbol and click the Reshape Points button. By manipulating the anchor points, you can change the shape of a symbol's outline. Figure 6.17 shows the anchor points along a polyline.

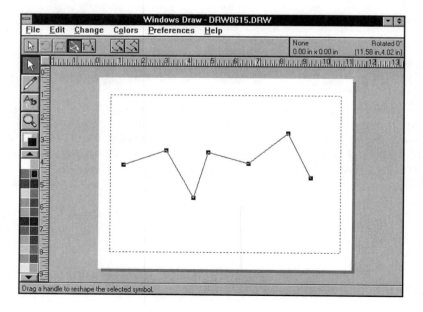

Fig. 6.17

The anchor points along a polyline.

Each anchor point has two control points that determine the angles of the line or curve segments on either side of the anchor point. One control point determines the angle at which the first line or curve segment approaches the anchor point. The other control point determines the angle at which the second line or curve segment departs from the anchor point. By dragging the control points, you can change the angles at which line and curve segments pass through anchor points. Figure 6.18 shows the control points along a curve.

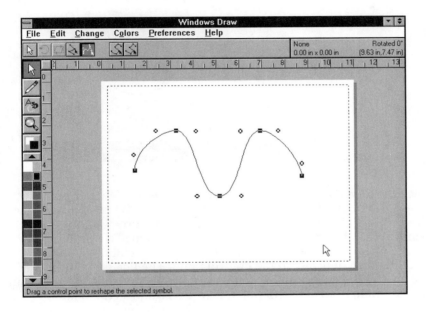

Working with Anchor Points and Control Points

To see the anchor and control points in some typical symbols, you can try a simple exercise. Draw a diagonal line and an ellipse side by side on a blank Draw page. Select the Draw tool from the toolbox and click the Select button in the Ribbon. When you click the line, handles surround the line. By dragging any of the handles, you can move and resize the line. No matter how you move the handle, however, the line remains a diagonal line. When you click the Reshape Points button, anchor points appear at either end of the line (see fig. 6.19). By dragging the anchor points, you can position either end of the line anywhere in the drawing area. You now have full control over the length, angle, and positioning of the line.

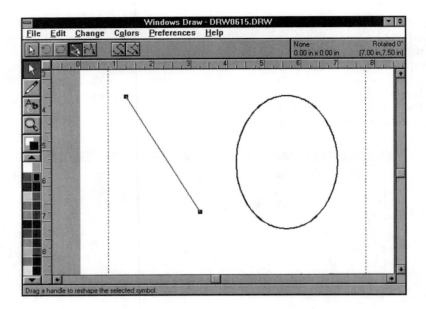

Fig. 6.19

The anchor
points of a line.

Click the Reshape Bézier button in the Ribbon. The anchor points at
either end of the line are replaced with small *x*'s. When you click one of
the *x*'s, hold the mouse button and drag in any direction, the line
bends. When you release the mouse button, a small round control
point appears and the line bends toward the control point as if it is
attracted magnetically to the control point. The line is still anchored at
the end by the anchor point, but it approaches the anchor point from
the direction of the control point. Figure 6.20 shows the bent line. Notice the small *x* at the lower end of the line. It indicates that you haven't
yet dragged the control points off the anchor point.

Select the Select tool from the Ribbon and click the ellipse. Handles
appear around the ellipse. When you click the Reshape Points button,
however, four anchor points appear along the curve of the ellipse, as
shown in figure 6.21.

The anchor points show that the ellipse is composed of four curves
joined end to end, which makes sense because you also can create an
ellipse by drawing four arcs joined end to end.

When you click the Reshape Bézier button in the Ribbon, a pair of control points flanking each anchor point appear. Because each anchor
point is at the intersection of two curves, two control points are near
each anchor point. Just as with lines, the control points determine the
angles at which the curves approach each anchor point. Figure 6.22
shows the pair of control points near each anchor point.

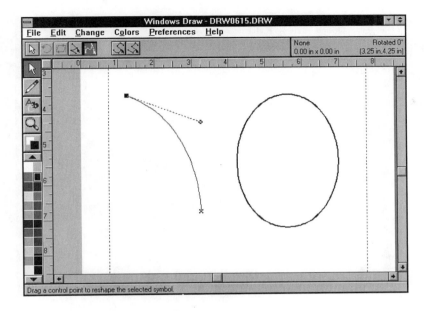

Fig. 6.20

The bent line.

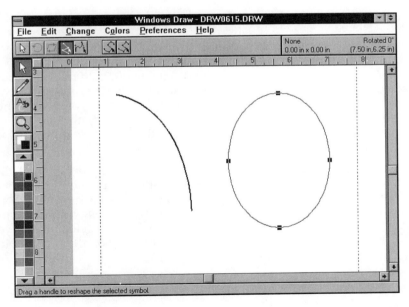

Fig. 6.21

The anchor points along an ellipse.

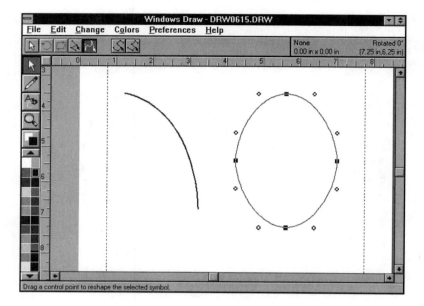

Fig. 6.22

The anchor
points and
control points of
an ellipse.

Moving More Than One Anchor Point

By selecting a symbol with the Select tool and then choosing the Reshape Points tool from the Ribbon, you can move any of the anchor
points to reshape the symbol by simply clicking it, holding the mouse
button, and dragging the mouse. Because all the anchor points are selected, you can move all the points simultaneously by positioning the
pointer near the symbol (but not on any of the points) clicking and
holding the mouse button, and dragging. This procedure moves the
entire symbol.

To move only selected points, click a point, hold the Shift key and click
each of the other points you want to move. Position the cursor somewhere in between all the points, click and hold and the mouse button,
and drag. You also can select several points by drawing a rubber band
box around them with the pointer. Several points are selected, but you
still can move one of the points by clicking directly on the point, holding the mouse button, and dragging.

When you place the pointer on an anchor or control point, the
pointer appears as a single point to indicate that you can move the
anchor or control point. When you place the pointer near a group of
selected anchor points, the pointer appears as a four-way arrow to
indicate that you can move the selected points as a group.

When the Reshape Points button is selected, you can choose **S**elect All from the **E**dit menu or press F2 to select all the points in the symbol with which you are working.

TIP

Adding Anchor Points

By adding an anchor point along the outline of a symbol, you can break a single line or curve segment into two connected segments that you can reshape individually. To add an anchor point, follow these steps:

1. Make sure that the Reshape Points button or the Reshape Bézier button is pressed.

2. Choose Duplicate from the Edit menu or press Ctrl-D. The cursor shows that you are in duplicate mode by displaying a pair of tiny rectangles.

3. Click along the line or curve where you want the additional point to appear.

If the Reshape Points button is selected when you duplicate a point, an anchor point appears. If the Reshape Bézier button is selected when you duplicate a point, an anchor point and its two control points appear.

With this method, you could "raise the roof" of a rectangle to create the outline of a house. Follow these steps:

1. From the toolbox, select the Draw tool.

2. In the Ribbon, click the rectangle button.

3. Draw a rectangle on the page that is taller than it is wide.

4. From the toolbox, select the Pointer tool.

5. In the Ribbon, click the Reshape Points button. All the anchor points of the rectangle are now selected, as shown in figure 6.23.

6. Press Ctrl-D to put Draw into duplicate mode. (The Reshape Points button must be selected when you press Ctrl-D to duplicate points.)

7. Click at the middle of the line between the top two points.

8. Click somewhere on the page away from the rectangle to deselect the points.

9. Click the point you have added, hold the mouse button, and drag the pointer up to "raise the roof," as shown in figure 6.24.

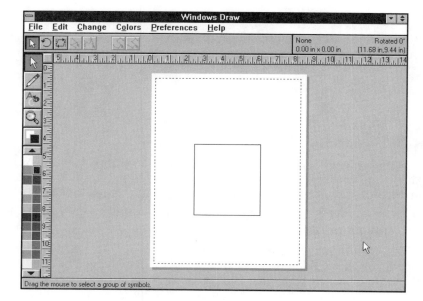

Fig. 6.23

All the anchor points are selected after you click the Reshape Points button.

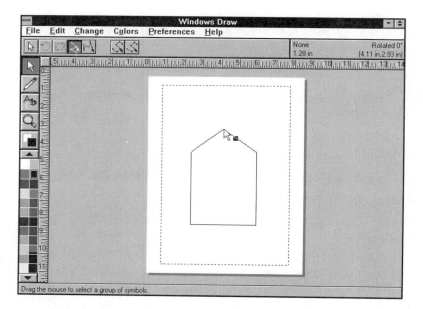

Fig. 6.24

Raising the roof of a rectangle.

Deleting Anchor Points

By deleting an anchor point, you replace two line segments or curves with a single segment. You can select a single point to delete, or you can select several anchor points to delete simultaneously. To delete an anchor point or points, follow these steps:

1. Make sure that the Reshape Points button or the Reshape Bézier button is pressed.

2. Select the point or points to delete.

3. Press the Delete (Del) key on the keyboard.

By deleting an anchor point, you can turn a perfect square into a perfect triangle. Follow these steps:

1. From the toolbox, select the Draw tool.

2. In the Ribbon, click the Rectangle button.

3. Press and hold the Ctrl key while you draw a rectangle.

4. From the toolbox, select the Pointer tool.

5. Click the square to select it.

6. Select the Reshape Points button. Figure 6.25 shows the Selected square with its anchor points.

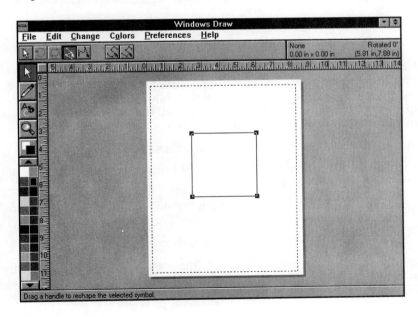

Fig. 6.25

The Selected square.

7. Click the upper right corner point.

8. Press the Del key to remove a side from the square and create a triangle, as shown in figure 6.26.

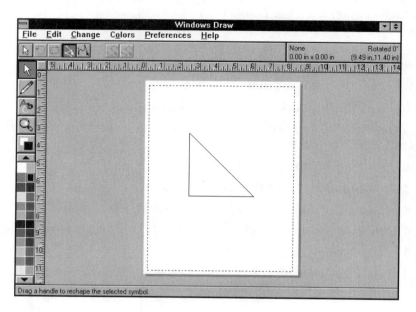

Fig. 6.26

The triangle formed by removing a side from a square.

Smoothing a Symbol

Draw provides a easy way for you to quickly smooth a symbol so that its anchor points are joined by curves rather than straight lines. The Smooth button causes the outline of a symbol to curve smoothly through all the selected anchor points. If all the points are selected, all the lines in the symbol look like one smoothly flowing curve.

To smooth the lines in a symbol, follow these steps:

1. Make sure that the Reshape Points button or the Reshape Bézier button is selected.

2. Select the points through which the line should pass as a smooth curve.

3. In the Ribbon, click the Smooth button.

To try using the Smooth button, use the Draw tool to draw a rectangle on the page. Select it with the Pointer tool and click the Reshape Points button. Finally, click the Smooth button to convert its lines to curves that pass smoothly through all four points. Figure 6.27 shows the rectangle before and after smoothing.

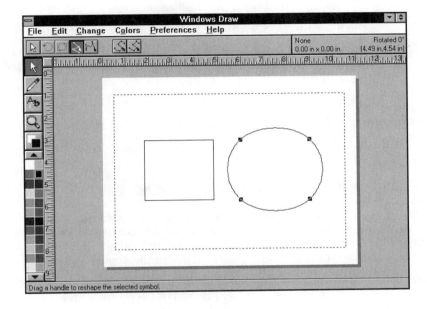

Fig. 6.27

A rectangle
before and after
smoothing.

Remember that you can smooth only a portion of a symbol by selecting only some of the symbol's anchor points.

Unsmoothing a Symbol

When you unsmooth a symbol, you convert the curves that connect the symbol's points to straight lines. To unsmooth a symbol, follow these steps:

1. Make sure that the Reshape Points or Reshape Bézier button is selected.

2. Select the points that should be connected with straight lines.

3. In the Ribbon, click the Unsmooth button.

You can try unsmoothing a curve by drawing a wavy line across the page with the Curve button and then unsmoothing it. Follow these steps:

1. Select the Draw tool and click the Curve button in the Ribbon area.

2. Draw a wavy line across the screen. (Click and drag alternately up to the right diagonally and then down and to the right diagonally.)

3. Select the Pointer tool from the toolbox.

4. Click the Select button in the Ribbon area.

5. Click the wavy line to select it. When you select the curve, all its anchor points appear. You can move any of the anchor points to reshape the curve.

6. In the Ribbon, click the Unsmooth button.

Unsmoothing a curve converts it to straight lines that run from anchor point to anchor point.

Reshaping a Symbol's Béziers

In the previous section, you learned to move, add, and delete line or curve segments by changing a symbol's anchor points with the Reshape Points button. The next button over, the Reshape Bézier button, allows you to make fine-tuning adjustments to the segments.

 A Bézier is a line or curve that is shaped by control points. A control point is next to the anchor point at the end of each line. It determines the angle at which the line approaches the anchor point. If the line or curve is composed of several segments, the anchor points along the line are flanked by pairs of control points. One control point determines the angle at which the first segment approaches the anchor point and the other control point determines the angle at which the next line departs from the anchor point.

Draw gives you unlimited control over the positioning of control points and, therefore, unlimited control over the angles of curving lines.

Grabbing Control Points

To work with the control points of a symbol, select the symbol with the Select tool and then click the Reshape Bézier button. Control points appear along with anchor points. If the symbol is a curve, the control points are easy to see as small, round circles on either side of the anchor points. The beginning and end points of the curve have only one control point nearby. Figure 6.28 shows a curve after it has been selected with the Reshape Bézier button.

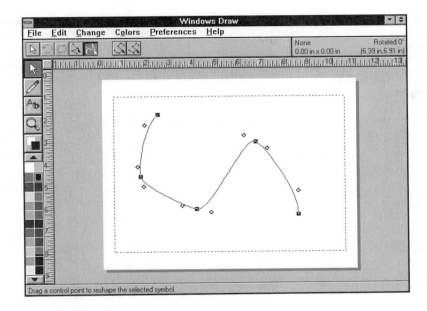

Fig. 6.28

A curve and its control points.

If the symbol you have selected is a shape composed of straight lines rather than curves, such as a rectangle or polyline, the control points are on top of the anchor points. Draw displays a small *x* at the anchor points rather than the usual small box. Figure 6.29 shows a rectangle that has been selected with the Reshape Bézier button.

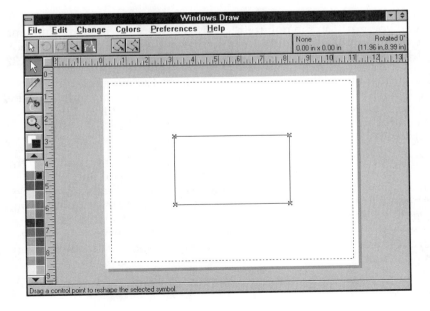

Fig. 6.29

A rectangle showing its control points on top of the anchor points.

You can pull out the control points by clicking the x, holding the mouse button, and dragging the mouse pointer away from the anchor point, as shown in figure 6.30. Click the x a second time and drag away to pull out the second control point. Figure 6.31 shows the rectangle after the pair of control points has been pulled away from one of the anchor points.

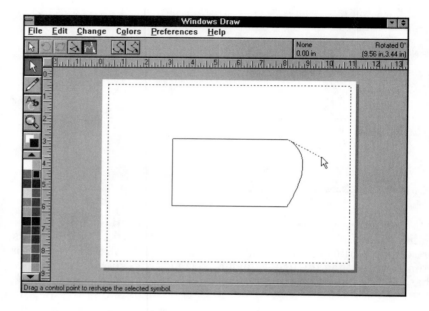

Fig. 6.30

Pulling the control points out from one of the anchor points of a rectangle.

When you position the pointer directly on one of the control points of a curve, a straight dashed tangent line that passes from one control point to the other through the anchor point appears, as shown in figure 6.32.

By clicking one of the control points, holding the mouse button, and dragging the mouse, you can drag the control points in tandem around the anchor point and change the angle of the tangent line. The angle of the curve follows the angle of the tangent line. Figure 6.33 shows the curve after the angle of the tangent line is changed.

By moving one of the control points closer to or farther away from the anchor point, you can change the length of the tangent line, which changes the bend of the curve as it arrives from or heads toward another anchor point. You can change the length of both ends of the tangent line independently. The farther away the control point is, the greater the bend in the curve. Figure 6.34 shows a curve segment before and after a control point is dragged to a greater distance from an anchor point.

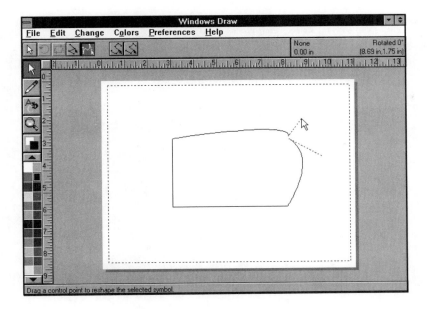

Fig. 6.31

The rectangle after two control points have been pulled out from one anchor point.

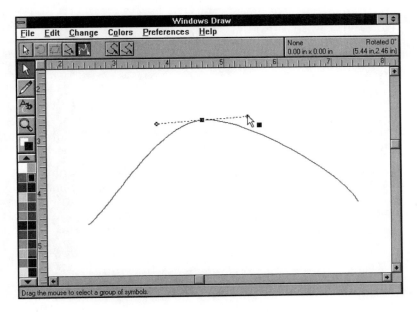

Fig. 6.32

A straight line that passes through the anchor point extends from one control point to the other.

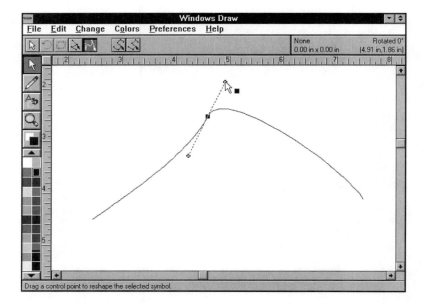

Fig. 6.33

Changing the angle of the tangent line by moving the control points.

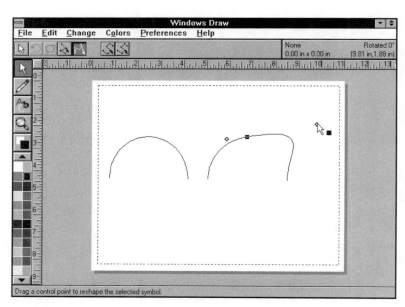

Fig. 6.34

A curve segment before and after a control point is dragged to a greater distance from an anchor point.

Moving Control Points Independently

Because the dashed tangent line that connects the control points is a straight line, the line curves smoothly through the anchor point. To move the control points independently, press and hold the Shift key before dragging a control point with the mouse pointer. When you press the Shift key, the control points no longer move in tandem around the anchor point. A corner is formed at the anchor point rather than a smooth curve. Figure 6.35 shows the curve after the control point on the right is moved independently.

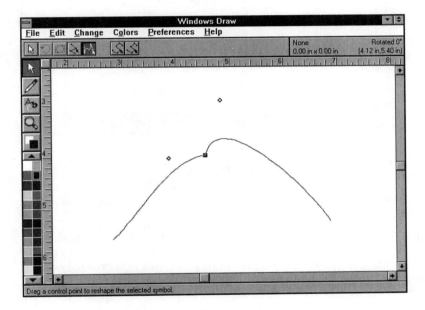

Fig. 6.35

The curve after the control point on the right is moved while the Shift key is pressed.

Creating an Even Curve

If you press the Shift key, you can move the two control points independently around an anchor point. Pressing the Ctrl key creates the opposite effect. When you move one control point, the other control point moves in an equal distance in the opposite direction. This ensures a perfectly even curve that has the same bend on either side of the anchor point. Figure 6.36 shows the curve after the control points are moved away from the anchor point while the Ctrl key is pressed.

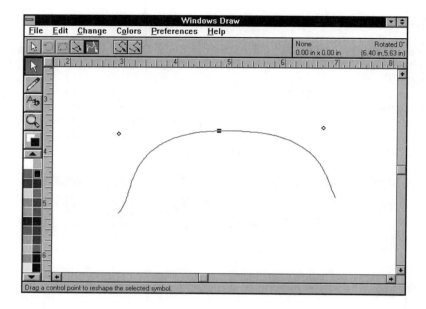

Fig. 6.36

The curve after the control points are moved away from the anchor point while the Ctrl key is pressed.

Working with Control Points

To try working with control points, follow this exercise: Draw a large rectangle and ellipse side by side on the page.

Click the ellipse with the Pointer tool and then select the Reshape Bézier button from the ribbon. Four anchor points appear on the circumference of the circle. Each anchor point has two control points. Position the pointer on the control point to the right of the anchor point at the top of the circle. Drag the control point up and away from the circle, as shown in figure 6.37. Notice how the shape of the curve changes.

Press the Shift key and drag the control point back down. Notice that the tangent line is no longer straight. You have created a sharp corner at the top of the circle by moving one of the control points independently. Figure 6.38 shows the new shape of the ellipse.

Click the control point to the right of the anchor point at the bottom of the circle. Press and hold the Ctrl key and move the control point straight to the right. Notice that the control point on the other side of the anchor point moves the same distance to the left, creating an even curve that passes through the anchor point. Fig. 6.39 shows the even curve that results.

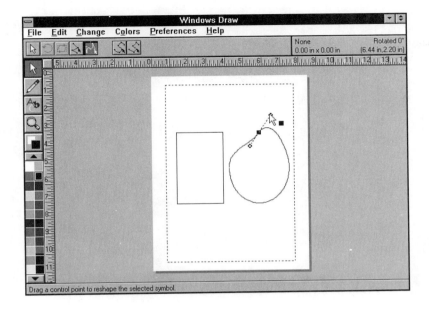

Fig. 6.37

The ellipse when a control point is moved.

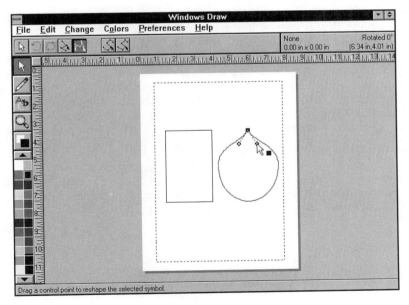

Fig. 6.38

The ellipse with a sharp corner created by moving a control point independently.

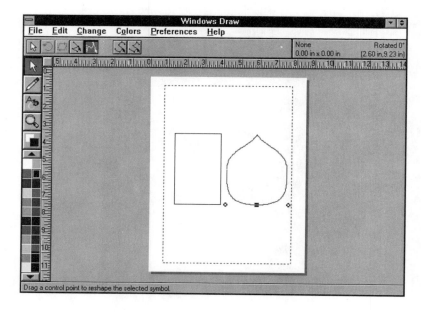

Fig. 6.39

An even curve
passing through
the bottom
anchor point.

Click the Select button in the ribbon and then click the rectangle. Select
the Reshape Bézier button in the ribbon. Click the x at the upper right
corner of the rectangle, hold the mouse button, and drag the mouse
pointer to the right. The first of the two control points is dragged off.
Click the same x again and drag the second control point straight up
and away from the anchor point. An anchor point and two control
points appear. You can manipulate the control points just as you would
manipulate the control points on a curve. Figure 6.40 shows the rectangle after you have dragged two control points from the anchor point.

Even the straight lines of a rectangle still can be curved when you use
the lines' control points. This exercise demonstrates that you can think
of every line in Draw as a curve. When you drag the control points off
the anchor points at the ends of a straight line, you can control the
amount of curve to apply to the line.

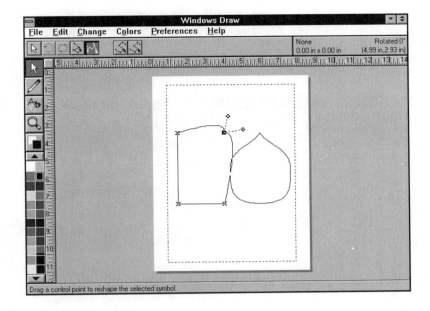

Fig. 6.40

Dragging two
control points
from an anchor
point on a
rectangle.

Exercise

This exercise enables you to try your hand at changing the shape of a
symbol by moving its anchor and control points. The new restaurant,
Rigley's, needs a logo. You create the logo by modifying the shape of
text that you convert to curves.

To begin creating the Rigley's logo, follow these steps:

1. Select the Text tool from the toolbox.

2. Select Dutch from the font list box and 60 pts from the font size
   list box in the ribbon.

3. Click the page and type **Rigley's**.

4. Position the text cursor between the character pairs and kern the
   characters so that they are tighter together, particularly the characters on either side of the apostrophe.

5. From the toolbox, select the Pointer tool.

6. Click the text you just entered.

7. From the **Change** menu, select **Convert to Curves** to convert the text to a series of curves. The page should look like the one shown in figure 6.41.

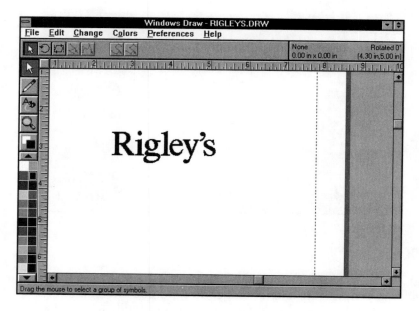

The logo text placed on the page and kerned.

Now you have on the page a group of independent graphic shapes. You can reshape the points of any of these shapes to add a little flair to the word. You may want to try stretching the right leg of the *R* in Rigley's to create an interesting look. To make it easier to see your work, click the View tool and then click the Zoom button. Draw a rubber band box around the *R* to zoom in on it.

To reshape the letters *R* and *Y* of Rigley's, follow these steps:

1. With the Pointer tool, click the *R* of Rigley's.

2. In the Ribbon, click the Reshape Points button.

3. Click the page away from the letter *R* to deselect all the points.

4. Draw a rubber band box around the three points at the bottom of the right leg of the letter, as shown in figure 6.42.

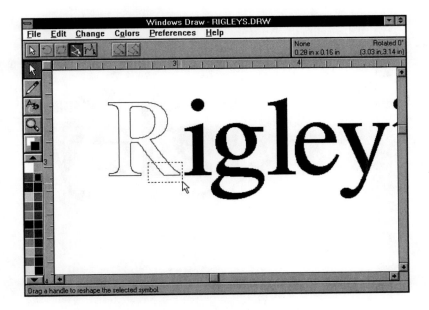

Fig. 6.42

Selecting the anchor points at the bottom of the right leg of the letter *R*.

5. Position the cursor somewhere among the three points. Make sure that the cursor shows a crosshair.

6. Click and hold the mouse button and drag down and to the right. The *R* should now look like the one shown in figure 6.43.

7. Press Esc to finish reshaping the symbol.

Use the same technique to stretch down the descender of the letter *Y* (the part that extends below the baseline). The revised drawing should match the drawing shown in figure 6.44.

In this next series of steps, you reshape the stretched leg of the letter R to give it a graceful curve.

1. With the Pointer tool, click the letter R and then click the Reshape Bézier button in the Ribbon. Notice the round control points to the left of the two anchor points at the bottom of the stretched leg, as shown in figure 6.45.

2. Click one of the control points, hold the mouse button, and drag the point up and to the left.

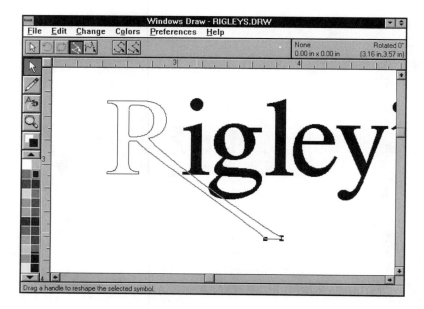

Fig. 6.43

The stretched leg
of the letter *R*.

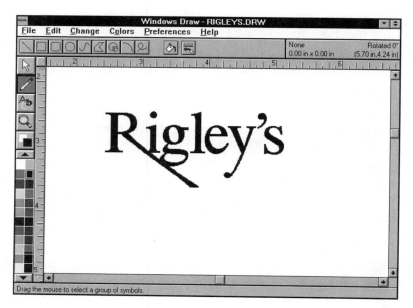

Fig. 6.44

The revised text
logo.

3. Click the other control point and drag it up and to the left also.
   The stretched part of the *R* should curve gracefully, as shown in
   figure 6.46.

If you have trouble getting exactly the curve you want, you can add
anchor points along the outline of the stretched leg. You then can move

the anchor points and their control points to make fine-tuning adjustments to the curve.

After you finish working with the text, you may want to make other changes to the appearance of the text. Figure 6.47 shows the original text and one possibility for a graphic text logo.

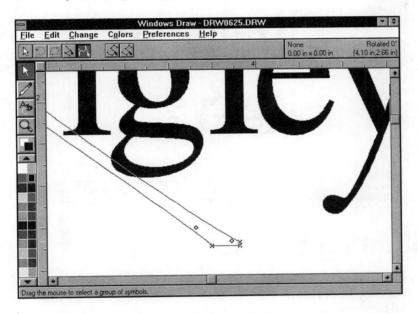

Fig. 6.45

The anchor and control points for the letter *R*.

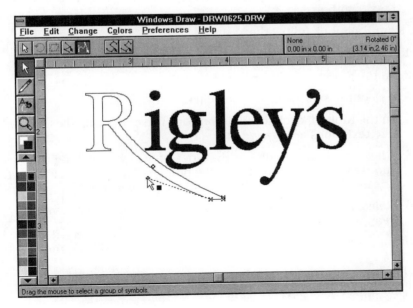

Fig. 6.46

The curved and stretched leg of the letter *R*.

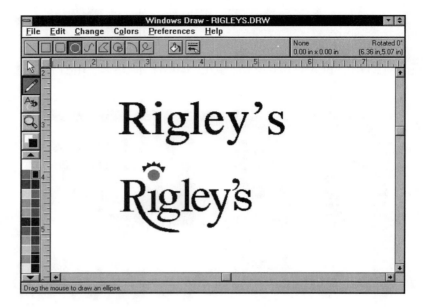

Fig. 6.47

The original text
and the revised
graphic text
logo.

Slanting Symbols

You can tilt graphic symbols by using the Slant button in the Ribbon. You cannot slant text or bitmap symbols, however. Tilting symbols is useful for creating a variety of effects. Figure 6.48 shows two sample tilted text symbols.

To slant a symbol, follow these steps:

1. From the toolbox, select the Pointer tool.

2. In the Ribbon, click the Select button.

3. Select the symbol to slant by clicking it.

4. In the Ribbon, click the Slant button. The corner handles around the text block are grayed out.

5. Click one of the handles at the sides of the symbol, hold the mouse button, and then drag the pointer. The status bar tells you the number of degrees the symbol has been slanted.

6. Release the mouse button when you are finished. The symbol reappears slanted.

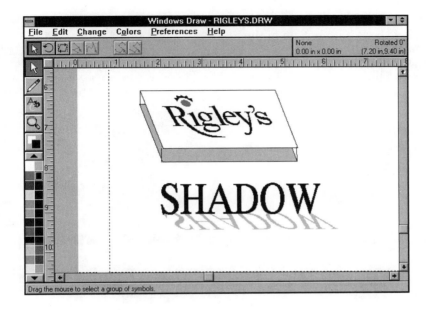

Fig. 6.48

Two sample
slanted text
symbols.

If you are unsatisfied with the slant angle, press Alt-Backspace or select
Undo from the Edit menu immediately before making another change.
Then try slanting the object again.

Although you cannot slant text symbols, you can convert a text
block to curves by using the **Convert to Curves** command on the
Change menu and then slanting the curves.

TIP

Rotating Symbols

You can rotate symbols around a pivot point by using the Rotate button. Draw places the pivot point at the center of the symbol so that the
symbol will rotate in place. You can move the pivot point to any position on-screen and rotate the symbol around that position, however.

To rotate a symbol, click the symbol with the Pointer tool and then select the Rotate button in the Ribbon. A pivot point appears at the center of the symbol. Place the cursor somewhere near the pivot point and move the pointer in a circular motion around the pivot point, either clockwise or counterclockwise. Figure 6.49 shows a symbol before and during rotation.

 When you rotate a symbol, the Status bar tells you the degree of rotation.

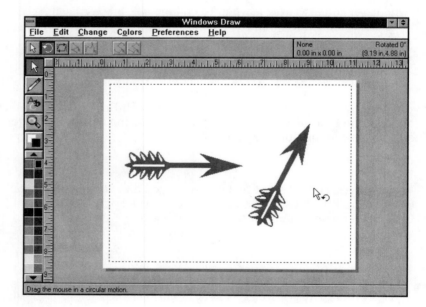

Fig. 6.49

A symbol before and during rotation.

⊕ Draw places the pivot point in the center of the symbol you are about to rotate, but you can move the pivot point anywhere on the page to rotate the symbol around that point. Click the pivot point, hold the mouse button, and drag the pivot point to the position you want.

After you select an object to pivot and then click the Rotate button, the pointer does not have to be on the symbol when you rotate it by dragging the pointer around the pivot point. For finer control of the angle of rotation, place the pointer out near the edge of the screen and move the pointer clockwise or counterclockwise around the pivot point.

TIP

Summary

This chapter explained how to change the fill and line style of symbols on the page. You also how learned to change the shape of symbols and how to slant and rotate them. The next chapter explains how to use Draw to arrange and align symbols on the page.

Arranging Symbols on the Page

Previous chapters in this book describe how to draw graphic symbols, place text on a page, and incorporate ClipArt symbols into your work. In using these techniques, however, you have only begun to tap the power of Draw.

You actually can accomplish such relatively simple tasks manually by using traditional graphic arts tools at a layout table. This chapter, however, describes techniques far beyond those of the traditional graphic artist. Only the combination of a computer and drawing software such as Windows Draw enables you to perform such tasks as aligning drawn objects automatically, flipping those objects over, changing the order in which the objects are stacked, and blending from one symbol design to another across the page.

All commands in this chapter require you first to select the symbols you want to arrange. You can use the techniques to select symbols described at the beginning of Chapter 6, "Changing the Appearance of Symbols."

Aligning Symbols

Draw provides a powerful and easy-to-use set of commands for aligning the symbols you create. **A**lign, on the **C**hange menu, enables you to align symbols with one another or in relation to the page. You can use the **A**lign command to center several lines of text under one another, for example, or to arrange symbols into a pattern.

You can use the Rulers, the Grid, and the Status bar to align symbols manually while still drawing them. After you have placed the objects on the page, however, you can use the **A**lign command to position these symbols.

To select symbols to align, click the symbols one by one while pressing the Shift key. A bounding box appears around the symbols after you select them. Handles to move or resize the objects appear at the boundaries of the bounding box. The **A**lign command aligns symbols against the sides or in the middle of this box.

You also can draw a rubber band box, as described in Chapter 6, "Changing the Appearance of Symbols," that completely encloses the symbols to be selected but encloses no other symbols. After you select the symbols, this rubber band box shrinks to a bounding box that tightly encloses the group of selected symbols. Figure 7.1 shows the rubber band box being drawn around a group of symbols. Figure 7.2 shows the symbols selected.

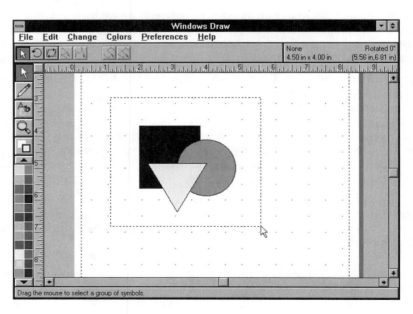

Fig. 7.1

A rubber band box being drawn around a group of symbols.

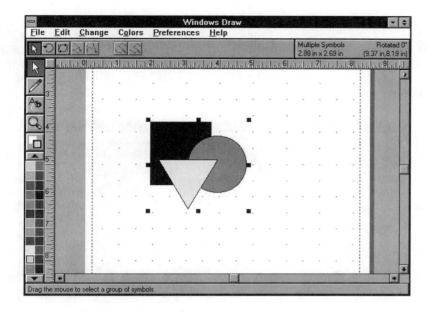

Fig. 7.2

The selected
symbols.

After you select the symbols to be aligned, choose **A**lign from the
Change menu. A pop-out menu appears displaying all the alignment
options, as shown in figure 7.3.

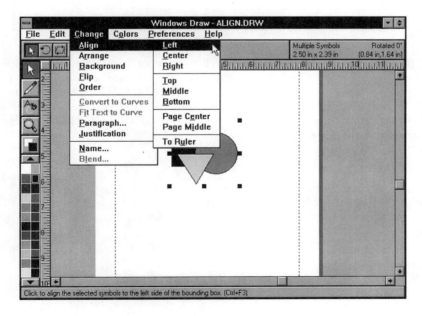

Fig. 7.3

The **A**lign menu.

The alignment options are divided into four groups. The first three options, **L**eft, **C**enter, and **R**ight, move symbols horizontally without disturbing their vertical positions. The next three options, **T**op, **M**iddle, and **B**ottom, move symbols vertically without disturbing their horizontal positions. Figures 7.4 and 7.5 show the effects of these horizontal and vertical alignment options.

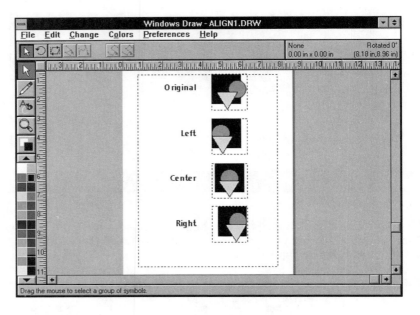

Fig. 7.4

The horizontal alignment options.

The third set of alignment options, Page **C**enter and Page **M**iddle, align the selected objects relative to the page. Page Center doesn't change an object's vertical position, but moves the object left or right to the horizontal center of the page. Page Middle doesn't change an object's horizontal position, but moves the object up or down to the vertical middle of the page, respectively.

TIP

To center a drawing you create on the page, select the entire drawing by choosing **S**elect All on the **E**dit menu. Then select the Page Center option on the **A**lign menu, followed by the Page Middle option.

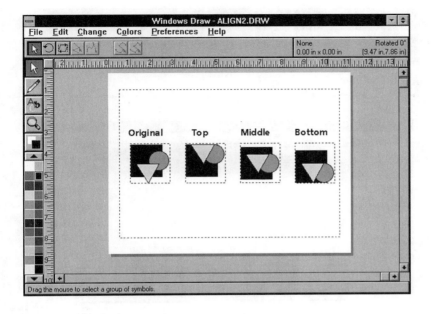

Fig. 7.5

The vertical
alignment
options.

The last option on the **A**lign menu, To R**u**ler, aligns the top left corner
of each selected object to the nearest Ruler division. With this option,
you can neatly space symbols in a pattern across the page.

To create the pattern of horizontal stripes 1/8 inch apart that is needed
for a business reply card, for example, simply draw the stripes on the
page in their approximate positions, align their left edges, set the ruler
for eight divisions per inch, and then align the objects to the ruler. Figure 7.6 shows the pattern of stripes before and after alignment. Notice
that the ruler is set to eight divisions per inch and that the stripes align
to the vertical ruler divisions.

The following table shows the keyboard shortcuts for each of the align
options:

Option	Shortcut
Align Left	Ctrl-F3
Align Center	Ctrl-F5
Align Right	Ctrl-F7
Align Top	Ctrl-F4
Align Middle	Ctrl-F6
Align Bottom	Ctrl-F8

Option	Shortcut
Align Page Center	Ctrl-F9
Align Page Middle	Ctrl-F10
Align To Ruler	Ctrl-F12

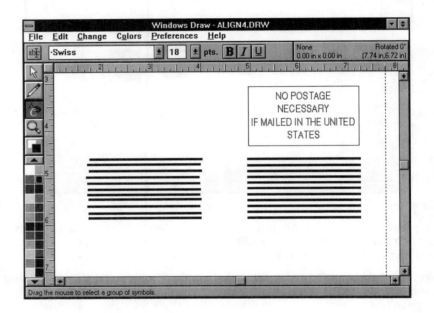

Fig. 7.6

Using the **A**lign To R**u**ler command to create the stripes for a business reply card.

Aligning Text within a Symbol

Draw provides an undocumented method of centering text both horizontally and vertically in a symbol, as shown in the examples in figure 7.7. This procedure places an insertion point at the center of the symbol so that the text you type is centered within the symbol.

To center text within any symbol, follow these steps:

1. Select the Text tool in the toolbox.

2. Click the Text Cursor button in the Ribbon area to deselect the button.

3. Click the symbol within which you want to type the centered text.

4. Press and hold the Shift key, and click the Text Cursor button. An insertion point appears at the center of the symbol.

5. Type the text. The text appears centered in the symbol.

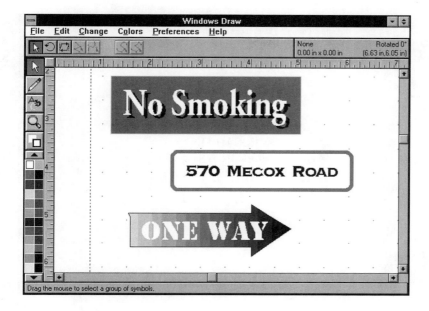

Fig. 7.7

Text centered
within symbols.

6. Press Esc or double-click the mouse after you finish typing the text.

To use the preceding procedure to create the *No postage necessary* part of a business reply card, as shown in figure 7.6, follow these steps:

1. Select the Draw tool in the toolbox, and click the Rectangle button.

2. Draw a square 2 1/2 inches across anywhere on the page. (To form a perfect square, hold the Ctrl key as you draw a rectangle.)

3. Click the Text tool in the toolbox.

4. Use the Font list box in the Ribbon area to select Swiss as the font and use the Font Size list box to select 20 points as the font size.

5. Click the Text Cursor button in the Ribbon area to deselect it.

6. Click the square to select it.

7. Press and hold the Shift key, and then click the Text Cursor button. An insertion point appears at the middle of the square.

8. Press the Caps Lock key and type **NO POSTAGE NECESSARY IF MAILED IN THE UNITED STATES**.

9. Press Esc or double-click the mouse after you finish typing the text.

The completed picture looks like the one shown in figure 7.8.

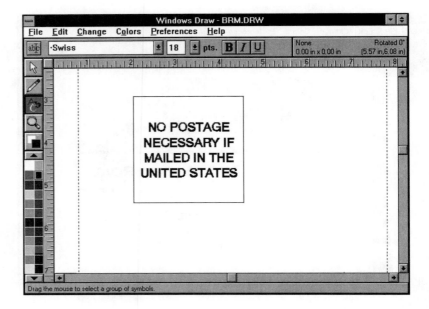

The completed
text of the
business reply
card.

Connecting Symbols

Draw provides a command expressly designed to connect the first and
last points of symbols that have distinct beginnings and endings.

Polylines, curves, arcs, and freehand symbols all have first and last
points that are not connected to one another. The Connect command
(found under Arrange on the Change menu) draws a straight line between these two points to close a symbol that previously was open. A
polyline that has been "connected" becomes a polygon. Figure 7.9
shows two symbols, a polyline and a curve, before and after being connected with the Connect command.

The Connect command also can be used to join two different objects
that have open endings. If you choose the Connect command after selecting two open symbols, such as two polylines, Draw joins the last
point of each symbol with the first point of the other symbol to form a
single closed symbol. Figure 7.10 shows a polyline and a curve before
and after being connected to each other with the Connect command.

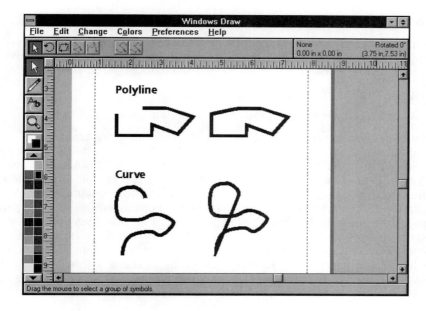

Fig. 7.9

A polyline and a curve before and after being connected.

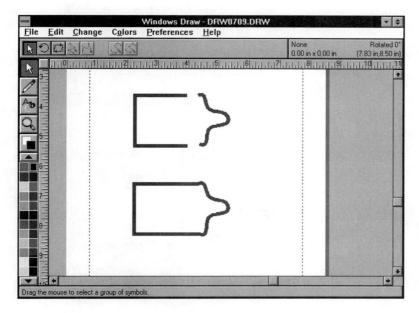

Fig. 7.10

A polyline and a curve before and after being connected to each other.

To connect two open symbols, follow these steps:

1. Select both symbols by clicking on the Select button and then clicking on each symbol with the Shift key pressed or by drawing a rubber band box that encloses the symbols.

2. From the Change menu, choose Arrange.

3. From the Arrange pop-out menu, choose Connect.

You can even use the Connect command to connect several closed symbols. The symbols do not need to be touching one another before being connected. After they are connected, they will be considered one symbol even though they are not physically connected. As when using the Group command (also on the Arrange pop-out menu under the Change menu and described in Chapter 3, "Working with ClipArt"), you no longer can select only one of the symbols that has been connected to other symbols. All the connected symbols are selected as a single symbol and take on the current fill and line settings. If a gradient is selected as the current fill setting, the gradient starts within one object and continues within the other connected objects. When objects are grouped instead of connected, however, each object has its own separate gradient. Figure 7.11 shows the difference between two grouped objects filled with a gradient and two connected objects filled with a gradient.

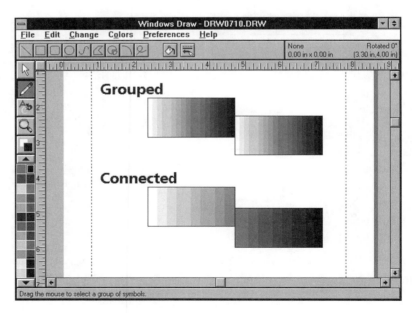

Fig. 7.11

Two grouped and two connected symbols filled with a gradient.

When two connected symbols overlap, the fill is removed within the region of overlap. Figure 7.12 shows two overlapping symbols filled with a solid color; the area of overlap appears unfilled. When three symbols overlap, the area overlapped by all three symbols is again filled, as shown in figure 7.13. A fourth symbol placed atop the existing three again turns off the fill in the region where all four symbols overlap.

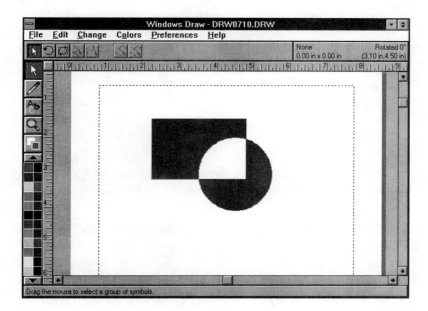

After you connect any number of symbols, you can add more symbols to the connection by simultaneously selecting the connected symbols and any new symbols. After you choose Connect, all the selected symbols, including the new symbols, are connected.

To disconnect symbols, simply select the connected symbols and choose Arrange on the Change menu and Disconnect on the Arrange pop-out menu.

Even after symbols are connected by the Connect command, those symbols maintain their original anchor points. If you connect two simple curves, for example, Draw adds new lines between their existing anchor points to create the new closed curve, as shown in figure 7.14. You can read all about anchor points in Chapter 6, "Changing the Appearance of Symbols."

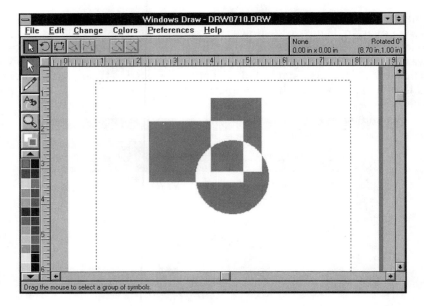

Fig. 7.13

Three overlapping connected symbols.

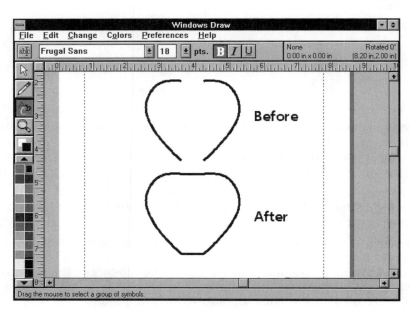

Fig. 7.14

Two simple curves before and after being connected.

Because all their original anchor points are still available, you can independently manipulate the shapes of connected symbols by using the Reshape Points and Reshape Bézier buttons. If you combine two symbols by grouping them, however, you cannot independently manipulate the shapes of the individual symbols in the group. After you group symbols, you no longer have access to the Reshape Points or Reshape Bézier buttons, because you cannot make changes to only one of the symbols in a group. You learned about the Reshape Points and Reshape Bézier buttons in Chapter 6, "Changing the Appearance of Symbols."

The following exercise demonstrates how to use the Connect command to create a line of text that fades from one color to another.

Because a gradient travels across all connected symbols, you can use the Connect command to create text with a smooth gradient from one end to another. To apply a gradient to text, you must first convert the text to curves by using the Convert to Curves command of the Change menu. (If you merely select the text and choose a gradient, the full gradient appears within each character.) Then you select all the characters of the text, connect them with the Connect command, and apply a horizontal gradient to the text. The resulting gradient runs from the start of the text to the finish.

To create a line of text fading from one color to another, start by creating a new landscape page, as described in Chapter 2, "Getting Started," and then follow these steps:

1. Select the Text tool from the toolbox.

2. Select Latin Wide from the Font list box and 72 points from the Font Size list box.

3. Click at the left side of the newly created page and type **FADE OUT**.

4. Click the Pointer tool in the toolbox.

5. Click on the text and choose Convert to Curves from the Change menu.

6. From the Change menu, choose Arrange.

7. From the Arrange menu, choose Connect.

Because the text characters are closed symbols, Draw connects them without making any changes to their appearance. If the symbols had been open instead (the first and last points not connected by a line), then Draw would have connected them with lines.

8. Click the Draw tool and then the Fill Style button in the ribbon area.

9. Choose **G**radient from the Fill Style menu and select a horizontal gradient.

10. Click the Color tool in the toolbox.

11. Click the Background color button, and choose a dark color from the palette as the Fade from color.

12. Click the Fill Color button, and choose white as the Fade to color.

13. Click the Line Style button, and choose **I**nvisible to remove the outlines from the characters and leave only the color gradient. The result is shown in figure 7.15.

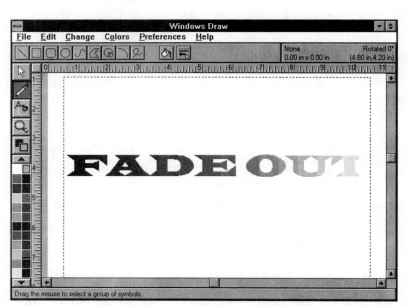

Fig. 7.15

The connected text, displaying a horizontal gradient.

Flipping Symbols

With Draw's **F**lip command, located on the **C**hange menu, you can turn symbols over on the page, either horizontally or vertically. When you flip a symbol horizontally, its left side becomes its right side. When you flip a symbol vertically, its top becomes its bottom. Figure 7.16 shows two symbols from the ClipArt library at the top of the screen; at the bottom are the same two symbols after the left symbol is flipped horizontally to fit a design.

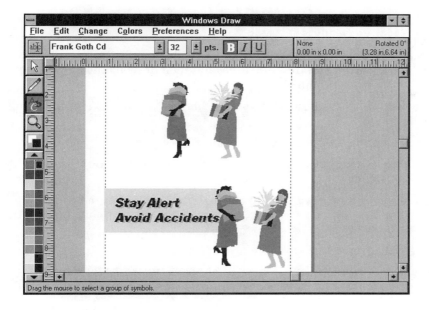

Fig. 7.16

Flipping a
ClipArt selection
horizontally to fit
a design.

To flip a symbol, follow these steps:

1. Select the symbol with the Pointer tool.

2. Choose **Flip** from the **C**hange menu. A pop-out menu provides two options: **H**orizontally and **V**ertically.

3. Choose either Horizontally or Vertically and the symbol will flip accordingly. You also can press F7 to flip a selected symbol horizontally and Shift-F7 to flip the symbol vertically.

You may need to flip ClipArt symbols to fit the needs of a logo or design (refer to fig. 7.16), but you also can use the **F**lip command to create a pair of symmetrical objects or to create the second half of an object with two symmetrical sides. One of the hardest objects to draw is one with identical left and right halves. One solution is to draw one half of the object, duplicate that half, and then flip the duplicate horizontally to create an equal but opposite copy. Then you can join the two symbols with the Connect command to create a single symbol.

The following exercise uses the **F**lip command to create a symmetrical vase. To begin creating the vase, first draw a vertical line to mark the center of the symbol by following these steps:

1. Select the Draw tool from the toolbox.

2. Click the Line button in the Ribbon.

3. Press and hold the Ctrl key to constrain the line you're about to draw vertically.

4. Draw a vertical line on the page by selecting the Draw tool, the Line button in the ribbon area, and then drawing the line on the page while holding the Ctrl key.

Now use the Curve button to draw the left half of the vase by following these steps:

1. Select the Curve button from the Ribbon.

2. Press and hold the Ctrl key to constrain the line you'll draw vertically.

3. From a point near the top of the vertical line, draw a horizontal line that extends to the left from the vertical line while holding the Ctrl key (see fig. 7.17).

4. Release the Ctrl key.

5. Draw the curve of the vase, as shown in figure 7.17. Chapter 5, "Adding Symbols," describes how to draw a curve.

6. Press and hold the Ctrl key while drawing the horizontal line that runs from the bottom of the curve back to the vertical line.

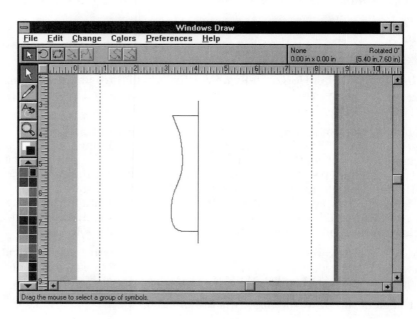

Fig. 7.17

The vertical line and the left half of the vase.

Now duplicate the curve to the right and flip the curve by following these steps:

1. Press and hold the Shift key and Ctrl keys to drag off a duplicate while constraining its movement horizontally.

2. Click the curve and drag a copy to the right. Make sure that the left edge of the curve touches the center line so the symbol will be properly positioned when flipped.

3. From the **Change** menu, choose **Flip**.

4. Choose **Horizontally** from the **Flip** menu. The right half of the vase flips to meet the left half.

Finally, delete the line and connect the two halves of the vase by following these steps:

1. Delete the vertical line by selecting it and then pressing the Delete key.

2. Select both halves of the vase.

3. From the **Change** menu, choose **Arrange Connect**. Now the two halves become one symbol.

Now you can fill the vase with color or a pattern by choosing from the Fill Style menu, as shown in figure 7.18.

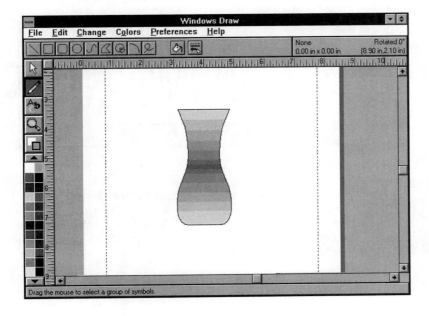

Fig. 7.18

The completed vase.

Changing the Order of Symbols

In Draw, each symbol is a separate entity that can be selected and moved. You can even drag a symbol out from underneath another symbol that overlaps it.

Draw provides a command that enables you to move a symbol that is overlapped by other symbols to the top of the stack without changing the symbol's placement on the page. This command, Move to **F**ront, is one of the two options on the **O**rder menu. The other option, Move to **B**ack, places an overlapping symbol underneath every other symbol it overlaps. Figure 7.19 shows the result of selecting a group of symbols and choosing Move to **B**ack.

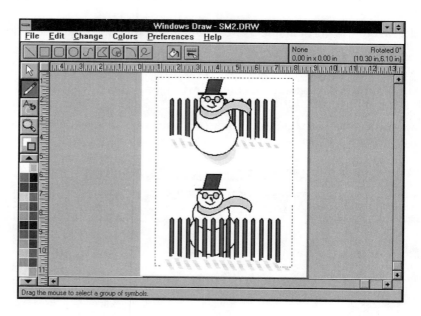

Fig. 7.19

Moving objects to the back with the Move to **B**ack command.

 NOTE If you select an object that is apart from other objects and then choose Move to **B**ack, the object will be placed behind other objects if you try to move it on top of other objects. You can use this knowledge to slide an object behind others by using Move to **B**ack on it first.

To use the Move to **F**ront or Move to **B**ack commands, follow these steps:

1. Select the object you want moved to the top or bottom of a stack of objects.

2. From the **C**hange menu, choose **O**rder.

3. From the **O**rder menu, choose Move to **B**ack or Move to **F**ront.

Moving an object to the back is easy. You simply select an object in the pile and choose Move to **B**ack. Moving an exposed object to the front is easy if it is not partially or totally obscured by other objects. But what if the object you want to move to the front is entirely hidden behind another object?

In this case, you have two choices: You can move the top object to the back instead, or you can click as many times as necessary atop the stack in which the object is positioned until the object you want is selected. Then you can choose Move to **F**ront. Each time you click a stack of objects, you select the item down in the stack. Clicking after the bottom object is selected selects the top object again.

By clicking twice at the position of the pointer shown in figure 7.20, you can select the symbol that happens to be hidden underneath. (Notice where the handles appear.)

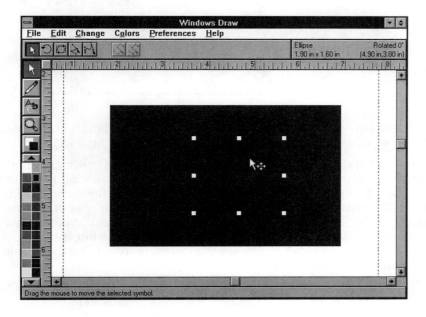

Fig. 7.20

Selecting a symbol that is underneath a rectangle.

Blending Symbols

You can create a sensational effect with Draw's Blend command, located on the **C**hange menu. After you select two symbols and choose Blend, Draw analyzes the shapes and colors of the two symbols and then creates additional symbols between the two originals that display a gradual metamorphosis. Figure 7.21 shows an ad created with the Blend command.

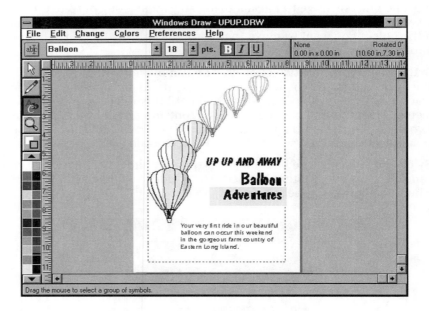

Fig. 7.21

An ad created
with the Blend
command.

To blend two symbols, select the symbols and then choose Blend from the **C**hange menu. The Blend dialog box appears (see fig. 7.22).

The Blend dialog box requests the number of steps to use in creating the blend. Type the number of intermediate images you want in the text box section of the **B**lend Steps selection box, or click the up- and down-arrow buttons to the right of the text box to set the number of intermediate images. The **R**everse Points option flips the second symbol before creating the blend. Using **R**everse Points can create an interesting effect. Figure 7.23 shows two blends, the top one without and the bottom one with **R**everse Points activated.

Fig. 7.22

The Blend dialog box.

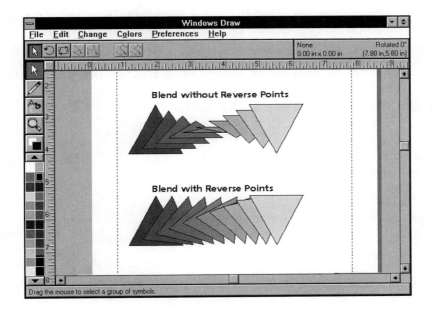

Fig. 7.23

Two blends, one without and one with **R**everse Points selected.

If you don't like the result of the settings on the Blend dialog box, press Alt-Backspace immediately to undo the blend. Then you can try a different setting on the Blend dialog box.

TIP

You can blend drawn graphic shapes such as polylines, polygons, circles, and curves, but you cannot blend text, grouped objects (this rules out most ClipArt selections), or objects filled with a bitmap pattern.

Theoretically, Draw does not blend text. In practice, however, you can blend text by first converting the text to curves using the **Change Convert to Curves** command and then connecting the curves into a single symbol with the **Connect** command. Draw does not blend grouped symbols either, but if you ungroup and then connect them, you actually can blend such grouped symbols as ClipArt selections.

In the following exercise, you'll use two ellipses and Blend to make an ellipse appear three dimensional, like a sphere:

1. Select the Draw tool from the toolbox.
2. Click the Fill Style button in the ribbon area and choose **Solid** from the Fill Style menu.
3. Click a dark color in the color palette.
4. Click the Line Style button.
5. Select **Invisible** from the Line Style menu.
6. Click the Ellipse button in the Ribbon.
7. Draw an ellipse on the page.
8. Select the Pointer tool from the toolbox.
9. Press the Shift key and drag off a copy of the ellipse.
10. Reduce the size of the copy, and select white from the color palette.
11. Position the smaller ellipse within the original ellipse, as shown in figure 7.24.
12. Select the two ellipses by drawing a rubber band box around them.
13. From the **Change** menu, choose Blend.
14. Choose **35** as the number of blend steps. Figure 7.25 shows the result.

Creating a Circular Pattern of Symbols

By using the Rotate button and a keystroke combination, you can create a circular arrangement of symbols for various designs.

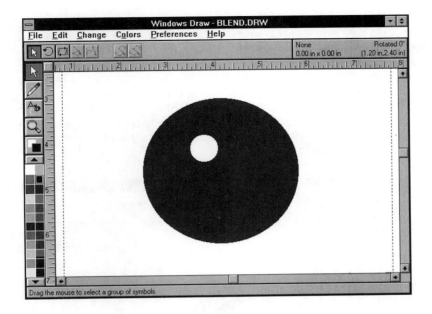

Fig. 7.24

Positioning two overlapping ellipses.

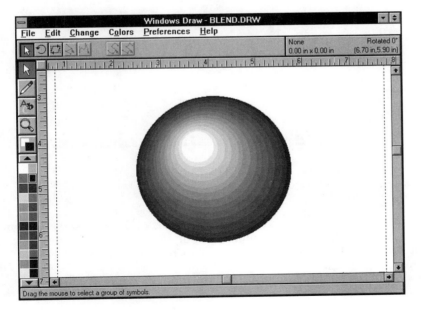

Fig. 7.25

Creating a three-dimensional effect with Blend.

To create a circular arrangement with the Rotate button, first create a symbol. Select that symbol, and click the Rotate button in the ribbon area. Before you begin rotating, however, drag the pivot point to the center of the circle in which you want the pattern of symbols to be arranged. Hold the Shift key and drag a duplicate symbol away from the original. The duplicate aligns itself along the circumference of the circle. Continue to drag off duplicates, placing them at equal distances along the circle until you've created a complete pattern. Figure 7.26 demonstrates one such circular pattern, using the sphere created in figure 7.25 and a pattern of stars.

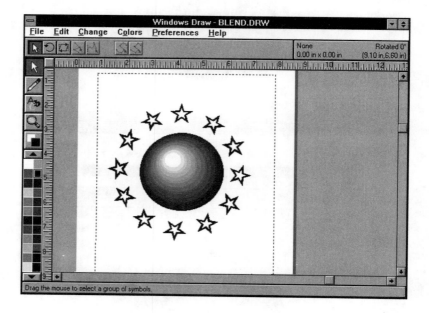

Fig. 7.26

A circular pattern of symbols surrounding a sphere.

Summary

In this chapter, you used the special controls of Draw to arrange symbols on the page, aligning, connecting, flipping, reordering, and blending symbols. The next chapter discusses how to change and edit Draw's color palette.

Working with Color Palettes

T he standard color palette in Windows Draw offers a selection of more than 50 hues and shades of color and gray. Concerning colors, however, no single palette can ever be broad enough. While one Draw user may want to create a landscape drawing that requires a palette of mostly blues and greens, another may need a broad array of reds and yellows for a client's advertising needs, and a third Draw user may require a specific violet color, the one his company has standardized for all its printed materials.

To accommodate such varying needs, Draw provides users with tools to modify each color in the palette and thus create custom combinations of colors. These customized hues can be saved in your very own color palettes.

In this chapter, therefore, you can learn not only about Draw's standard color palette, but how to edit colors and save and load the color palettes that you create for specific purposes.

Using the Color Palette and Your Video Card

The exact colors you see when you inspect the Draw color palette on-screen depend very much on the video display system installed in your computer. VGA video display systems currently are the most popular because VGA systems are built into most IBM PS/2 computers. Most PC clone computers also use VGA video systems. The VGA video system, however, can display only 16 solid colors. These colors are created by changing *pixels* (dots) on your monitor from one color to another. The resolution of a VGA display is 640 pixels in 480 rows across the screen. This resolution is usually referred to as "640 by 480."

Because standard VGA systems can display only the 16 solid colors, every gradation between those 16 is created in Draw by mixing pixels of two colors together on-screen. Mixing pixels of two colors to create a third is called *dithering*.

Many other computers use a video display system called Super VGA. Super VGA systems vary widely in their capabilities, from brand to brand, but many provide a full 256 on-screen colors at resolutions of up to 1024 by 768 pixels. A resolution of 800 by 600 is a common standard. These additional pure colors, rather than additional colors created by dithering, can greatly augment the appearance of your on-screen drawings—especially those that use gradients or many subtle shades of only a few colors.

If you are uncertain whether you own a Super VGA system, inspect the color palette on the Draw screen. If each color seems pure, without visible dot or line patterns, your video system is probably a Super VGA. If you see 16 solid colors at the top of the color palette, but the other colors appear to be composed of mixtures of dots, then your system is probably a standard VGA.

Some very expensive, specialty video systems incorporate an extremely high resolution card capable of displaying an especially broad array of colors. Such video systems are usually installed in computers used for intensive graphics work, such as computer-aided design (CAD) or photographic retouching. Many such systems can display up to 32,000 different colors on-screen. Some can even display as many as 16 million colors. (Whether our eyes can distinguish among 16 million colors, however, is another story.)

Changing the Color Palette

Windows Draw comes with two ready-made color palettes in addition
to its standard palette. To load a color palette, choose **O**pen Palette
from the **C**olors menu. Figure 8.1 shows the **C**olors menu. After you
choose **O**pen Palette, the Open Palette dialog box appears, as shown in
figure 8.2.

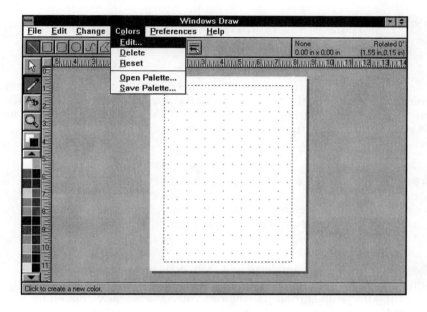

Fig. 8.1

The Colors menu.

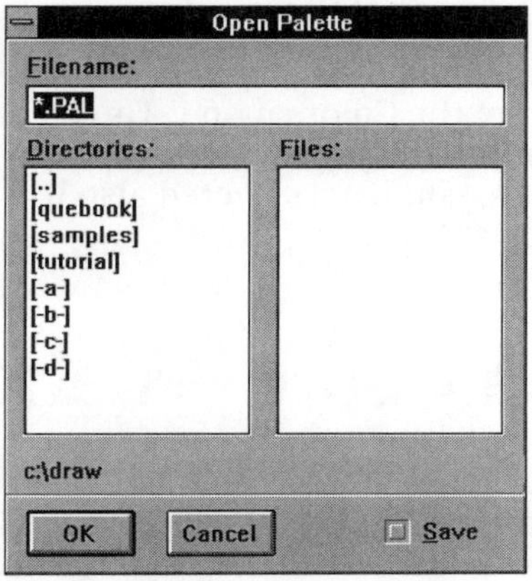

Fig. 8.2

The Open Palette
dialog box.

The Open Palette dialog box accesses only those files with the file extension PAL (palette files). The two sample palettes provided with Draw are located in the SAMPLES directory. To access these palettes, select the directory name SAMPLES in the **D**irectories list box. The file names of the two palettes, ARTIST.PAL and CRAYON.PAL, appear in the **F**iles list box. Choose the file name of one of these two palettes to open the palette you want or simply type the file name into the **F**ilename text box and click OK.

 To have Draw return to the same directory when you try to open a palette again, click the **S**ave check box before clicking OK.

The ARTIST.PAL palette contains a small collection of richly saturated colors. As you place the pointer on each color, its name appears in the hint line at the bottom of the screen. The CRAYON.PAL palette contains 64 colors of varying hues and intensities.

 A fourth palette, TUTORIAL.PAL, is located in the TUTORIAL directory. Although this palette is meant to be used only with the tutorial found in the Draw user manual, the file's simple palette includes a variety of gray shades that can be useful in other Draw applications.

Even after you select a palette, you can switch to a different palette simply by opening the new palette. Opening a new palette replaces the current palette on-screen. The colors you have already chosen for a symbol, however, remain the same on-screen even if the new color palette does not contain any of those colors.

To switch back at any time to the standard color palette for Windows Draw, select **R**eset from the **C**olors menu. The color palette resets back to the standard color palette. If you don't return to the standard color palette, the new palette you have selected also will be opened the next time you start Windows Draw.

Editing the Color Palette

No matter how many colors are contained in a palette, the time will come when none of them is sufficient for your needs. Fortunately, Draw enables you to create additional colors beyond those in the existing palettes.

Understanding How Colors Are Defined

Draw's color palette editing capabilities enable you to easily make subtle changes to existing colors in a color palette, modifying one of the red tones to match a client's primary logo color, for example, or even making very pronounced changes, such as replacing an entire series of colors with various shades of blue.

To alter any color in the current color palette, click that color's square on the palette and choose Colors Edit. The Edit Color dialog box appears, as shown in figure 8.3. If you want a new shade of blue, you may want to click an existing shade of blue to serve as a basis for the change. When you have created the new color, you can have Draw replace the color you have selected or add the color as a new selection in the color palette.

 NOTE   Draw's color palettes can hold an unlimited number of colors, but you probably will want to limit the color selections to less than 100 so you don't have to scroll through the palette endlessly to find the colors you need.

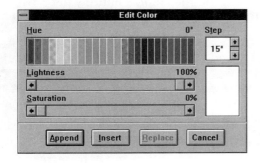

Fig. 8.3

The Edit Color dialog box.

The Edit Color dialog box contains four controls for changing the appearance of the selected color: Hue, Lightness, Saturation, and Step. (Step is explained in the next section.) The vertical rectangle at the right side of the dialog box, the *color swatch*, displays the color you have selected and the changes to the color as you alter it.

The *hue* of a color is its color value—that is, its position along the color wheel. The hue of a certain color may be blue, for example, or red. The *color wheel* displays the full spectrum of colors in a circle. The first color, for example, at the 0-degree position, is pure red; the last color, at the 359-degrees position, is near red.

The *lightness* of a color is determined by the amount of white or black that is mixed into the hue. Lightness is measured as a percentage. Table 8.1 shows how the lightness percentage works.

Table 8.1 The Effect of the Lightness Control	
Lightness Percentage	**Effect on Color**
0% lightness	The color is entirely black.
25% lightness	The color is 50% black and 50% pure.
50% lightness	The color is pure with neither white nor black mixed in.
75% lightness	The color is 50% white and 50% pure.
100% lightness	The color is entirely white.

The *saturation* of a color is the amount of gray mixed in. Saturation, like lightness, is measured as a percentage. When the saturation is 0 percent, no pure color is mixed in, and the color is entirely gray. When the saturation is 100 percent, the color is entirely pure, with no gray. Table 8.2 shows how the saturation percentage works.

Table 8.2 The Effect of the Saturation Control	
Saturation Percentage	**Effect on Color**
0% Saturation	The color is entirely gray.
50% Saturation	The color is 50% gray and 50% pure.
100% Saturation	The color is entirely pure.

Changing the Values of a Color

To change the appearance of a color, use the **H**ue, **L**ightness, and **S**aturation scroll bars. The **L**ightness and **S**aturation scroll bars operate just like any other horizontal scroll bar; drag the scroll box or click on the bar or arrows to adjust the percentage of lightness or saturation (refer to fig. 8.3). The **H**ue scroll bar, however, has an extra twist: the **S**tep selection box.

The Step selection box, located to the right of the **Hue** scroll bar, determines how big a step there should be between each of the colors shown in the Hue display. The bigger the step, the fewer the colors. The step is measured in degrees (the distance traveled around the color wheel to the next color). The default setting, 15 °, shows the colors that appear at 15-degree intervals around the color wheel. If you change the **Step** setting to 10 ° by clicking the down arrow at the right of the Step box, the **Hue** section displays more colors. When the number of colors displayed doesn't fit into the Hue display, a scroll bar appears so you can scroll to the colors that don't fit.

The possible **Step** settings are: 1 °, 5 °, 10 °, and 15 °. You must use the up and down arrows next to the current Step setting to increment or decrement the Step setting.

To select a specific hue, click that hue in the **Hue** section. Then adjust the lightness and saturation percentages to get the exact new color you want. The measurement at the top right corner of the Hue display shows the distance around the color wheel of the selected color.

Another way to select a hue is to press Alt-H and then use the left- and right-arrow keys to highlight the desired hue.

Saving the Revised Color

After you finish revising the **Hue, Lightness,** and **Saturation** values of a color, you can save the revised color in the color palette. The palette colors are ordered in rows rather than columns (like reading). The buttons at the bottom of the dialog box give you the following choices:

- *Append* adds the newly revised color to the color palette after the currently selected color.

- *Insert* adds the newly revised color to the color palette before the currently selected color.

- *Replace* substitutes the selected color with the newly revised color.

- *Cancel* closes the Edit Color dialog box without saving your changes to the current color.

After you choose a button (other than Cancel), the new color appears on the palette in the appropriate position.

Deleting a Color from the Color Palette

When your color palette grows larger with colors that you rarely use, you may want to delete unnecessary colors to leave behind a smaller, more easily accessible set of colors.

To delete any color from a color palette, select the color by clicking it, and choose Colors Delete. The color is removed from the color palette. You must save the color palette to remove the color permanently. Saving a palette is described next.

Saving a Color Palette

After you finish revising the color palette, you can save the revised palette as a new palette file. You can re-open the saved palette file at any time while using Draw to gain access to the revised colors you created.

To save a revised palette, follow these steps:

1. From the Colors menu, choose Save Palette. The Save Palette dialog box appears, as shown in figure 8.4.

2. Select the directory in which you want to save the revised color palette from the directory selection box. If the directory in which you want to save the file does not appear in the box, scroll down until that directory name is visible.

   If you skip this step, the palette is saved in the last directory that was selected as a default directory for color palettes (with the Save check box).

3. Type a DOS file name for the palette in the Save File As text box. Use a standard file name of up to eight characters. Draw supplies the three-letter extension PAL.

4. Click the Backup check box to uncheck it if you do not want to create a copy of the previous version of the palette you just edited. The copy is assigned the extension BAK.

> **CAUTION:** The **B**ackup check box is active by default, so unless you click it, a backup of the unedited palette is saved every time you modify a palette. Be careful not to save a palette file with the same name as one of your backup drawings; if you do, the backup palette file replaces the backup drawing.

5. Click Save, or press Enter. (If you decide not to save the revised palette, click the Cancel button instead.)

The revised palette is now saved in the designated file of the selected directory, and you can access the palette at any time when working in Draw.

Fig. 8.4

The Save Palette dialog box.

Summary

In this chapter, you learned how to modify color palettes and create your own custom combinations of color. The next chapter explains how to print your finished work.

Printing Your Work

A t some point you may want to transfer the work you have done on the computer screen to paper. If you're like most artists, you probably will not print until you have revisited the drawing many times for adjustments and polishing. Even after you print, you may feel the need to return to the drawing again to adjust colors or gray shades before reprinting.

Working with your drawing on-screen is different from printing it. Rather than working with bits and bytes inside your computer, you may be working with a mechanical device. You also must understand that your printer may print different shades of gray or different colors than you see on-screen. This chapter offers some helpful tips in getting hard copy of your work.

Printing with Windows

Microsoft Windows has made printing your work easy by introducing *device independence* to the printing process. Device independence means that you can create a drawing in Draw or any other Windows graphics program without regard to the output device you will be using. Windows worries about the output devices for you. You can print your work on any printer that prints graphics and has a printer driver for Windows.

Printer drivers are small software translators that are installed in Windows—they translate Draw's pictures into a language the printer can understand. Printer drivers for all the most popular printers come with Windows. When you choose a printer during the Windows installation process, you also choose and install the appropriate printer driver from the Windows installation disks. Printer drivers for more unusual printers often are available directly from the printer's manufacturer. After you install a printer driver in Windows, the driver informs Windows how to prepare the image so the printer properly reproduces it. Windows makes the adjustments to the image behind the scenes.

After you finish a drawing, you can print it on a dot matrix printer to see a draft image or on a laser printer to get a higher quality reproduction. Later in this chapter, you will learn that you can even print a Draw illustration on a very high resolution *imagesetter*. These expensive devices produce extraordinary results. Your images are professionally produced with rich gray shades and razor sharp lines. Few people have imagesetters, though, so most of us prepare a special output file, then take it to a service bureau. For a moderate per-page charge, service bureaus can print your file with their imagesetters. This chapter later describes how to prepare an output file for imagesetting.

Choosing and Setting Up a Printer

When you're ready to print your work, you should save it as a file on disk with the **S**ave or Save **A**s command. Of course, you should save your work often while in progress, but you should certainly save your work before printing. You probably will not encounter any technical problems while printing, but you don't want to take any chances when you have spent a long time creating your work.

Your first step is to confirm that the correct printer is chosen on the printer setting. After you choose a printer, that printer remains selected so you can simply print the drawing if no one has changed the printer setting in your Windows system. To confirm the printer setting, follow these steps:

1. Choose Printer Setup from the File menu. The Printer Setup dialog box appears, as shown in figure 9.1.

2. Scroll through the list of printers and click the printer you want to use.

Fig. 9.1

The Printer Setup
dialog box.

3. Click OK or click the Setup button to set special options for the printer. When you click Setup, a dialog box appears with settings for the printer you have chosen. These options are described in the next few sections. Figure 9.2 shows the Printer Setup dialog box for the Hewlett-Packard LaserJet Series II.

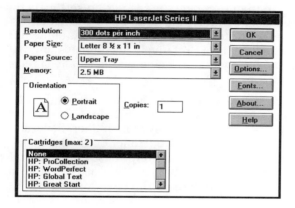

Fig. 9.2

The Printer Set-up dialog box for a Hewlett-Packard LaserJet Series II.

Changing the Printer's Resolution

In general, you should set the *Resolution* control in the Printer Setup dialog box to the highest available setting. If you're using a laser printer, choose 300 dots per inch (dpi). The higher you make the dpi setting, the sharper lines and text appear and the smoother gray areas look. When an image is composed of more dots, the dots are smaller and less noticeable.

Most laser printers have 512 kilobytes (512K) of memory and a maximum resolution of 300 dpi, with alternate settings of 150 dpi and 75 dpi. Choosing 150 dpi (half the standard resolution) is usually enough to print even the largest, darkest drawings. You probably will never need to use 75 dpi.

NOTE   If you try to print a drawing with many dark or black regions and your black and white laser printer displays an out-of-memory error, then you must either reduce the resolution setting or add more memory to the printer. Laser printers create printed images by first building the image as a pattern of dots in their memory then sending the dot pattern to the page. The more dots in the image, the more memory is used inside the laser printer. Large areas of black are created with heavy concentrations of dots, so they require large amounts of memory. By choosing a lower resolution setting, you instruct the Windows printer driver to construct an image in the printer's memory that requires fewer dots and less memory.

A better solution than reducing the resolution setting is to add more memory to the laser printer. Many add-on memory boards are available for standard laser printers, and because the cost of memory chips has decreased, these boards are relatively inexpensive. Increasing a 512K laser printer to 1.5 megabytes of memory is usually sufficient to print any drawing you create.

The newest laser printers have greater resolutions than the standard 300 dpi. These printers are capable of 600 dpi so the images they create are noticeably sharper and the grays much finer. Several companies even make special laser printer controller cards designed to use with Windows and a standard laser printer. These controller cards augment your printer's resolution to as high as 800 dpi. Computer magazines are the best source for information on the latest printer advancements.

Setting the Page Orientation

The Printer Setup dialog box offers two choices for Orientation: *Portrait* and *Landscape*. As you can see by examining the small page preview in the dialog box, portrait pages are oriented vertically and landscape pages are oriented horizontally.

When you have a drawing on-screen and you change the Orientation setting in the Printer Setup dialog box, you see the warning message displayed in figure 9.3. This message warns you that the drawing is larger than your printer can print and gives you the option to set the drawing to match the printed page. You will not see the warning if you also choose a paper size that is large enough at the same time.

Fig. 9.3

The page
orientation
warning
message.

If you choose **Yes**, Draw changes the page orientation as though you
had gone to the Preferences menu, chosen Page, and then changed the
orientation manually. The page changes orientation, but the symbols
you have placed on the page do not change. You may have to rearrange
the placement of the symbols to fit them on the new page orientation.

If you try to print a drawing when Draw's page orientation and the
Printer's page orientation do not match, the warning message shown in
figure 9.4 appears.

Fig. 9.4

The page
orientation
warning mess-
age after page
orientation is
changed.

Draw gives you the choice to reduce the drawing so it fits on one page
(choose the One Page button) or to split the drawing to fit on multiple
pages (choose on the **Multiple Pages** button). If you choose Multiple
Pages, Draw prints as much of the image as it can fit on the first page,
then prints the remainder of the image on the next page. To see the
entire image, you can arrange and then tape together the pages in a
tiled pattern.

You can use the Multiple Pages technique to print a drawing that is
much larger than your printer can accommodate, such as a large
sign directing people to a special event. Choose **P**age from the
Preferences menu, then choose a large page size in the Page dialog
box. When you choose **P**rint, the warning message in figure 9.4
appears. Choose **M**ultiple Pages and Draw prints parts of the image
on several pages that you can tape together to reconstruct the large
image.

Other Options

The Paper Source option on the Setup dialog box for most printers enables you to choose Manual Feed rather than the standard paper tray. This capability enables you to feed special paper or labels into the manual feed slot of the printer.

The Copies option enables you to print more than one copy. Simply enter the number of copies you want the printer to create.

Changing the Windows Dithering and Intensity Options

A pair of important and often overlooked controls in the Printer Setup dialog box become available when you choose the **O**ptions button. The Options dialog box enables you to adjust the Dithering and Intensity settings for your printing (see fig. 9.5).

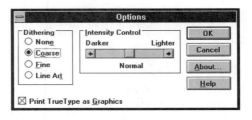

Fig. 9.5

The Options dialog box.

The *Dithering* setting determines how a laser printer creates shades of gray by mixing dots of white and black. Figure 9.6 shows a pattern of symbols with various gray shades and a gray-shade gradient.

Figure 9.7 displays the result when the Dithering control is set to None. This setting prevents dithering so a laser printer prints only pure black. The result is a black and white drawing that loses the grays. In figure 9.7, dark grays are translated to black, and light grays are translated to white.

Figure 9.8 shows the result when the Dithering control is set to Coarse. Coarse is the recommended setting when the image has gradients and you are using a standard laser printer with a resolution of 300 dpi or greater.

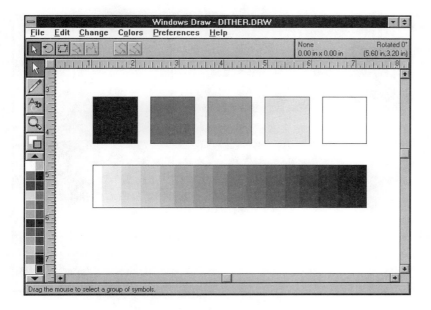

Fig. 9.6

Various shades and a gradient as they appear in Draw.

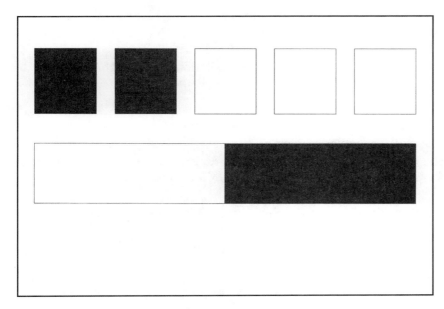

Fig. 9.7

The pattern when Dithering is set to None.

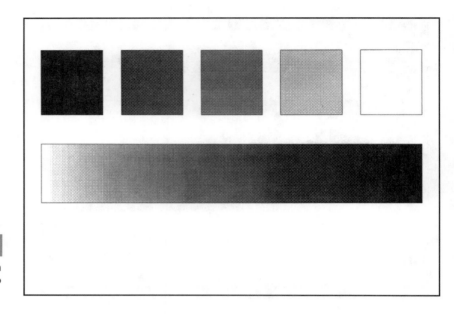

Fig. 9.8

The pattern when Dithering is set to Coarse.

If your drawing contains gradients and you are using a dot matrix or other printer with a resolution of 200 dpi or lower, choose the **F**ine setting for Dithering. Choose Line Art instead if:

- You're using a printer with a resolution of higher than 200 dpi (most laser printers are at least 300 dpi).

- Your image doesn't contain gradients.

- The image is composed entirely of black, white, and shades of gray.

The Intensity Control enables you to vary the lightness or darkness of the entire image. Modify the Intensity Control only after you examine an actual printout from your printer.

The Print TrueType as Graphics check box is checked by default, which causes the printer driver to print text that you created with a TrueType font as a graphics image, provides faster printing time, and uses less printer memory.

Table 9.1 summarizes the Dithering settings.

Table 9.1 The Settings for the Dithering Control

None	Does not dither black and white dots to create shades of gray. Do not use this setting unless the images you want to print are entirely black and white.
Coarse	Creates gray shades by dithering black and white dots. This setting is recommended for use with images that have gradients and printers that are capable of 300 dpi resolution or greater.
Fine	Creates gray shades by dithering black and white dots. This setting is recommended for use with images that have gradients and printers that print 200 dpi or less.
Line Art	Produces black, white, and shades of gray. This setting is recommended for images with solid black and gray areas.

Printing All or Part of Your Drawing

When you're ready to print your work, you can print the entire page or only a portion of the page. This capability can be helpful when you create several logo design alternatives side by side and you want to print only one of them.

Printing the Page

To print the entire page of your drawing, choose **P**rint from the **F**ile menu. Then choose **P**age from the pop-out Print menu that appears (see fig. 9.9).

TIP

You also can press Shift-F4 to print the page.

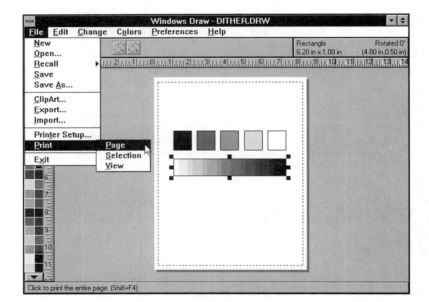

Fig. 9.9

The pop-out Print
menu.

Printing Selected Symbols

To print only selected symbols, click the Pointer tool and select the
symbols you want to print (press and hold the Shift key while you click
each symbol, or draw a rubber band box around a group of symbols).
Choose **P**rint from the File menu and then choose **S**election from the
Print menu. Only those symbols that are selected will print. The symbols you select do not need to be in the same region of the page. Draw
prints the symbols you select even if they are scattered around the
page.

Printing a View

Another way to print a portion of a drawing is to choose **View** from the **Print** menu. After you choose View, a special cursor appears that enables you to drag a rubber band box around a rectangular area of the drawing. The rectangular region you select is enlarged to fill the entire page.

With this technique, you can create several variations of a logo on a page, for example, then select only one logo to print. When printed, that logo enlarges to fill the page. Figure 9.10 shows a rubber band box drawn around a rectangular region to be printed.

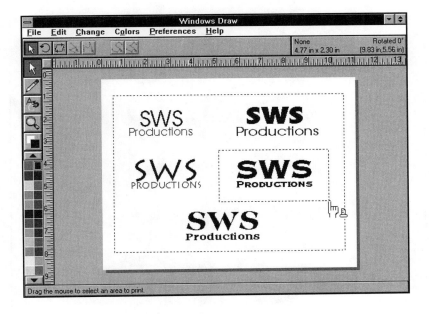

Fig. 9.10

Selecting a view to print.

Figure 9.11 shows the resulting printout on a landscape page.

You can press Ctrl-F4 to print the current view.

TIP

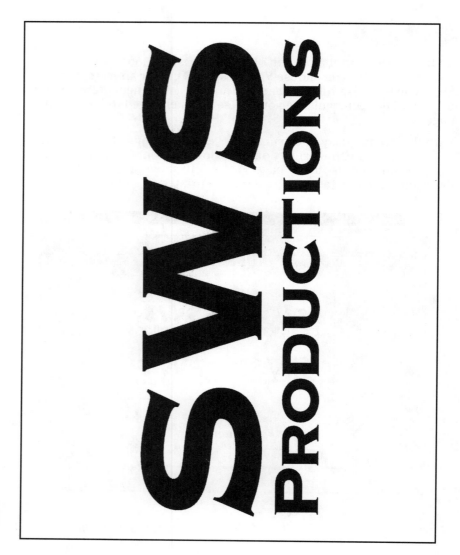

Fig. 9.11

The printed view.

Printing to a PostScript Printer

If your output device is a black and white PostScript printer (such as
the Apple LaserWriter II NT or the NEC Silentwriter) or a color
PostScript printer (such as the QMS ColorScript, Tektronix Phaser, or
NEC Colormate), you should use the special *PostScript driver* provided
with Draw. This PostScript printer driver supports all these printers
and many more. The Micrografx PostScript driver provides better

results when used with Draw than the PostScript driver that comes with Windows. During the Draw installation process the Micrografx PostScript driver is automatically installed in Windows.

Before you can use the driver, you must use the Windows *Control Panel* to establish a proper connection between the driver and an output port. To accomplish this step, double-click the Control Panel icon in the Windows Program Manager. Then double-click the Printers icon. Choose the Micrografx PostScript Driver ("PostScript (Micrografx) on None") on the list of installed printers, then choose the **C**onnect button. The Connect dialog box appears in figure 9.12. Choose an LPT (parallel) or COM (serial) port for the printer according to the way the printer is connected to your computer, then choose OK. Choose the Close button, then choose E**x**it from the **S**ettings menu to exit the Control Panel.

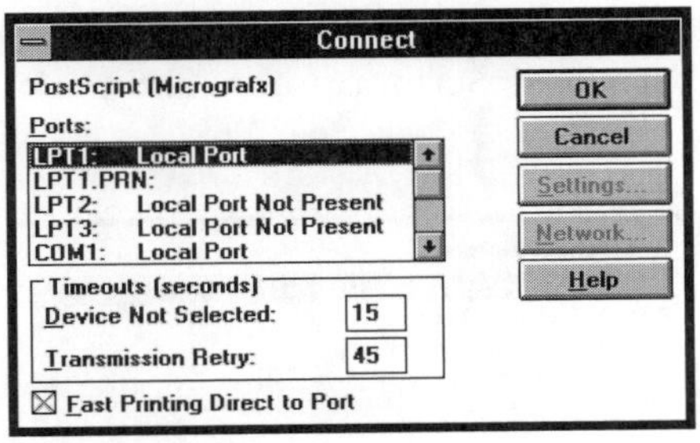

Fig. 9.12

The Connect dialog box.

When you return to Draw and choose **F**ile Printer Setup, you see the Micrografx PostScript driver connected to the port you specified. Now you can choose the PostScript driver from the list.

Choosing a PostScript Driver and Printer

Before using the PostScript driver for the first time, you should set up the driver. Follow these steps:

1. Choose Printer Setup from the File menu.

2. Choose the Micrografx PostScript driver.

3. Choose the **S**etup button. The PostScript Setup dialog box appears, as shown in figure 9.13.

   The Title Bar of the PostScript Setup dialog box tells you the currently selected PostScript printer. (Figure 9.13 shows the Apple LaserWriter II NT.) If the printer displayed is not the printer you have in your system, choose **S**elect from the **P**rinter menu. The PostScript Printers dialog box opens, as shown in figure 9.14.

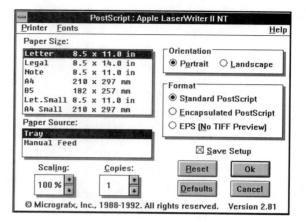

Fig. 9.13

The Setup dialog box for the Micrografx PostScript driver.

4. At the top of the PostScript Printers dialog box, scroll through the alphabetical list of PostScript printers and click your printer model.

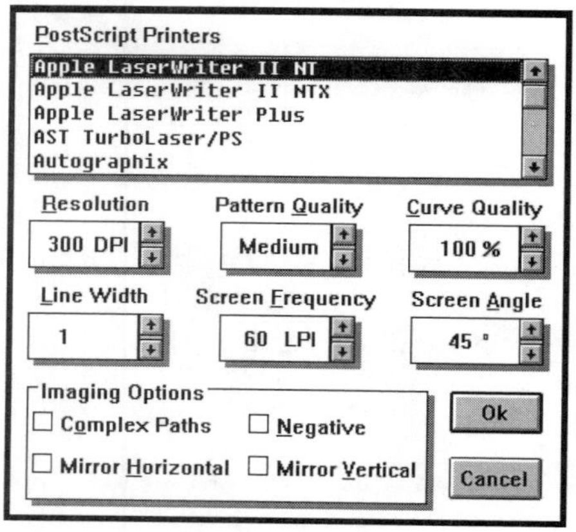

Fig. 9.14

The PostScript Printers dialog box.

Selecting the Options

The six controls below the printer list show the default settings for the selected printer. You can change any of these settings by using the scroll bar next to each control. The controls are described in the following list:

Resolution

Enables you to choose from the printer's resolution settings. Resolution is measured in dots per inch.

Pattern **Q**uality

Enables you to choose Coarse, Medium, or Fine for the quality of printed PostScript patterns. The finer the pattern quality, the slower the printing and the better the printed result. While creating draft prints of your drawing, you may want to choose Coarse or Medium for Pattern Quality. To create final output, choose Fine.

Curve Quality

Enables you to choose the precision with which the curves in your drawing are reproduced. You can choose any setting from 1% to 100%, although the higher the percentage, the better the quality. 100% produces the best curve quality, but it also creates more complex PostScript information so your printer may not print properly. If your printer displays a PostScript error and refuses to print, try reducing Curve Quality by several percentage points then trying again.

Line Width

Enables you to increase the width of lines in the output file if the lines fade or fail to print in high resolution, such as 1200 dpi on an imagesetter. The Line Width setting is measured in pixels. If lines seem to be missing from your print, increase the line width setting by a few pixels and try again.

Screen **F**requency

Enables you to choose a screen frequency for the print. The greater the screen frequency, the more gray levels appear in your drawing, but the lower the resolution. Screen frequency is measured in lines per inch. Try the default screen frequency first. Modify the setting only if the gradients in your drawing appear as stripes of grays rather than a continuous blend of shades.

Screen **A**ngle

Enables you to change the angle at which pixels are printed on the page. The default screen angle usually produces the best results. You may want to try different screen angles and inspect the results to see if the quality of the print improves.

Setting Imaging Options

At the bottom of the PostScript Printers dialog box are four *Imaging Options* settings. As with the other settings in this dialog box, the default settings probably give you the best results. The controls are described in this list:

Complex Paths	Causes the printer driver to break each complex line into a series of shorter, simpler lines. You should turn on Complex Paths only if you are having trouble printing a very complex drawing with many lines. Turning on Complex Paths rasterizes the lines so they are sent to the printer as an image rather than a complex mathematical description.
Negative	Reverses the image and creates a negative. Light areas are printed as dark areas, and vice versa. You should turn on Negative only when you need to create a negative image for a printing company. When you turn on Negative while printing a color image, black is printed as white, cyan is printed as red, magenta is printed as green, and yellow is printed as blue.
Mirror Horizontal	Prints an image that is flipped horizontally. You also can use the Flip command in Draw to mirror an image before printing it.
Mirror Vertical	Prints an image that is flipped vertically. You also can use the Flip command in Draw to mirror an image before printing it.

After choosing a printer or changing options in the PostScript Printers dialog box, choose OK to return to the main dialog box.

Setting Printing Format

From the main PostScript Setup dialog box, you can choose a paper size, page orientation, and paper source for the printer. For paper size, select the size of paper you are using. For page orientation, select whether you will print the image on a portrait or landscape page. For paper source, select from the options that are available for your printer. Many printers have an Upper Tray setting that pulls paper from the standard paper tray. Many printers also have a Manual Feed option that enables you to feed special paper one page at a time.

You also can choose a *Format* from among three options:

Standard PostScript	Choose this option if you are printing a file to a PostScript printer or you need to create a standard PostScript output file.
Encapsulated PostScript	Choose this option if you want to create an Encapsulated PostScript (EPS) file that you can import into a desktop publishing or word processing program. EPS files are useful only when you eventually print the file in a desktop publishing or word processing program on a PostScript printer. Otherwise, you should choose another export format for transferring a drawing into another application.

For detailed steps on generating an EPS file, follow the instructions in Chapter 10, "Exporting and Importing Graphics."

When you choose the EPS option to generate an EPS file on disk, a bit-mapped header is included in the file (a TIFF representation of the image) so you can view the image in a desktop publishing program. If the image does not include the header, the image appears as a rectangle with a large X inside.

EPS (No TIFF Preview)	This option also generates an EPS file, but the bit-mapped header (the TIFF Preview) is not included in the EPS file. This reduces the size of the EPS file. You may be able to use an EPS file without a TIFF header in another application that does not import files created in the EPS format.

Understanding the Printer and Fonts Menus

The Printer and Fonts menus on the PostScript Setup dialog box give you special controls you can use with PostScript printers. The printers and font menus follow:

- **Printer Select** enables you to choose a different PostScript printer.

- **Printer Form** enables you to create custom page sizes.

- **Printer Initialize** enables you to change how the driver communicates with the printer. (The default setting should work fine.)

- **Printer Status** enables you to instruct the printer to print a report about its status. When the Fonts Samples check box is checked, the printer also prints samples of the fonts it has in memory.

- **Fonts Default** enables you to select a default font when the Windows application you're using doesn't let you change fonts. Draw lets you change fonts, though, so you don't need to use this command.

- **Fonts Download** enables you to download selected PostScript fonts to the printer before a session so they don't need to be downloaded when each file is printed. This capability can save printing time. Downloading PostScript fonts to the printer only saves time when you plan to print many pages with many fonts. Because the work you do in Draw usually requires printing few characters, you will not derive much benefit from downloading fonts.

Saving the New Options

After you choose options for your PostScript printer, make sure that the Save Setup check box is checked before you click OK. This action ensures that the same options are in effect the next time you use Draw. If you make changes to the settings but decide to discard the changes, choose **R**eset. To automatically select the default settings for the currently selected printer, choose **D**efaults.

Creating a PostScript Output File for Imagesetting

A standard laser printer produces images at 300 dots per inch (dpi). This resolution is high enough to create clean shapes and text, but 300 dpi does not compare to the clarity of professional output devices called *imagesetters*. These sophisticated devices produce output at 1200 dpi, 2400 dpi, and even higher. Text is sharp, lines are straight, and edges are clear, unlike the slightly jagged edges produced by laser printers.

Imagesetters use a photographic process to produce extremely high resolutions, and they are capable of producing images on heavy-weight photographic paper and clear film. When you print to film rather than paper, you can deliver the film to a professional printer and save a step in pre-printing preparation. The printer does not need to photographi- cally shoot the printed pages to create film for the printing equipment. Printing to film provides two advantages: First, the printer doesn't need to photograph the pages and should pass the cost savings to you. Sec- ond, because the pages are not photographed to generate film, you can avoid the slight loss in resolution that inevitably results. The printed output is one generation closer to your source materials.

Although many large corporations have imagesetters in their graphics, printing, or art departments, very few individuals have imagesetters because of their expense and size. An imagesetter often is called a *lino* because one popular brand of imagesetter is the Linotronic (just as tissues often are called Kleenex). Fortunately, businesses called *service bureaus* can output your work on their imagesetters for a per-page charge, usually under $10 per page. To transfer your work to a service bureau, you must create a PostScript output file. Then you can copy the file to a diskette and deliver the diskette to the service bureau. All service bureaus can accept a file on diskette and many can accept a file sent by modem.

In this section, you learn how to print your work to a PostScript file that can be delivered to a service bureau. Before you learn the step-by- step mechanics, though, you should understand what to expect when you output a Draw file on an imagesetter.

Understanding Resolution

The more dots used to compose an image, the sharper the image. Because the dots are smaller, the image is less coarse.

When you view a drawing in progress on-screen, you see a reproduction of the image in very low resolution. Common VGA screens (640 pixels across and 480 pixels down) have a resolution of only about 60 dpi. SuperVGA screens (up to 1,024 pixels across and 768 pixels down) increase on-screen resolution to about 100 dpi. The resolution varies depending on the size of the monitor and the capabilities of the graphics system in your computer. Figure 9.15 shows a portion of an image displayed on a VGA monitor at approximately 64 dpi.

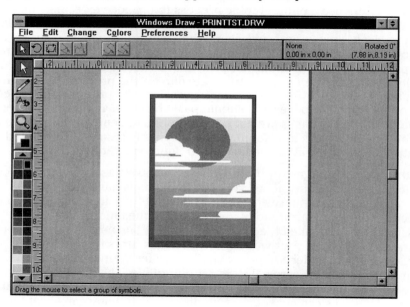

Fig. 9.15

An image displayed on a VGA monitor.

The printed resolution from a standard printer of 300 dpi is much higher than the on-screen resolution. Therefore, your images look much better when they're printed. Figure 9.16 shows the image in figure 9.15 printed at 300 dpi on a Hewlett-Packard LaserJet Series II.

When the same image is produced with a high-resolution imagesetter, the increase in quality is again dramatic. The edges of shapes are exceptionally sharp and areas of gray are smooth, unlike the coarse dots you see in gray areas on a laser printout.

Fig. 9.16

The image printed on a laser printer.

Printing the PostScript File

Windows has a special provision for printing to file that you can use to generate a *PostScript file*. You must use the Windows Control Panel to set up this process, but you do not need to have Draw loaded. To set up printing to a PostScript file, follow these steps:

1. Double-click the Control Panel icon in the Program Manager.

2. Double-click the Printers icon in the Control Panel to open the Printers dialog box.

3. Choose the Micrografx PostScript driver from the list of printer drivers.

4. Choose the **S**etup button.

5. Choose **P**rinter in the next dialog box, then choose **S**elect from the Printer menu.

6. Choose the imagesetter model that you or the service bureau will use to generate the output.

7. Change the resolution setting, if necessary. (1200 dpi is usually sufficient for professional results. 2400 dpi is usually more expensive because more printing time is required, but the output is a step better).

8. Choose OK.

9. Choose OK again to close the PostScript Setup dialog box.

10. Choose the Connect button.

11. Scroll down the list of ports in the Connect dialog box and choose FILE, as shown in figure 9.17.

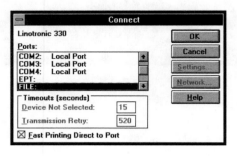

12. Choose OK to close the Connect dialog box.

13. Choose the Close button to close the Printers dialog box.

14. Exit the Control Panel.

When you're ready to produce a PostScript output file, choose Printer Setup from the **F**ile menu and make sure the Micrografx PostScript driver is selected. Then choose **P**rint from the **F**ile menu and choose

Page, Selected, or View depending on your needs. The Print To File dialog box opens, as shown in figure 9.18. Type the filename of the file you want to create. You can use any three-letter file extension, but you may want to use .OUT to designate the file as a PostScript output file. After you type a filename, choose OK and Windows prints your work to the file you have specified.

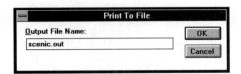

Fig. 9.18

The Print To File dialog box.

Because PostScript files tend to be very large, you may want to use a file compression program such as PKZIP to compress the file after you have printed it to disk. A word of advice: Before submitting the file to the service bureau, make sure they have the software to decompress it.

TIP

Understanding Fonts in Windows

Before Windows, fonts for text were troublesome in most software programs. Software had to support both bit-mapped fonts for LaserJet printers and scalable fonts for PostScript printers. Windows has solved these troubles by supporting bit-mapped LaserJet fonts and scalable PostScript fonts. Windows also has added its own font technology, TrueType, that provides the best advantages of bit-mapped fonts and scalable fonts.

Bit-Mapped Fonts

Bit-mapped fonts create each printed character with a pattern of dots. A complete set of characters makes up one font file. To print the same typeface at a larger size, you need another font file in which each character is built with more dots. Therefore, you need a different bit-mapped font file for each typeface in each point size. Figure 9.19 shows a magnified view of the letter A in a bit-mapped font. Because bit-mapped font files become rather large when the typeface is bigger than 12 or 14 points, you quickly end up with a collection of bit-mapped font files that consumes a lot of disk space and printer memory. You need these files, however, to have flexibility in choosing typefaces and font sizes for printing.

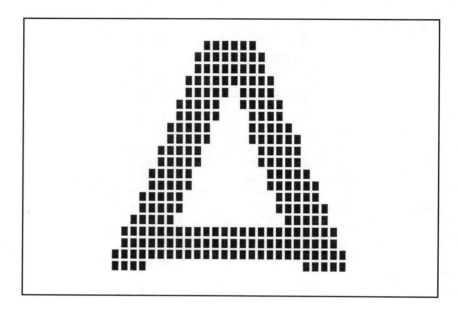

To see on-screen what your output will look like, you need another collection of bit-mapped fonts that the software can display on-screen. These fonts are specially designed for your screen's much lower resolution. Many different PC graphics standards exist, so software packages need to include numerous screen fonts in different resolutions if the fonts are to work properly with any system.

Trying to support bit-mapped fonts is a difficult proposition for software makers. To give LaserJet users even a modest array of fonts, makers need to provide disks of fonts that can be downloaded to the printer and displayed on-screen.

Scalable Fonts

Windows supports *scalable* fonts that can be stretched to any point size for both the screen and printer. One scalable font file provides a typeface in any size you choose. Scalable fonts represent each character's outline mathematically. Figure 9.20 shows the outlines of a scalable font.

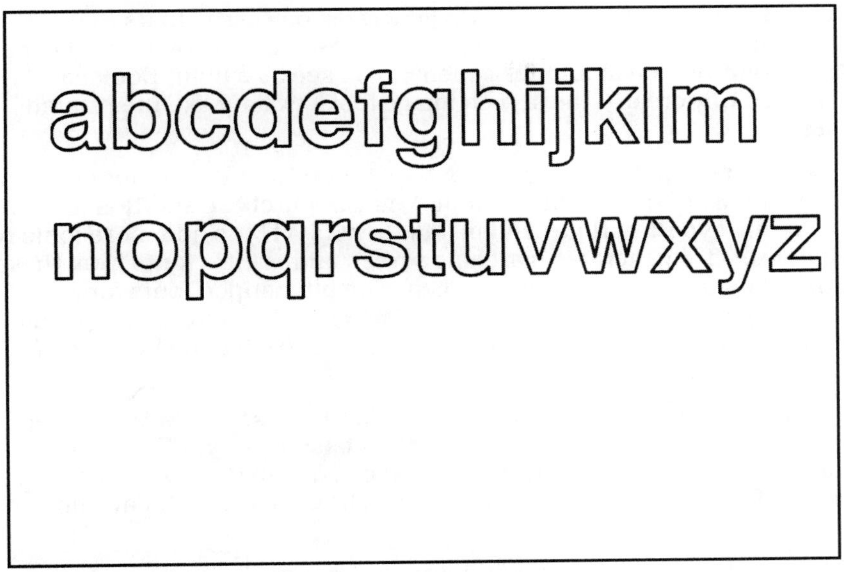

abcdefghijklm
nopqrstuvwxyz

Fig. 9.20

A magnified view of the outlines of a scalable font.

By changing the scaling factor in the equation for the font, you can stretch the outlines to create a larger or smaller version of the font. Because scalable fonts are outlines of font shapes rather than patterns of dots, the software that scales the fonts can use more dots to fill the outlines when the printer or the screen is higher resolution. Likewise, fewer dots are used if the printer or screen is low resolution. Scalable fonts, therefore, are independent of the resolution of the output device or the graphics system you use.

Because one file provides both screen and printer fonts in any point size, the disk space requirements for scalable fonts are far less than the requirements for bit-mapped fonts. Scalable fonts are resolution independent, so you can hook up virtually any printer and monitor to a system that uses scalable fonts and get the same results. Only the clarity of the text changes at different resolutions, both on-screen and on the printed page.

PostScript Scalable Fonts

One scalable font technology is the *PostScript* page description language. PostScript printers come with a starter set of font outlines. Software programs that support PostScript printers can instruct the printer to generate fonts in any common size (usually up to 128 points). Windows supports PostScript fonts when you purchase and install the

Adobe Type Manager (ATM). ATM generates on-screen fonts that match the fonts the printer generates. For example, if you have chosen a 29.5 point Bookman font for a memo, you see 29.5 point Bookman displayed on-screen—the screen image looks exactly like the printed image.

ATM requires PostScript Type 1 outline fonts. Most PostScript printers come with 35 of these fonts built in. You can purchase additional PostScript Type 1 outlines and install them in ATM to add more fonts to Windows. ATM generates matching screen and printer fonts from these additional outlines. ATM also can generate bit-mapped fonts for LaserJet printers from PostScript outline fonts. Therefore, even if you don't have a PostScript laser printer, you still receive the benefits of scalable fonts.

Draw works with ATM and PostScript Type 1 fonts. If ATM is installed in your Windows system, you see all the PostScript Type 1 fonts installed in ATM in the Font List box. You can do anything with these fonts that Draw is capable of doing: stretch them, rotate them, and even convert them to curves.

ATM is included with many Windows software packages, so you already may have ATM on your system. Figure 9.21 shows the ATM Control Panel that enables you to add and remove PostScript fonts, among other options.

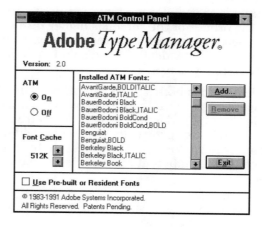

Bitstream Speedo Scalable Fonts

A second scalable font technology is Bitstream Speedo fonts. Speedo fonts work with any printer. When you purchase and install Bitstream's scalable font software, *Bitstream FaceLift*, you can add Bitstream

Speedo fonts to your system. Just as ATM generates matching printer and screen fonts from PostScript Type 1 fonts, FaceLift generates matching printer and screen fonts from Speedo fonts.

NOTE Because you're using Draw, you don't need to buy Bitstream FaceLift—Draw incorporates Bitstream's technology. The fonts preceded by a dot in the Font List box are Bitstream Speedo fonts that come with Draw. When you choose one of these fonts (Dutch, Swiss, or Vivaldi, for example) the Bitstream software built into Draw manipulates the on-screen fonts for you.

TrueType Scalable Fonts

The newest scalable font technology, *TrueType*, comes built into Windows 3.1. TrueType outline fonts generate matching screen and printer fonts for any printer you have installed in Windows.

Windows comes with several TrueType outline typefaces: Arial (a version of Helvetica), Times New Roman (a version of Times Roman), Courier New (a version of Courier), and Symbol and Wingdings fonts (which provide common symbols and shapes). For each typeface, you get four TrueType fonts (one bold, one italic, one bold and italic, and one normal). The TrueType typefaces are listed on the font menu of every Windows application you use in Windows 3.1, including Draw.

When you install Windows Draw 3.0 into Windows 3.1, 32 additional TrueType fonts are available in every Windows application you use. Appendix B displays these fonts.

The number one advantage of TrueType is that it's built right into Windows 3.1. In addition, TrueType is fast. When you print a drawing that contains TrueType fonts, TrueType sends to the printer only the individual characters you need rather than every character in the font. This process speeds printing considerably. Another advantage is that TrueType fonts are readily available at low cost. Most type companies sell inexpensive collections of TrueType fonts that you can install easily in Windows. In addition, many Shareware TrueType fonts are available for downloading from large information services such as CompuServe and small bulletin board systems (BBSs) in your local area. You pay only a modest fee to use these fonts.

If you use a PostScript printer, TrueType sends PostScript Type 1 font information to your printer when you use the Windows PostScript printer driver. Therefore, you can use the TrueType fonts with a PostScript printer or when you create a PostScript output file.

Viewing the TrueType Fonts in your System

Windows 3.1 provides an easy way to inspect the TrueType fonts that are installed (see fig. 9.22). Open the Windows Control Panel and then select the Fonts icon.

Control
Panel

The Control Panel icon.

Fonts

The Fonts icon.

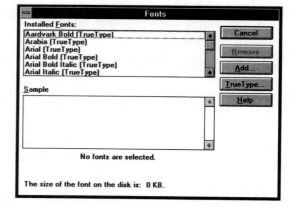

Fig. 9.22

The Fonts dialog box.

The Installed Fonts list offers an alphabetical list of all the fonts installed in your copy of Windows. TrueType fonts are designated on the list by TrueType in parentheses. When you click any of the TrueType fonts, a sample of the font appears in the Sample section, as shown in figure 9.23.

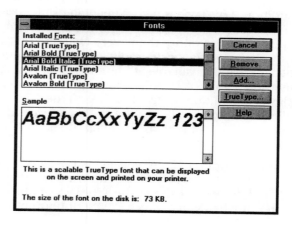

Fig. 9.23

The Sample preview of the selected font.

Controlling TrueType Fonts

Choosing the TrueType button in the Fonts dialog box opens the TrueType dialog box (see fig. 9.24). You can choose whether to accept the default setting, Enable TrueType Fonts, which displays TrueType fonts in the Font List box of all Windows applications. If you also choose Show Only TrueType Fonts in Applications, only True-Type fonts will display in the Font List box. You can turn off Enable TrueType Fonts if you want to display only Windows fonts and non-TrueType fonts, such as PostScript fonts. You may choose to disable TrueType fonts if you want to use only PostScript Type 1 fonts in a drawing you're preparing for image setting at a service bureau.

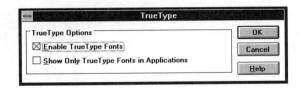

Fig. 9.24

The TrueType dialog box.

Adding and Removing TrueType Fonts

Some TrueType font packages come with an installation program that automatically installs the fonts in Windows 3.1. The Microsoft True-Type Font Pack for Windows comes with such an installation program, for example.

To install TrueType fonts that don't come with an installation program or fonts you have downloaded from an electronic service, follow these steps:

1. If the fonts are on a floppy disk, insert the disk in the A or B drive.

2. Double-click the Control Panel icon in the Main group of the Program Manager.

3. Double-click the Fonts icon.

4. Choose the Add button. The Add Fonts dialog box opens, as shown in figure 9.25.

5. Using the Drives and Directories controls, choose the disk drive that contains the font disk or choose the directory on your hard disk that holds the fonts. The fonts on the disk or in the directory appear in the List of Fonts.

6. Highlight the fonts to install. You can drag across the font names or press and hold the Ctrl key then click just the names you want. You also can choose the Select All button to select all the fonts on the disk or in the selected directory.

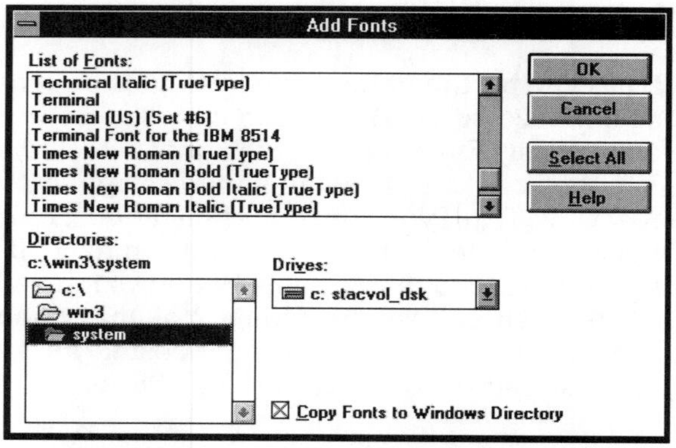

Fig. 9.25

The Add Fonts
dialog box.

7. Make sure the Copy Fonts to Windows Directory option is
    checked. If not, click the option to turn it on.

8. Choose the OK button.

9. Choose the Close button after the fonts are installed.

To remove TrueType fonts, select the fonts to remove, choose the **Re**-
move button in the Fonts dialog box, and then click Yes. Click Yes to All
if you have selected more than one font and you want all the selected
fonts removed. Leave **D**elete Font File From Disk unchecked only if you
want to remove the TrueType file from its installation in Windows and
without deleting it from your disk.

CAUTION: Be careful not to remove the MS Sans Serif screen
font. Windows uses this font to display text in the Program
Manager.

Summary

In this chapter, you learned to print your work on your system's printer
and to prepare an output file for printing on an imagesetter at a service
bureau. You also learned about fonts in Windows, particularly how to
view, add, and remove TrueType fonts.

In the next chapter, you learn to create a different form of output—
exporting your work as a file to use in other programs. You can take
advantage of the special powers of Windows 3.1 to use your drawings
in other Windows applications.

Exporting and Importing Graphics

I f you plan to use your drawings in other programs, the information in this chapter will help you. You will learn how to transfer the drawings you have created in Draw to other software, such as word processing and desktop publishing programs. You also will learn how to import graphics into Draw so you can incorporate in your drawings work you have done elsewhere.

Windows makes the transfer easy, especially if the other program is also a Windows application. For example, you easily can copy a company logo made in Draw to the masthead of a company newsletter created in Aldus PageMaker. With Windows 3.1 and the latest version of Draw (Windows Draw 3.0 + OLE), you even can establish a link between Draw and other Windows applications so any changes to the original drawing occur on all the duplicates placed in other Windows applications. In addition, if you're working on a file in another Windows application, you can jump to Draw temporarily and create a drawing intended expressly for use in that file.

Exporting a Draw drawing as a graphic file on disk also is easy to accomplish. Exporting makes the drawing available for use in any other software program that can import graphics files, even if the program is not a Windows application, such as WordPerfect for DOS.

In this chapter, you learn about copying and pasting Draw illustrations into other Windows applications and how to set up links between the copies and their originals. You learn also how to export a drawing as a graphics file that you can import into another non-Windows software program.

What Is OLE?

The arrival of Windows 3.1 added a new capability to the already-impressive list of capabilities in Windows. The new feature, *Object Linking and Embedding*, usually is recognized by its acronym, *OLE* (pronounced just as a bullfighter would: *oh-lay*). In general, OLE makes it easy to copy an element created in one Windows application to another Windows application. That element can be a graph created in a chart program, an image created in a paint program, a segment of text created in a word processing program, or a table of numbers placed in a spreadsheet, among other possibilities. What's special about OLE is that it can maintain a *link* between the original and the copies. If you change the original, OLE automatically updates the copies, too. Linking keeps the original and its copies uniform and alleviates the need to find and update every copy after you have updated the original.

Windows Draw 3.0 + OLE takes advantage of OLE. Draw can act as an OLE Server, supplying drawings for inclusion in other programs, but it cannot act as an OLE Client. Therefore, you cannot use OLE to include an item from another program in a Draw drawing. Earlier versions of Windows Draw do not include support for OLE.

Draw uses OLE to copy a symbol, a collection of symbols, or even a complete drawing into another Windows application. After you have finished copying, you can update the original in Draw and know that the copies in other applications are updated, too. OLE takes care of this work for you behind the scenes.

Maintaining agreement between the original drawing in Draw and duplicates in other applications is only the linking side of Object Linking and Embedding. *Embedding* offers other advantages. Rather than copying a drawing into another application as a linked object, you can copy the drawing as an embedded object. An embedded object doesn't maintain a link with the original, but the object is self-contained and fully editable. After you open a document containing an embedded drawing, you can alter the drawing by double-clicking it to open a temporary version of Draw. You then can make changes to the drawing with all of Draw's tools and commands. After you revise the object and close the temporary version of Draw, the embedded object in the other application is revised. Essentially, you are adding Draw's capabilities to the other application by embedding a Draw object. Draw's tools become available whenever you need to change the drawing.

Another way to embed an object from Draw is to choose the Insert Object command in the application. A dialog box displays a list of the objects you can create. (The list shows objects created by applications that can produce objects for embedding.) When you choose one of the objects, the application used to create the object appears in a window. Create the object, then choose Exit and return to the first application from the File menu. The application used to create the object closes and leaves behind an embedded object in the first application.

Using the Insert Object command is handy when you're creating a document and you find that you need a drawing. By choosing Insert Object, you can load Draw temporarily to create the object you need. When you finish, you can exit Draw, and the drawing you have created remains embedded in the document.

Because object linking and object embedding seem so similar (they do overlap each other's capabilities somewhat), understanding which method to use can be difficult. If you have created an object in Draw that you're likely to update, and you want a copy in another application, you should use object linking. Object linking updates the copy when the original changes. If you don't think the original drawing will change, you can use object embedding. After a drawing has been embedded, you can double-click it to open a temporary Draw window to edit the copy without changing the original. This method can be helpful when you want to maintain a master, unchanged copy of a drawing.

You can use OLE only if the application to which you want to copy a drawing can act as an OLE *client*. An OLE client is a program that can receive both linked and embedded objects from an OLE *server*. Draw is an OLE server. Most new versions of Windows programs provide full OLE capabilities.

Linking an Object

To link an object to another Windows application, follow these steps:

1. Copy the object to the Windows Clipboard.

2. Switch to the other Windows application.

3. Use the Paste Link command to paste the object into the application. This step pastes a copy of the object into the application and also sets up an OLE link.

You can double-click the object at any time to return to the original application and edit the object. When you finish making changes and save the newly edited object, the copy in the second application is updated with the changes.

To change the way the object is linked to the second application, use the Links command in the second application (usually found on the Edit menu). In the Links dialog box that appears, you see any objects that are linked to the application (see fig. 10.1). Choose an object on the list; then choose **A**utomatic or **M**anual for the Update option. Automatic causes the copy to update whenever the original is modified then saved. Manual updates the copy only when you choose the **U**pdate Now button in the Links dialog box.

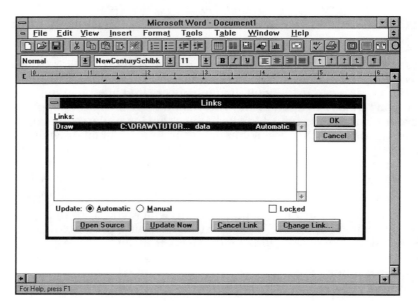

Fig. 10.1

The Links dialog box in Word for Windows.

Choosing the **Ch**ange Link button enables you to choose a different object to link to the second application. Choosing the **C**ancel Link button cancels the link, severing the connection between the original object and its duplicate in that application. If you edit the original of the object, the copy does not update.

Embedding an Object

To embed an object in an application, you first copy the object to the
Windows Clipboard, just as you do when you link an object. In the second application, choose Paste Special rather than Paste Link. A Paste
Special dialog box opens that enables you to choose the item to paste
(see fig. 10.2). Click the item that includes the word object on the list.
If you are attempting to embed a Windows Draw drawing, click the item
labeled Windows Draw Drawing Object. Then choose the **P**aste button.

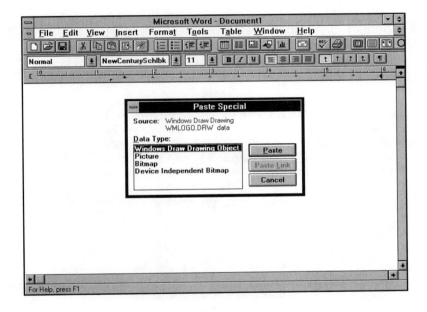

Fig. 10.2

The Paste
Special dialog
box in Word
for Windows.

After the object has been pasted into place, you can double-click it to
return to the original application and edit the object. You see no Save
option on the File menu of the original application; instead, a new option, Exit and Return to (the second application) appears. When you
choose this option, the original application closes and the object in the
second application is updated.

When you double-click a linked or embedded object, you can change
the object using the capabilities of the application that created it. But
editing linked and embedded objects actually accomplishes quite different tasks. Editing an embedded object does not change the original.
When you edit a linked object, however, you are actually editing the
original, and the edits transfer to the copy on which you double-
clicked.

Linking a Drawing to a Windows Application

To link a Draw picture to another Windows application, you must have the drawing loaded in Windows Draw. Then follow these steps:

1. Select the drawing or symbols you want to copy to the other application. To select the entire drawing, draw a rubber band box around it with the Pointer tool or choose **S**elect All from the **Edit** menu.

2. Choose **C**opy from the **Edit** menu to place a copy of the drawing on the Windows clipboard.

3. Switch to the other application (pressing Ctrl-Esc will give you a list you can use to switch to another running application).

4. Choose **Edit Paste Link**. If Paste Link does not appear on the **Edit** menu, choose Paste Special. Choose Picture in the Paste Special dialog box then choose the Paste Link button. For specific information about how to paste a link into your application, consult your application's user manual. Figure 10.3 shows the Paste Special dialog box in Microsoft Word for Windows.

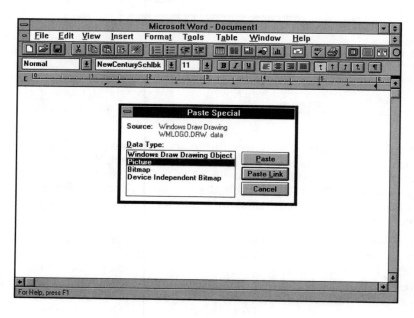

Exercise: Linking a Drawing to Another Application

To try linking a drawing to another application, complete the following exercise. You will be linking a drawing to a memo in Windows Write.

First, load the Water Mill Symphony logo you created in Chapter 4. The logo is in the file WMLOGO.DRW. (If you didn't create the Water Mill Symphony logo, then any logo drawing will do.) Then follow these steps:

1. Select the logo by clicking it.

2. Choose **Edit C**opy to copy the logo to the Windows clipboard. To confirm that the drawing has been copied to the Clipboard, you can load the Clipboard Viewer by double-clicking the Clipboard icon in the Accessories group of the Windows Program Manager. You see the logo in the Viewer, as shown in figure 10.4. Close the Viewer by choosing Exit from the **F**ile menu.

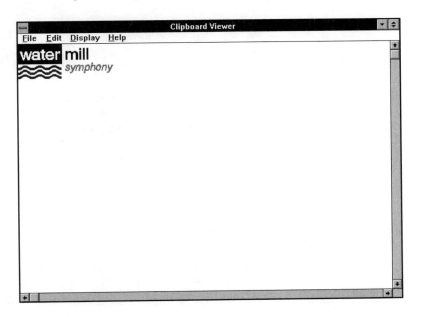

Fig. 10.4

The Water Mill Symphony Logo in the Clipboard Viewer.

3. Load Windows Write by double-clicking the Write icon in the Accessories group of the Program Manager.

Write

4. Choose Edit Paste Link. In other applications, you must choose Edit Paste Special then choose the Paste **L**ink button.

5. The Water Mill Symphony logo appears in Windows Write (see fig. 10.5). Now you can type the text of the memo using the word processing controls of Windows Write.

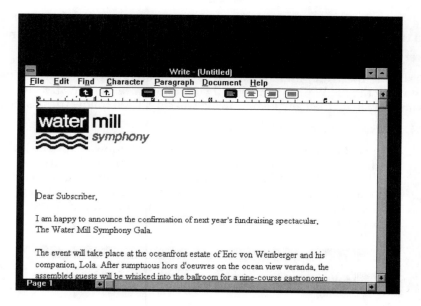

Fig. 10.5

The Water Mill Logo in a Windows Write document.

To try editing the logo, double-click it in Windows Write. A copy of Draw opens with the logo loaded. Click the water portion of the logo and change its color to red. Then save the drawing using **S**ave from the **F**ile menu. The logo in Windows Write updates instantly with the new color red. Switch back to Windows Write to see the revised logo.

Embedding a Drawing in a Windows Application

To embed a Draw picture in another Windows application, you must have the drawing loaded in Windows Draw. Then follow these steps:

1. Select the drawing or symbols you want to copy to the other application. To select the entire drawing, draw a rubber band box around it with the Pointer tool or choose **E**dit **S**elect All.

2. Choose **E**dit **C**opy to place a copy of the drawing on the Windows clipboard.

3. Switch to the other application.

4. Choose **E**dit Paste Special. If you do not see Paste Special on the Edit menu, consult your application's user manual to see whether it is OLE compatible. The equivalent command may be on another menu.

5. Select Windows Draw Drawing Object from the Paste Special dialog box then choose the Paste button. Figure 10.6 shows the Paste Special dialog box in Word for Windows.

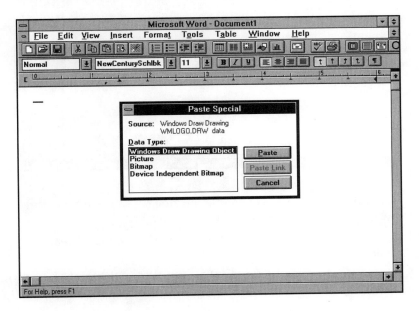

Fig. 10.6

The Paste Special dialog box in Word for Windows.

Exercise: Embedding a Drawing

To try embedding a drawing in another application, complete the following exercise. You will be embedding a drawing in a memo created with Windows Write.

First, load the Snowman picture you created in Chapter 5. (If you did not create and save the Snowman picture, any other drawing will do just as well.) Then, follow these steps:

1. Select the drawing by clicking it.

2. Choose **E**dit **C**opy to copy the drawing to the Windows clipboard. To confirm that the drawing has been copied to the Clipboard, you can load the Clipboard Viewer by double-clicking the Clipboard icon in the Accessories group of the Windows Program Manager. You see the drawing in the Viewer, as shown in figure 10.7. Close the Viewer by choosing E**x**it from the **F**ile menu.

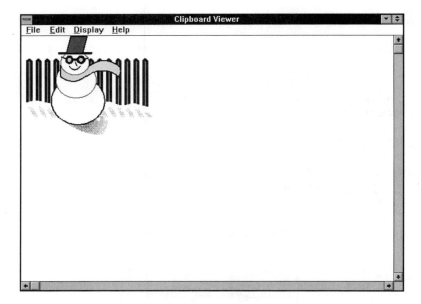

Fig. 10.7

The Snowman
drawing in
the Clipboard
Viewer.

3. Load Windows Write by double-clicking the Write icon in the Accessories group of the Program Manager.

4. Choose **E**dit Paste Sp**e**cial. The Snowman drawing appears in Windows Write.

5. Now you can type the text of the memo using the word processing controls of Windows Write.

To try editing the drawing, double-click it in Windows Write. A copy of Draw opens with the drawing loaded. Make any changes to the snowman picture then choose Exit and Return to Write. The drawing in Windows Write updates instantly but the original Snowman file is unaltered.

Creating Draw Objects in Other Applications

Another way to embed a drawing you have created in another application in Draw is to use the Insert Object command on the other application's menu. The Insert Object dialog box appears, which displays all the objects you can create using OLE server applications (applications that can provide objects to embed). Follow these steps:

1. Select Windows Draw Drawing from the list. Windows Draw opens so you can create an object.

2. Create the drawing you need in Draw.

3. Choose **E**xit and return to the first application. The object appears in the first application as an embedded object. Now you can double-click the embedded drawing to edit it any time you need to use the full powers of Windows Draw.

Exercise: Embedding Objects by Using the Insert Object Command

To try embedding an object with the **Insert Object** command, follow these steps:

1. Open Windows Write, usually found in the Accessories group of the Program Manager.

2. Choose **E**dit **I**nsert Object. The Insert Object dialog box opens, as shown in figure 10.8.

3. Select Windows Draw Drawing from the list.

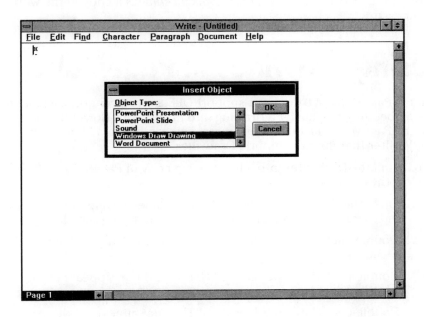

Fig. 10.8

The Insert Object dialog box in Windows Write.

4. When the Draw window opens, create a simple drawing by combining a few objects.

5. Choose File Exit and return to Write. The drawing you created is embedded in Write. You can double-click the drawing to return to Draw for editing.

Using Drawings in Word for Windows, AmiPro, and WordPerfect for Windows

All three of these Windows word processing programs can act as OLE clients—they can receive linked or embedded objects that you create in Draw.

If you want to incorporate a drawing you already have made in Draw, then open Draw in its own window and copy the drawing onto the Windows Clipboard. Switch back to the word processor and choose Edit Paste Link or Paste Special. Remember, choosing Paste Link *links* a copy to the word processor; Paste Special *embeds* a copy in the word processor.

Using Drawings in PageMaker

Aldus PageMaker 4.0 does not support OLE, so you cannot use linking or embedding to transfer a drawing into PageMaker. However, as part of the PageMaker installation process, you can install a Micrografx DRW filter that directly imports Draw files.

To install the DRW filter into a functioning copy of PageMaker 4.0, follow these steps:

1. Open the Windows File Manager by double-clicking the File Manager icon in the Main group of the Windows Program Manager.

2. Double-click the folder labeled ALDUS in the left panel of the File Manager.

3. Double-click the folder labeled USENGLSH that appears in the ALDUS directory.

4. Double-click the folder labeled SETUP that appears in the USENGLSH directory.

5. Double-click the program ALDSETUP.EXE on the right panel of the File Manager.

6. If a Select file window appears that asks you to select a CTL file, select the file on the list that starts with PM4 (see fig. 10.9).

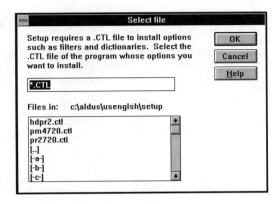

Fig. 10.9

The Select file window.

7. Choose OK.

8. On the Aldus Setup Main window, choose Filters on the list then choose the **S**etup button. The setup program advises you to install only the filters you need. Choose OK to acknowledge the warning.

9. Scroll through the list of filters and select Micrografx Designer Import (.DRW). (Both Micrografx Designer and Micrografx Draw use the same DRW file format.) Figure 10.10 shows the Select filters window with the correct filter selected.

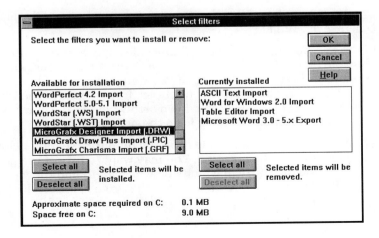

Fig. 10.10

The Select filters window with the correct filter selected.

10. Choose OK.

11. The setup program asks for a drive designation. Type the drive name in which you will place the PageMaker installation diskette with the filter. Then choose OK. The Draw import filter is installed.

TIP

If you plan to use a PostScript imagesetter or a PostScript printer to output documents created in PageMaker, you may want to export an Encapsulated PostScript (EPS) file from Draw and import the file into the desktop publishing program. You can learn how to export an EPS file later in this chapter.

Exporting to a Graphics File for a Non-Windows Program

If the program in which you want to use a Draw picture is not a Windows application, you must save the picture as a graphics file then import the file into the other program. The graphics file format you choose depends on which graphics file format the other application can accept.

To export a drawing as a graphics file, follow these steps:

1. Select the symbols you want to export. If you don't select symbols first, the entire drawing is exported.

2. Choose Export from the File menu to open the Export File dialog box (see fig. 10.11).

3. In the text box section labeled Export file as, type a standard filename up to eight characters. Do not type a file extension; Draw supplies the extension for you. If you want a different file type than the current one, make your choice from the File Type list (see fig. 10.12) by clicking the down arrow next to the current file type name and then selecting from the pull-down list.

4. Choose a directory for the file from the directory section below the File Type text box section. You may want to export the graphics file to the directory in which you will want to find the file later. To export to a diskette, choose the drive name on the list ([-A-] or [-B-]).

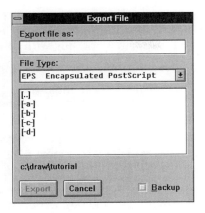

Fig. 10.11

The Export File
dialog box.

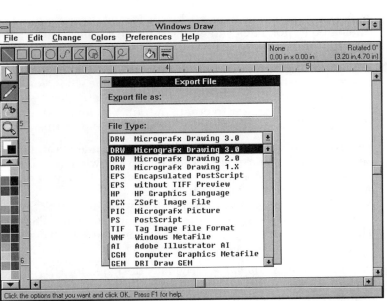

Fig. 10.12

The File Type list
in the Export File
dialog box.

When you export a file, you must choose an appropriate file type. The
file type must match one of the file types supported by the program
to which you are importing the file. The file type also must provide
enough information to transfer the special characteristics of the drawing, such as curves and fonts.

Windows Draw provides both *vector* and *bit-mapped* file types. Vector
files are composed entirely of lines and curves, and they can be resized
without losing or gaining resolution. Bit-mapped files are composed

entirely of patterns of dots. When a bit-mapped file is resized, its resolution changes. Generally, you want to use a vector format whenever possible, but some programs can work only with bit-mapped files.

The following list provides information about each file type.

- *DRW—Micrografx Drawing 3.0.* The most recent version of the Micrografx DRW format. This file type also is used by Micrografx Designer 3.0 and Micrografx Charisma.

- *DRW—Micrografx Drawing 2.0.* An earlier version of the DRW format. Use this format if you need to export a file that can be read by Micrografx Designer 2.0.

- *DRW—Micrografx Drawing 1.X.* An even earlier version of the DRW format. Use this format if you need to export a file that can be read by Micrografx Windows Draw Plus and versions of Micrografx Designer earlier than 2.0. In this format, Bézier curves are translated to polylines and gradient fills are translated to solid fill patterns.

- *EPS—Encapsulated PostScript.* A PostScript vector file format with an embedded bit-mapped preview. Use this file when you need to export a drawing to a desktop publishing program and you plan to use a PostScript printer to create output. You must install the Micrografx PostScript driver before you can export this file type.

- *EPS without TIFF Preview.* A PostScript file format without the embedded bit-mapped preview. Use this format when the program you use to import the file does not recognize the standard Encapsulated PostScript format with an embedded TIFF preview file. EPS files with TIFF previews are substantially larger than EPS files without TIFF previews, so not all programs can read EPS files with TIFF previews properly. See TIFF below for more information about the TIFF file format.

- *HP—HP Graphics Language.* Originally designed for Hewlett Packard Plotters, this vector file format is rarely used. Try this format only as an export file format if you can't get other, more popular vector file formats like CGM to work.

- *PCX Zsoft Image File.* A very popular bit-mapped file format created by Zsoft, the makers of PC Paintbrush and Publisher's Paintbrush PC painting programs. Virtually all graphics programs can import PCX bit-mapped files. PCX files are compressed so they're a good choice when you want to transfer an export file to a floppy disk or when your hard disk space is limited.

- *PIC—Micrografx Picture.* The earliest version of the Micrografx file format used by Micrografx In*A*Vision, Graph Plus, Windows

Draw 1.0, and Windows Graph. This vector file format does not provide support for Bézier curves and gradient fills so these attributes of drawings are not carried over. Curves are changed to polylines.

■ *PS—PostScript.* Files without a TIFF Preview and without a binary header. You can export a PostScript file to a disk, then take the disk to a PC with a PostScript printer. To print the file, copy it from disk to the printer with the DOS Copy command.

■ *TIFF—Tagged Image File Format.* The other popular bit-mapped file format (PCX is the first). TIFF files are widely used to transfer images into desktop publishing programs. Many scanning programs generate TIFF files, too. When you choose TIFF as the export file type, a dialog box with configuration options opens:

The *Format* option enables you to determine how many colors or gray scales will be in the exported image. You can choose from the following options:

Monochrome	Black-and-white
4-bit Gray Scale	16 grays
8-bit Gray Scale	256 grays
24-bit RGB Color	16.7 million colors
8 Fixed Colors	8 default Windows colors
16 Fixed Colors	8 default Windows colors and a darker shade of each color
256 Fixed Colors	256 predefined colors (the IBM 8514 display adapter specification)
Device Colors	The colors supported by the display or printer selected in the Device section

The *Device* setting enables you to choose the resolution of the export file. Choose **S**creen to export the file at the resolution of your current graphics display system. Choose **P**rinter to export the file at the resolution of the currently selected printer. **P**rinter provides better printed results but usually takes longer and creates a larger export file.

The *Compression* setting enables you to choose whether to apply compression to the exported file. Compressing a TIFF file greatly reduces the amount of disk space it requires. Test a sample file to make sure that the graphics program you will use to import the file can read the compressed TIFF files Draw creates.

■ *WMF—Windows Metafile.* The file format used internally by Windows to transfer graphics from one program to another. You can get good results using a Windows Metafile to transfer a drawing to another Windows application.

To create a Windows Metafile that gives you the best results, choose the printer you will be using *before* you export the WMF file. (Use the Printer Setup command from the File menu.) This technique generates a WMF that is customized for the printer. Following is a list of printer options.

■ *AI—Adobe Illustrator.* The native file format for the Adobe Illustrator drawing program. AI does not support gradients or bit-mapped fills, so drawings that contain gradients will not export properly. When you choose AI as the export file format, a dialog box opens with customization options:

File Format enables you to choose the version of Adobe Illustrator for which to customize the file.

Target Environment enables you to choose a Macintosh or PC version file.

Pattern Color enables you to decide how bit-mapped and hatch patterns are portrayed in the file. (AI does not support these two Draw capabilities.)

Size Area enables you to determine the size of the drawing area when the image is brought into Adobe Illustrator. The default setting of 100 produces an image of the same size. A setting smaller than 100 reduces the image size, and a setting larger than 100 increases the image size.

■ *CGM—Computer Graphics Metafile.* The most popular vector file format, but many varieties of CGM exist. When you choose CGM as the export file type, a dialog box opens that presents CGM export options.

CGM Output enables you to customize the output for use in a specific program. If you don't choose the appropriate CGM Output setting, your image may have scaling and color-matching problems.

Curve Quality determines how many polylines are used to represent Bèzier curves in Draw drawings. (CGM does not support Bézier curves.) The higher the Curve Quality, the better the picture quality, but the larger the CGM file.

Scale Factor sets the size of the drawing in the output file. A setting of 100 produces the default image size. A setting larger than 100 increases the image size; a setting smaller than 100 decreases the image size.

Font information is not supported in CGM files; therefore, the fonts in the output file may not match the original fonts.

If you import a CGM file into Harvard Graphics, the symbols may appear smaller than they were in the original Draw file. You need to resize the symbols to make them larger.

■ *GEM—DRI Draw GEM.* Creates GEM Version 3.1 vector metafiles. GEM metafiles support only 16 colors. Other colors are mapped to the closest of the 16 GEM colors, so gradients do not translate well. DRI Draw GEM files are limited to 128 points in a curve or polyline and 128 points in a Bézier curve.

■ *GEM—DRI Artline GEM.* Creates another variety of GEM Version 3.1 vector metafiles. GEM metafiles support only 16 colors. Other colors are mapped to the closest of the 16 GEM colors, so gradients do not translate well. DRI Draw GEM files are limited to 255 points in a curve or polyline and 255 points in a Bézier curve.

■ *PCT—Macintosh PICT.* The vector file format used by the Macintosh computer. When you choose PICT as the export file type, a dialog box opens with special PICT options:

Output File Format enables you to choose either PICT Version 1 (a black-and-white file format) or PICT Version 2 (a color format).

Scale Factor enables you to increase or decrease the size of the drawing. 100% is the default size. You can increase the drawing size up to 1000% or decrease the size down to 0% (using 5% increments).

■ *WPG—WordPerfect Graphics.* Produces the vector file format used by the clip art selections included with WordPerfect. When you choose WPG, a dialog box opens that provides special WPG options:

Curve Quality enables you to choose a quality setting for curves. WPG files do not support Bézier curves, so curves are translated to polylines. The higher the Curve Quality, the closer the result is to the original, but the larger and slower the file.

Scale Factor determines the size of the drawing in the WPG file. 100% produces the default drawing size. A setting larger than 100% increases the drawing size; a setting less than 100% decreases the drawing size.

Importing Graphics and Clip Art

If you have created a graphic or drawing in another Windows program, you can select the graphic or drawing, and then copy it into Draw via the Windows Clipboard. Following are the specific steps.

1. In the other application, select the graphic or drawing and then choose **C**opy from the **E**dit menu.

2. Switch to Draw.

3. Choose **P**aste from Draw's **E**dit menu. The drawing will appear on the Draw page.

You also can import a graphic file stored on disk into Draw and incorporate it in a Draw picture. You will need to use this method when the program in which you have created the file is not a Windows application. To import a graphic file, follow these steps:

1. Choose **I**mport from the **F**ile menu. The Import File dialog box appears, as shown in figure 10.13.

Fig. 10.13

The Import File dialog box.

2. Choose a file type from the File **T**ype selection box.

3. From the **D**irectories display, choose the directory where the file resides.

4. Choose the file name from the F**i**les display. If you know the full pathname to the file, you can type it into the **F**ilename text section. To load a file called SUMMER.CGM that is located in the HG directory on the hard disk, type the following name into the Filename text section:

C:\HG\SUMMER.CGM

Choosing Import File Types

Windows Draw can import all the file types shown on the File Type list. Following is specific information about each of these file types:

- *DRW—Micrografx Drawing.* The standard file format for drawings created by the Micrografx family of graphics products. Another way to import named symbols from DRW files is to use the **C**lipArt command from the **F**ile menu. See Chapter 2, "Using ClipArt," for more information about the **C**lipArt command.

- *GRF—Micrografx Graph.* The file format for Micrografx Charisma and Graph Plus. GRF imported files are snapshots of graphs created in Charisma or Graph Plus. These files do not contain the data that is graphed; therefore, you cannot edit the data to update the graph.

- *PCX—Zsoft Image File.* The bit-mapped file format used by Zsoft's Paintbrush series of painting programs. You can import a PCX file into Draw, but you cannot edit the objects displayed. Bit-mapped files can only be moved, resized, and cropped. For information about cropping bit-mapped files, see the following section, "Cropping a Bit-Mapped Graphic in Draw."

- *PIC—Micrografx Picture.* Choose PIC to import a file created by Micrografx In*A*Vision, Windows Draw 1.X, or Windows Graph.

- *TIFF—Tagged Image File Format.* Draw can import and display bit-mapped TIFF files, but it cannot edit their contents. As with PCX files, TIFF files can only be moved, resized, and cropped. For information about cropping bit-mapped files, see the following section, "Cropping an Imported Bit-Mapped Graphic in Draw."

- *WMF—Windows Metafile.* The standard format used by Windows applications to transfer graphic images. You can transfer a graphic from another Windows application in one of two ways: copy the image to the Clipboard by using the **C**opy command in the other application and paste the image into Draw using the **P**aste command; or export a Windows Metafile and import the WMF file into Draw.

- *AI—Adobe Illustrator AI.* Use this format to import files created with Adobe Illustrator. However, Draw does not import Illustrator pattern fills.

- *EPS—Adobe Illustrator EPS.* Use this format to import Encapsulated PostScript files generated by Adobe Illustrator.

- *CGM—Computer Graphics Metafile.* Many graphics programs can export vector CGM files, so you may find CGM one of the best ways to transfer a graphic from a graphics program into Draw.

Many clip art collections provide selections in CGM, so you can purchase libraries of CGM clip art and augment the ClipArt provided with Draw.

- *GEM—Digital Research GEM.* Use GEM to import vector files created with the Digital Research GEM graphics applications such as GEM Draw and GEM Graph.

- *PCT—Macintosh PICT.* Use this format to import a Macintosh graphics file that has been transferred to a PC.

- *WPG—WordPerfect Graphics.* Choose this format to import a clip art file from the collection of files provided with WordPerfect.

Cropping an Imported Bit-Mapped Graphic in Draw

After you have imported or pasted a PCX or TIFF bit-mapped file into Draw, you cannot edit the file's contents. You cannot change the color of an area, for example, or change the size of a graphic shape. The file is bit-mapped, and Draw only works with vector images. You can, however, stretch the size of the entire bit-mapped image and move it as you would any other symbol by dragging the handles surrounding it.

You also can *crop* the image, displaying only one rectangular area. To crop an image, follow these steps:

1. Click the image with the Pointer tool.

2. Choose the Reshape Points button.

3. Drag the points to change the size of the rubber band box so it outlines one rectangular region of the image.

4. Press Esc or click the Select tool. The portion of the image you have selected remains on-screen. Figure 10.14 shows a bit-mapped graphic being cropped. Figure 10.15 shows the resulting cropped graphic.

Importing Text

Rather than type text directly onto the Draw screen, you can import an ASCII text file. The text appears on the Draw page as though you had typed the text after clicking the Text tool, and the text has the current text settings.

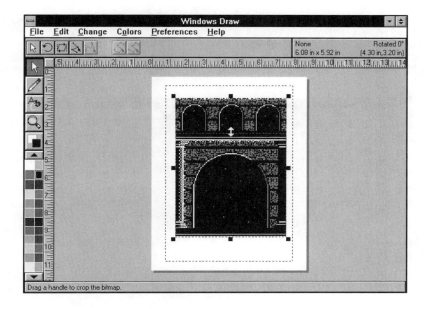

Fig. 10.14

Cropping a bit-
mapped graphic.

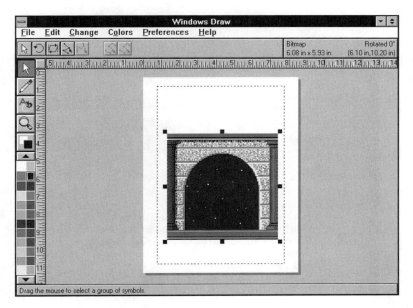

Fig. 10.15

The resulting
cropped graphic.

To import text, choose **F**ile Import. Then choose TXT ANSI Text from
the File **T**ype list. Use the **D**irectories and **F**iles control to find the text

you would like to import. When you choose the file, its contents appear on the Draw screen.

Figure 10.16 shows a block of text in the Windows Notepad. Figure 10.17 shows the same text after it has been imported into Draw.

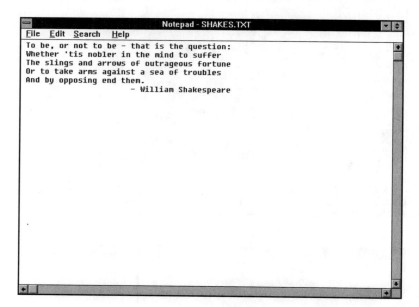

Fig. 10.16

Text in the Windows Notepad.

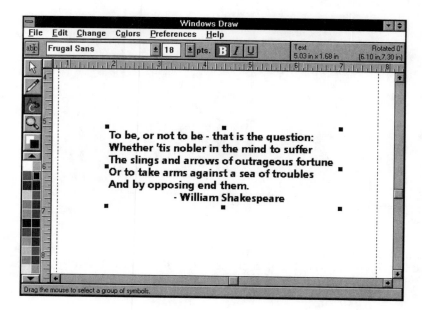

Fig. 10.17

The text after it has been imported into Draw.

Summary

In this chapter, you learned how to transfer your drawings to other software applications. You also learned how to incorporate graphics and text from other sources in your drawings.

Good luck with Draw!

Installing Draw

This appendix describes the system requirements for running Draw and how to install the Draw software.

Running Draw

Before you can install Draw, you should have the following hardware and software:

■ An IBM PC or PS/2 compatible desktop or laptop computer. A 386sx or better is the practical minimum for running a graphics program under Windows.

■ A hard disk.

■ At least one megabyte of RAM. The more memory you add to your system, the better. Memory now has become relatively inexpensive, so you may want at least four megabytes for running Windows. Set aside one megabyte for the SmartDrive disk cache that the Windows installation program installs. Eight megabytes is better if you plan to run other Windows applications simultaneously.

■ A mouse.

■ A video system (video card and monitor) compatible with Windows. VGA or SuperVGA is recommended, although the software works with EGA systems, too. A 16-bit graphics card or a card with a special Windows accelerator chip is highly recommended.

- DOS 3.1 or higher installed. DOS 5.0 or higher is recommended because of the additional memory 5.0 makes available.

- Microsoft Windows Version 3.0 or Version 3.1 installed. Although Windows Draw can run on Windows 3.0, Windows 3.1 is strongly recommended for its additional speed and stability, its TrueType fonts, and its Object Linking and Embedding (OLE). Windows 3.1 enables you to easily transfer pictures created in Draw to other Windows applications.

Installing the Draw Software

The software on the Windows Draw disks is in compressed files, so you must use the Windows Draw installation program to copy the software to your hard disk and decompress it. The installation program automatically copies and decompresses the software.

To install the Draw software, follow these steps:

1. Start Windows. (Usually, you can type **win** to start Windows.) The Program Manager appears, as shown in figure A.1.

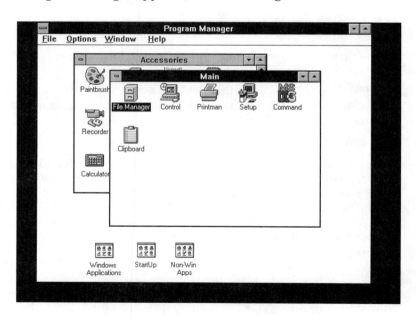

2. Insert the Windows Draw disk labeled *Installation Disk #1* in the disk drive of your computer.

3. Choose **F**ile from the Program Manager's menu, then choose **R**un from the File menu. The Run dialog box appears, as shown in figure A.2.

4. Type **A:INSTALL** or **B:INSTALL,** depending on whether you inserted the disk in the A or B drive, and press Enter.

5. When the Micrografx Installer window appears, choose **C**ontinue (see fig. A.3).

6. After you read the copyright warning information on the next screen, choose **C**ontinue again. Another screen appears with a place for you to enter the serial number on your Windows Draw registration card. Type the serial number, then choose OK.

7. Another screen appears to inform you that a Help window has opened behind the current screen with special installation information. You can click the exposed portion of this window, then

read its contents. After you finish, close the Help window by double-clicking the window control button in the upper left corner of the window. Or you can minimize the window by clicking the down-arrow button in the upper right corner of the window.

8. Choose the Continue button to see a description of the three installation options.

9. Choose the Continue button on this screen to open the Micrografx Installer Main Menu (see fig. A.4).

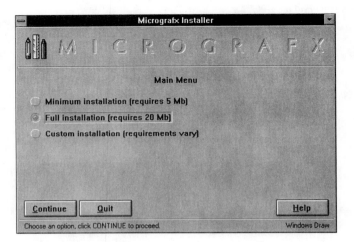

Fig. A.4

The Micrografx Installer Main Menu.

The Main Menu provides three options:

- *Minimum installation* installs only the software you need to run Windows Draw and a few sample Draw files. ClipArt files and translators that enable you to import and export graphics are not installed. Choose Minimum installation and choose Continue only if you are limited by disk space. If you perform a minimum installation, no ClipArt files are installed, so you cannot follow many of the example exercises in this book. Figure A.5 shows the Minimum installation screen.

- *Full installation* installs all the Windows Draw software, including the Draw program files, sample drawings, special output device drives, ClipArt files, and import/export translators. Choose Full installation and choose Continue if you have enough disk space. Figure A.6 shows the Full installation screen.

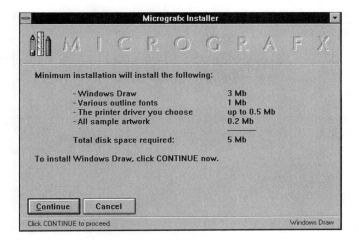

Fig. A.5

The Minimum installation screen.

Fig. A.6

The Full installation screen.

■ *Custom installation* enables you to pick and choose the parts of the program to install. Choose Custom installation and click **Con**tinue this option if you are an experienced PC user and you want to limit the installed software to only those components you need. Figure A.7 shows the Custom installation screen.

Now that you have chosen an installation option, a window appears asking you to accept or change the location for Draw.

1. To accept the default location (in a directory called DRAW under the Windows directory), choose OK. If you want the Draw files in a different directory, type the path name to the directory. For example, to install the Draw files in a directory called DRAW under the root directory, type **C:\DRAW**. Then choose OK.

2. If you're performing a Full or Custom installation, another window opens asking for the directory in which you want to install the Micrografx libraries. Choose OK to accept the suggested directory name.

3. If you're performing a Full installation or a Custom installation and you have chosen to install ClipArt, another window opens asking for the directory in which to install the ClipArt catalogs. Choose OK to accept the suggested directory name.

4. The next set of screens asks you to select the outline fonts to install. You should choose **All** to select all the outline fonts unless you're severely limited in disk space. If you're using Windows 3.1, the TrueType fonts that you installed become available to every Windows application—an excellent bonus. Click **Continue**.

5. The next screen asks you to choose a special printer driver. Scroll down the list by pressing the down-arrow key, by pressing the PgDn key, or by using the scroll bar to the right of the list. Choose the name of your currently installed printer, then choose **Accept**.

If your printer doesn't appear on the list, you don't need to install a special printer driver for it, and you can choose **S**kip. The printer driver you selected when you installed Windows will be used instead. The Hewlett-Packard LaserJet Series II is one of those printers that doesn't appear in the list because you do not need to install a special driver for it. Instead, you can press **S**kip.

6. If you're performing a Custom installation and you have chosen to install translators, the next screen enables you to select the translators to install. Translators convert files from DRW format to a generic graphics format that other programs will accept. Choose the translators for the graphic file types that you expect to use with Draw and then choose **A**ccept.

7. If you're performing a Custom installation, the next screen asks which sample Draw drawings to install. Choose the samples to install or choose All or None. Then choose **A**ccept.

8. If you're performing a Custom installation, the next screen enables you to choose only certain ClipArt subjects and files. Select the subjects you want by clicking them on the list and then click Continue.

9. The next-to-last screen enables you to choose whether to automatically add the Windows Draw icon to the Program Manager. Choose **A**ccept.

10. The final screen enables you to review your choices and make changes, or install the choices you have made. If you want to change any of your earlier selections, choose Review; otherwise, choose Install.

The installation process informs you of its progress and instructs you to place each of the diskettes in the drive when needed. Follow the instructions that appear on-screen.

When the program is installed, a window appears asking whether to start Draw or return to the Main Menu of the installation program. To see Draw in action immediately, you can choose the **S**tart button.

If you choose to have Draw add an icon to the Program Manager, the installation program sets up a special group called Micrografx with the Windows Draw 3.0 icon inside. To start Draw, you double-click this icon or move the highlight to it with the arrow keys and press Enter. Figure A.8 shows the Micrografx group.

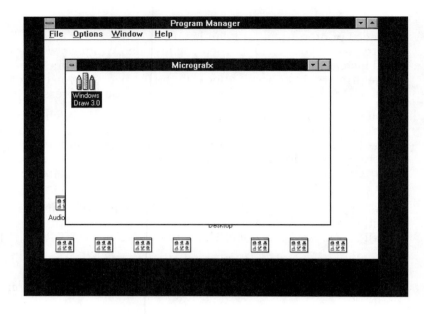

Fig. A.8

The Micrografx group in the Program Manager window.

Updating a Draw Installation

After you've installed Draw, you can change any of the installed options by starting the installation program again, as described earlier, and choosing Update Windows Draw at the Main Menu, as shown in figure A.9. The Installer automatically updates the installation.

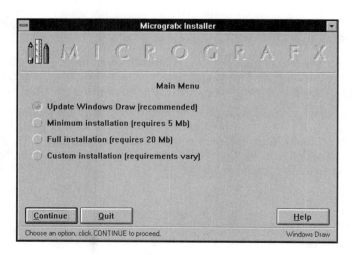

Fig. A.9

The Installer Main Menu with Update Windows Draw selected.

Draw's Fonts

The following pages provide examples of the fonts that come with Windows Draw. Each font is shown in both headline and body text sizes.

BALLOON

NORMAL

ABCDEFGHIJKLMNOPQRSTUVWXYZ

ITALIC

ABCDEFGHIJKLMNOPQRSTUVWXYZ

BOLD

ABCDEFGHIJKLMNOPQRSTUVWXYZ

BOLD AND ITALIC

ABCDEFGHIJKLMNOPQRSTUVWXYZ

IN THE PAST FEW HUNDRED YEARS THERE HAS BEEN AN EXTRAORDINARY
ENLARGEMENT OF MEN'S IDEAS ABOUT THE VISIBLE UNIVERSE IN WHICH THEY LIVE.
AT THE SAME TIME THERE HAS BEEN PERHAPS A CERTAIN DIMINUTION IN THEIR
INDIVIDUAL SELF-IMPORTANCE. THEY HAVE LEARNT THAT THEY ARE ITEMS IN A
WHOLE FAR VASTER, MORE ENDURING AND MORE WONDERFUL THAN THEIR
ANCESTORS EVER DREAMED OR SUSPECTED.

— H.G. WELLS

Bodoni

Roman

ABCDEFGHIJKLMNOPQRSTUVWXYZ
abcdefghijklmnopqrstuvwxyz

Roman Italic

ABCDEFGHIJKLMNOPQRSTUVWXYZ
abcdefghijklmnopqrstuvwxyz

Bold

ABCDEFGHIJKLMNOPQRSTUVWXYZ
abcdefghijklmnopqrstuvwxyz

Bold and Italic

ABCDEFGHIJKLMNOPQRSTUVWXYZ
abcdefghijklmnopqrstuvwxyz

In the past few hundred years there has been an extraordinary enlargement of men's ideas about the visible universe in which they live. At the same time there has been perhaps a certain diminution in their individual self-importance. They have learnt that they are items in a whole far vaster, more enduring and more wonderful than their ancestors ever dreamed or suspected.

-- H.G. Wells

Broadway

Normal

ABCDEFGHIJKLMNOPQRSTUVWXYZ
abcdefghijklmnopqrstuvwxyz

Italic

ABCDEFGHIJKLMNOPQRSTUVWXYZ
abcdefghijklmnopqrstuvwxyz

Bold

ABCDEFGHIJKLMNOPQRSTUVWXYZ
abcdefghijklmnopqrstuvwxyz

Bold and Italic

ABCDEFGHIJKLMNOPQRSTUVWXYZ
abcdefghijklmnopqrstuvwxyz

In the past few hundred years there has been an extraordinary enlargement of men's ideas about the visible universe in which they live. At the same time there has been perhaps a certain diminution in their individual self-importance. They have learnt that they are items in a whole far vaster, more enduring and more wonderful than their ancestors ever dreamed or suspected.

— H.G. Wells

Cooper Black

Normal

ABCDEFGHIJKLMNOPQRSTUVWXYZ
abcdefghijklmnopqrstuvwxyz

Italic

ABCDEFGHIJKLMNOPQRSTUVWXYZ
abcdefghijklmnopqrstuvwxyz

Bold

ABCDEFGHIJKLMNOPQRSTUVWXYZ
abcdefghijklmnopqrstuvwxyz

Bold and Italic

ABCDEFGHIJKLMNOPQRSTUVWXYZ
abcdefghijklmnopqrstuvwxyz

In the past few hundred years there has been an extraordinary enlargement of men's ideas about the visible universe in which they live. At the same time there has been perhaps a certain diminution in their individual self-importance. They have learnt that they are items in a whole far vaster, more enduring and more wonderful than their ancestors ever dreamed or suspected.

– H.G. Wells

COPPERPLATE BOLD

BOLD

ABCDEFGHIJKLMNOPQRSTUVWXYZ
ABCDEFGHIJKLMNOPQRSTUVWXYZ

BOLD AND ITALIC

ABCDEFGHIJKLMNOPQRSTUVWXYZ
ABCDEFGHIJKLMNOPQRSTUVWXYZ

IN THE PAST FEW HUNDRED YEARS THERE HAS BEEN AN
EXTRAORDINARY ENLARGEMENT OF MEN'S IDEAS ABOUT THE VISIBLE
UNIVERSE IN WHICH THEY LIVE. AT THE SAME TIME THERE HAS BEEN
PERHAPS A CERTAIN DIMINUTION IN THEIR INDIVIDUAL
SELF-IMPORTANCE. THEY HAVE LEARNT THAT THEY ARE ITEMS IN A
WHOLE FAR VASTER, MORE ENDURING AND MORE WONDERFUL THAN
THEIR ANCESTORS EVER DREAMED OR SUSPECTED.

-- H.G. WELLS

Dom Casual

Normal

ABCDEFGHIJKLMNOPQRSTUVWXYZ
abcdefghijklmnopqrstuvwxyz

Italic

ABCDEFGHIJKLMNOPQRSTUVWXYZ
abcdefghijklmnopqrstuvwxyz

Bold

ABCDEFGHIJKLMNOPQRSTUVWXYZ
abcdefghijklmnopqrstuvwxyz

Bold and Italic

ABCDEFGHIJKLMNOPQRSTUVWXYZ
abcdefghijklmnopqrstuvwxyz

In the past few hundred years there has been an extraordinary enlargement of men's ideas about the visible universe in which they live. At the same time there has been perhaps a certain diminution in their individual self-importance. They have learnt that they are items in a whole far vaster, more enduring and more wonderful than their ancestors ever dreamed or suspected.

– H.G. Wells

Eurostile Extended

Roman

ABCDEFGHIJKLMNOPQRSTUVWXYZ
abcdefghijklmnopqrstuvwxyz

Roman Italic

ABCDEFGHIJKLMNOPQRSTUVWXYZ
abcdefghijklmnopqrstuvwxyz

Bold

ABCDEFGHIJKLMNOPQRSTUVWXYZ
abcdefghijklmnopqrstuvwxyz

Bold and Italic

ABCDEFGHIJKLMNOPQRSTUVWXYZ
abcdefghijklmnopqrstuvwxyz

In the past few hundred years there has been an extraordinary enlargement of men's ideas about the visible universe in which they live. At the same time there has been perhaps a certain diminution in their individual self-importance. They have learnt that they are items in a whole far vaster, more enduring and more wonderful than their ancestors ever dreamed or suspected.
— H.G. Wells

Fette Engschrift

Normal

ABCDEFGHIJKLMNOPQRSTUVWXYZ
abcdefghijklmnopqrstuvwxyz

Italic

ABCDEFGHIJKLMNOPQRSTUVWXYZ
abcdefghijklmnopqrstuvwxyz

Bold

ABCDEFGHIJKLMNOPQRSTUVWXYZ
abcdefghijklmnopqrstuvwxyz

Bold and Italic

ABCDEFGHIJKLMNOPQRSTUVWXYZ
abcdefghijklmnopqrstuvwxyz

In the past few hundred years there has been an extraordinary enlargement of men's ideas about the visible universe in which they live. At the same time there has been perhaps a certain diminution in their individual self-importance. They have learnt that they are items in a whole far vaster, more enduring and more wonderful than their ancestors ever dreamed or suspected.

-- H.G. Wells

Franklin Gothic Condensed

Normal

ABCDEFGHIJKLMNOPQRSTUVWXYZ
abcdefghijklmnopqrstuvwxyz

Italic

ABCDEFGHIJKLMNOPQRSTUVWXYZ
abcdefghijklmnopqrstuvwxyz

Bold

ABCDEFGHIJKLMNOPQRSTUVWXYZ
abcdefghijklmnopqrstuvwxyz

Bold and Italic

ABCDEFGHIJKLMNOPQRSTUVWXYZ
abcdefghijklmnopqrstuvwxyz

In the past few hundred years there has been an extraordinary enlargement of men's ideas about the visible universe in which they live. At the same time there has been perhaps a certain diminution in their individual self-importance. They have learnt that they are items in a whole far vaster, more enduring and more wonderful than their ancestors ever dreamed or suspected.

-- H.G. Wells

Frugal Sans

Light

ABCDEFGHIJKLMNOPQRSTUVWXYZ
abcdefghijklmnopqrstuvwxyz

Light Italic

ABCDEFGHIJKLMNOPQRSTUVWXYZ
abcdefghijklmnopqrstuvwxyz

Bold

ABCDEFGHIJKLMNOPQRSTUVWXYZ
abcdefghijklmnopqrstuvwxyz

Bold and Italic

ABCDEFGHIJKLMNOPQRSTUVWXYZ
abcdefghijklmnopqrstuvwxyz

In the past few hundred years there has been an extraordinary enlargement of men's ideas about the visible universe in which they live. At the same time there has been perhaps a certain diminution in their individual self-importance. They have learnt that they are items in a whole far vaster, more enduring and more wonderful than their ancestors ever dreamed or suspected.

– H.G. Wells

Garamond

Roman

ABCDEFGHIJKLMNOPQRSTUVWXYZ
abcdefghijklmnopqrstuvwxyz

Roman Italic

ABCDEFGHIJKLMNOPQRSTUVWXYZ
abcdefghijklmnopqrstuvwxyz

Medium

ABCDEFGHIJKLMNOPQRSTUVWXYZ
abcdefghijklmnopqrstuvwxyz

Medium Italic

ABCDEFGHIJKLMNOPQRSTUVWXYZ
abcdefghijklmnopqrstuvwxyz

In the past few hundred years there has been an extraordinary enlargement of men's ideas about the visible universe in which they live. At the same time there has been perhaps a certain diminution in their individual self-importance. They have learnt that they are items in a whole far vaster, more enduring and more wonderful than their ancestors ever dreamed or suspected.

– H.G. Wells

Heritage Extra Bold

Normal

ABCDEFGHIJKLMNOPQRSTUVWXYZ
abcdefghijklmnopqrstuvwxyz

Italic

ABCDEFGHIJKLMNOPQRSTUVWXYZ
abcdefghijklmnopqrstuvwxyz

Bold

ABCDEFGHIJKLMNOPQRSTUVWXYZ
abcdefghijklmnopqrstuvwxyz

Bold and Italic

ABCDEFGHIJKLMNOPQRSTUVWXYZ
abcdefghijklmnopqrstuvwxyz

In the past few hundred years there has been an extraordinary enlargement of men's ideas about the visible universe in which they live. At the same time there has been perhaps a certain diminution in their individual self-importance. They have learnt that they are items in a whole far vaster, more enduring and more wonderful than their ancestors ever dreamed or suspected.

– H.G. Wells

Latin Wide

Normal

ABCDEFGHIJKLMNOPQRSTUVWXYZ
abcdefghijklmnopqrstuvwxyz

Italic

ABCDEFGHIJKLMNOPQRSTUVWXYZ
abcdefghijklmnopqrstuvwxyz

Bold

ABCDEFGHIJKLMNOPQRSTUVWXYZ
abcdefghijklmnopqrstuvwxyz

Bold and Italic

ABCDEFGHIJKLMNOPQRSTUVWXYZ
abcdefghijklmnopqrstuvwxyz

In the past few hundred years there has been an extraordinary enlargement of men's ideas about the visible universe in which they live. At the same time there has been perhaps a certain diminution in their individual self-importance. They have learnt that they are items in a whole far vaster, more enduring and more wonderful than their ancestors ever dreamed or suspected.

— H.G. Wells

Marriage

Normal

ABCDEFGHIJKLMNOPQRSTUVWXYZ
abcdefghijklmnopqrstuvwxyz

Italic

ABCDEFGHIJKLMNOPQRSTUVWXYZ
abcdefghijklmnopqrstuvwxyz

Bold

ABCDEFGHIJKLMNOPQRSTUVWXYZ
abcdefghijklmnopqrstuvwxyz

Bold and Italic

ABCDEFGHIJKLMNOPQRSTUVWXYZ
abcdefghijklmnopqrstuvwxyz

In the past few hundred years there has been an extraordinary enlargement of men's ideas about the visible universe in which they live. At the same time there has been perhaps a certain diminution in their individual self-importance. They have learnt that they are items in a whole far vaster, more enduring and more wonderful than their ancestors ever dreamed or suspected.

-- H.G. Wells

Optimum

Roman

ABCDEFGHIJKLMNOPQRSTUVWXYZ
abcdefghijklmnopqrstuvwxyz

Roman Oblique

ABCDEFGHIJKLMNOPQRSTUVWXYZ
abcdefghijklmnopqrstuvwxyz

Bold

ABCDEFGHIJKLMNOPQRSTUVWXYZ
abcdefghijklmnopqrstuvwxyz

Bold Italic

ABCDEFGHIJKLMNOPQRSTUVWXYZ
abcdefghijklmnopqrstuvwxyz

In the past few hundred years there has been an extraordinary enlargement of men's ideas about the visible universe in which they live. At the same time there has been perhaps a certain diminution in their individual self-importance. They have learnt that they are items in a whole far vaster, more enduring and more wonderful than their ancestors ever dreamed or suspected.

– H.G. Wells

Mural Script

Normal

ABCDEFGHIJKLMNOPQRSTUVWXYZ
abcdefghijklmnopqrstuvwxyz

Italic

ABCDEFGHIJKLMNOPQRSTUVWXYZ
abcdefghijklmnopqrstuvwxyz

Bold

ABCDEFGHIJKLMNOPQRSTUVWXYZ
abcdefghijklmnopqrstuvwxyz

Bold and Italic

ABCDEFGHIJKLMNOPQRSTUVWXYZ
abcdefghijklmnopqrstuvwxyz

In the past few hundred years there has been an extraordinary enlargement of men's ideas about the visible universe in which they live. At the same time there has been perhaps a certain diminution in their individual self-importance. They have learnt that they are items in a whole far vaster, more enduring and more wonderful than their ancestors ever dreamed or suspected.

-- H.G. Wells

Serpentine Bold

Normal

ABCDEFGHIJKLMNOPQRSTUVWXYZ
abcdefghijklmnopqrstuvwxyz

Italic

ABCDEFGHIJKLMNOPQRSTUVWXYZ
abcdefghijklmnopqrstuvwxyz

Bold

ABCDEFGHIJKLMNOPQRSTUVWXYZ
abcdefghijklmnopqrstuvwxyz

Bold and Italic

ABCDEFGHIJKLMNOPQRSTUVWXYZ
abcdefghijklmnopqrstuvwxyz

In the past few hundred years there has been an extraordinary enlargement of men's ideas about the visible universe in which they live. At the same time there has been perhaps a certain diminution in their individual self-importance. They have learnt that they are items in a whole far vaster, more enduring and more wonderful than their ancestors ever dreamed or suspected.
-- H.G. Wells

STENCIL

NORMAL

ABCDEFGHIJKLMNOPQRSTUVWXYZ

ITALIC

ABCDEFGHIJKLMNOPQRSTUVWXYZ

BOLD

ABCDEFGHIJKLMNOPQRSTUVWXYZ

BOLD AND ITALIC

ABCDEFGHIJKLMNOPQRSTUVWXYZ

IN THE PAST FEW HUNDRED YEARS THERE HAS BEEN AN EXTRAORDINARY ENLARGEMENT OF MEN'S IDEAS ABOUT THE VISIBLE UNIVERSE IN WHICH THEY LIVE. AT THE SAME TIME THERE HAS BEEN PERHAPS A CERTAIN DIMINUTION IN THEIR INDIVIDUAL SELF-IMPORTANCE. THEY HAVE LEARNT THAT THEY ARE ITEMS IN A WHOLE FAR VASTER, MORE ENDURING AND MORE WONDERFUL THAN THEIR ANCESTORS EVER DREAMED OR SUSPECTED.

— H.G. WELLS

STOP

NORMAL

ABCDEFGHIJKLMNOPQRSTUVWXYZ

ITALIC

ABCDEFGHIJKLMNOPQRSTUVWXYZ

BOLD

ABCDEFGHIJKLMNOPQRSTUVWXYZ

BOLD AND ITALIC

ABCDEFGHIJKLMNOPQRSTUVWXYZ

IN THE PAST FEW HUNDRED YEARS THERE HAS BEEN AN EXTRAORDINARY ENLARGEMENT OF MEN'S IDEAS ABOUT THE VISIBLE UNIVERSE IN WHICH THEY LIVE. AT THE SAME TIME THERE HAS BEEN PERHAPS A CERTAIN DIMINUTION IN THEIR INDIVIDUAL SELF-IMPORTANCE. THEY HAVE LEARNT THAT THEY ARE ITEMS IN A WHOLE FAR VASTER, MORE ENDURING AND MORE WONDERFUL THAN THEIR ANCESTORS EVER DREAMED OR SUSPECTED.

— H.G. WELLS

Draw Keyboard Shortcuts

The following table lists the commands that have keyboard short-cuts you can use.

Command	Keyboard Shortcut
Align Bottom	Ctrl-F8
Align Center	Ctrl-F5
Align Left	Ctrl-F3
Align Middle	Ctrl-F6
Align Page Center	Ctrl-F9
Align Page Middle	Ctrl-F10
Align Right	Ctrl-F7
Align Top	Ctrl-F4
Align to Ruler	Ctrl-F2
Connect	F11
Copy	Ctrl-Ins
Current Topic Help	F1
Cut	Shift-Del
Delete	Del

Command	Keyboard Shortcut
Disconnect	Shift-F11
Duplicate	Ctrl-D
Exit	Alt-F4
Flip Horizontally	F7
Flip Vertically	Shift-F7
Group	F5
Move to Back	F9
Move to Front	Shift-F9
Name	F12
Paste	Shift-Ins
Print Page	Shift-F4
Print View	F4
Redraw	F3
Save	Ctrl-S
Select All	F2
Undo	Alt-Backspace
Ungroup	Shift-F5
View Previous	Ctrl-V
Zoom	Ctrl-Z

INDEX

Symbols

5 Points Wide command (Line Style menu), 184

A

accessing Windows Task List, 58
Add ClipArt dialog box, 109
adding
    ClipArt symbols, 16-19,
      97-102, 108
      to existing files, 110-112
    fonts, TrueType, 159, 331-332
    gradients, 232-235
    points, anchor, 245
    text, 11-12, 38-46
      to ClipArt catalog, 51-52
Adobe PostScript Type 1 fonts,
  159-160
Adobe Type Manager for
  Windows 2.0 (ATM 2.0), 121,
  159, 328

AI—Adobe Illustrator file
  format, 350, 353
Aldus PageMaker 4.0, importing
  Draw files, 344-346
Align command (Change menu),
  270-273
Align menu, 16
aligning
    symbols, 270-274
    text, 15-16
      within symbols, 274-275
Alt key combinations (menus,
  choosing), 72
Alt-F4 keyboard shortcut
  (closing windows), 82
Always on Top button (Help
  window), 75
Ami Pro, as OLE client for Draw,
  344
anchor points, 34, 150-153,
  241-242
    adding, 245
    deleting, 247-248
    moving, 240-241, 244-245

C

U-V